*The Little Flowers of St. Francis* ~~was not written~~ [by St.?]
Francis of Assisi, but by Brother [Ugolino di Monte Santa?]
Maria, who lived a century after [the founder?] [This?]
work played an important part in the stormy early history of
the Franciscan order. There was a heated controversy among
Franciscans over the true nature of the Franciscan way of life;
this book was written to capture the true Franciscan spirit in
the lives and thoughts of the founder and his followers.

The original was written in Latin and called the *Actus*. The
bulk of the *Actus,* in turn, was translated into Italian and became the famous *Fioretti,* or Little Flowers. The anonymous
translator is an acknowledged master of Italian prose.

This edition, alone among those available in English, trans-
lates the complete *Actus,* while also making use of the *Fioretti*
whenever it would enhance the translation. It includes nineteen chapters which have never before appeared in English,
along with the following selections which over the years have
come to be included with the original *Little Flowers:* "The
Five Considerations on the Holy Stigmata"; "The Life of
Brother Juniper"; "The Life of Brother Giles"; and "The Sayings of Brother Giles."

Valuable extra features of this edition include an informa-
tive Introduction giving new data about the author; the
background of the book and its historical value and significance; a short biography of St. Francis; nineteen biographical
sketches of the principal persons appearing in the book; a useful map; and the full critical apparatus of notes, appendices,
references, and bibliography.

BOOKS BY RAPHAEL BROWN

The Life of Mary as Seen by the Mystics
Mary Communes with the Saints
World Survey of Catholic Leprosy Work

*Translations:*

Our Lady and St. Francis (*St. Francis Texts 1*)
Fifty Animal Stories of St. Francis
(*St. Francis Texts 2*)
The St. Francis Nobody Knows, A New Collection
of Unknown Stories (*St. Francis Texts 3*)
The Hermitages of St. Francis
(*St. Francis Texts 4*)
The Perfect Joy of St. Francis
*by Felix Timmermans*
The Revelations of St. Margaret of Cortona
*by Ange Marie Hiral,* O.F.M.
An Apostle of Two Worlds,
Good Father Frederic Janssoone, O.F.M.,
*by Romain Legaré,* O.F.M.

# THE LITTLE FLOWERS
# OF ST. FRANCIS

First Complete Edition
*An Entirely New Version*
*With Twenty Additional Chapters*

Also

THE CONSIDERATIONS ON
THE HOLY STIGMATA

THE LIFE AND SAYINGS
OF BROTHER GILES

THE LIFE OF BROTHER JUNIPER

*A Modern English Translation*
*From the Latin and the Italian*
*with Introduction, Notes, and*
*Biographical Sketches*
*by*
RAPHAEL BROWN
FRANCISCAN TERTIARY

**IMAGE BOOKS**
**DOUBLEDAY**
NEW YORK  LONDON  TORONTO  SYDNEY  AUCKLAND

AN IMAGE BOOK
PUBLISHED BY DOUBLEDAY
a division of Bantam Doubleday Dell Publishing Group, Inc.
1540 Broadway, New York, New York 10036

IMAGE, DOUBLEDAY, and the portrayal of a deer drinking
from a stream are trademarks of Doubleday, a division of
Bantam Doubleday Dell Publishing Group, Inc.

NIHIL OBSTAT:    Edward J. Montano, S.T.D.
                 *Censor Librorum*

IMPRIMATUR:    ✠ Francis Cardinal Spellman
               *Archbishop of New York*
               *April 2, 1958*

ISBN 0-385-07544-8

# Contents

**6** *Contents*

## PART TWO: THE CONSIDERATIONS ON THE HOLY STIGMATA

## PART FIVE: THE SAYINGS OF BROTHER GILES

## PART SIX: ADDITIONAL CHAPTERS

## Contents

# INTRODUCTION

For the last hundred years the *Fioretti,* or *The Little Flowers of St. Francis,* has been the most widely read book about the "Poverello," the Little Poor Man of Assisi, who is the most popular figure in the history of Christianity after Jesus Himself and the Blessed Virgin. But the true story of this great classic of world literature and of its author, as revealed by modern Franciscan research, has not yet been told.

We shall therefore briefly survey in the Introduction the life of St. Francis and of the author of this book, the crucial role which it played in the turbulent early history of the Franciscan Order, its historical value, its Latin and Italian versions with their various additional parts, its rise to world-wide popularity in modern times, the special features of this new edition, and lastly the literary and spiritual qualities of the *Fioretti.*

At the outset it may be advisable to dispel a fairly common misconception: *The Little Flowers* was not written by St. Francis himself, but by an Italian Franciscan who lived a hundred years after the Saint died.

### St. Francis of Assisi

This extraordinary man whom all the world loves and honors as a faithful mirror of Christ began life as a gay playboy. He was born in Assisi in central Italy in 1182, the son of a wealthy middle-class linen merchant, Pietro di Bernardone. Francis was a gentle, likable, and fun-loving boy. He learned to read and write Latin at St. George's Church school, and his father, who often traded in France, taught him some French.

In his youth he was deeply influenced by the high ethical ideals of medieval chivalry as reflected in the great epic poems which he heard the troubadours sing: selfless devotion to a lofty goal, loyalty to a liege lord, considerate courtesy toward all persons, and generous compassion for the poor and the weak. Young Francis dreamed of winning fame and glory as a valiant knight in armor.

But his military career was brief and disappointing. Captured during a battle between Assisi and Perugia, he spent a frustrating year as a cheerful and popular prisoner of war. After a period of illness he set out to fight for the Pope, but a revelation which he received in nearby Spoleto urged him to serve the Lord rather than man, so he went home and began to turn to Christ in solitary prayer. At this time he was also granted an unforgettable vision of Jesus suffering His Passion on the Cross.

Characteristically, Francis then began to help poor priests and the needy and even to associate with paupers. During a pilgrimage to St. Peter's Tomb in Rome, he spent a day dressed as a beggar. Later near Assisi he embraced a man who had leprosy. While he was praying fervently for divine guidance in the old chapel of San Damiano, Christ in the Crucifix said to him: "Francis, go and repair My Church which, as you see, is falling into ruins."

Soon his greedy father, exasperated by his son's extravagant generosity and strange vocation, summoned him before the Bishop's court in order to recover the money he had spent. But Francis stripped himself naked to symbolize his complete renunciation of the world for God. This climax of his conversion, which occurred in 1206, when he was about twenty-five, marked the beginning of his twenty years of knightly service to his true liege lord, Christ the King.

Dressed in a hermit's robe, he spent over two years nursing victims of leprosy and repairing three small churches near Assisi: San Damiano, San Pietro, and the Portiuncula or St. Mary of the Angels. There on February 24, 1209, the Holy Spirit revealed to him in the Gospel of the Mass (Matt. 10:9 ff.) the specific way of life to which God was calling him. He then began to preach brief, informal sermons in Assisi.

Within a few weeks three companions—Bernard, Peter

Catani, and Giles—joined him. Soon they set out on a first mission journey, Francis and Giles going to the Marches of Ancona while the other two took another direction. After eight more volunteers had taken up the new life, in 1210 they wrote a simple Rule based on the Gospels and traveled to Rome, where Pope Innocent III gave them his verbal approval. Probably at this time Francis was ordained a deacon; out of humility he never became a priest.

On returning to Assisi the twelve Friars Minor lived for a while in extreme destitution in a shed at Rivo Torto and then, as their numbers increased, they moved to the Portiuncula, which was given to them by the Benedictines of Mount Subasio. In that chapel in 1212 Francis gave the religious habit to an aristocratic eighteen-year-old girl of Assisi named Clare, who thereby became the Foundress of the Second Order of cloistered nuns.

St. Francis was the first founder of an Order to include in its Rule a chapter dealing with foreign missions. In 1212 and again a year later he tried in vain to reach the Moslems in North Africa and Spain, with the hope of preaching to them —and of dying as a martyr. While attending the Lateran Council in Rome in 1215, he formed a lasting friendship with St. Dominic. The following year he obtained from Pope Honorius III the Portiuncula Indulgence. In 1217, when the General Chapter organized provinces and missions in European countries and the Holy Land, he volunteered to go to France. But Cardinal Hugolin (later Pope Gregory IX) persuaded him to remain in Italy, where he preached throughout 1218. The next year, however, he left two Vicars to govern the Order and sailed to join the Crusaders at the siege of Damietta in Egypt. There at the risk of his life he preached to the Sultan.

The Saint's return to Italy in 1220, suffering from malaria and glaucoma, marked the beginning of the great spiritual trial in his life when (according to his first biographer) he complained that some of his friars were "piercing me with a hard sword and stabbing it into my heart all day." Within a few months he obtained from the Holy See the appointment of Cardinal Hugolin as Protector of the Order, and then he proceeded to resign as its effective administrator, naming in his place Peter Catani and (after the latter's death in 1221) the famous Brother Elias. Next he wrote the long, eloquent Rule of 1221, but found that he must revise and rewrite it twice before it was formally approved in 1223.

In order to understand the nature of this great trial, this "dark night of the spirit," which the Poverello suffered for over two years, we must have a clear idea of the novel form of the religious life which he introduced into the traditional mold of monastic chastity, poverty, and obedience. In his mind the basic conception of the Order of Friars Minor was quite simple: it was the literal, deliberate imitation of the way of life of Christ and His Apostles as described in the Gospels. In practical application this meant an itinerant life divided almost equally between prayer and preaching and supported by work (if possible manual) or by begging, with the greatest stress laid on voluntary self-denial and renunciation of property—all for the single purpose of enabling oneself and inducing others to live a life of ever closer union with Christ in His Church.

Now an objective study of early Franciscan documents definitely reveals that some friars, represented by the two Vicars of 1219 and later by Brother Elias, failed to grasp or accept this ideal. In its stead they advocated a combination of traditional monastic asceticism and conventual life with a more active and especially a more intellectual apostolate. As a result, St. Francis found an influential group within the Order trying to modify the way of life which he was convinced that God had inspired him to adopt.

In the end, while retaining as much of his original ideal as he could, he humbly submitted to the prudent mediation and guidance of his friend, Cardinal Hugolin, who persuaded him that some degree of adaptation was essential so that the Order might most effectively "repair the Church" by contributing a full measure of co-operation to the educational and missionary apostolates which were so sorely needed at that time. With the Cardinal he also instituted the lay Third Order in 1221.

The Poverello regained his peace of soul when in a crucial revelation he received divine assurance that Christ Himself would always remain the principal head of the Order and that all friars who sincerely wished to follow their Founder would do so. On emerging from this "dark night," the Saint experienced the mystical joy of holding in his arms the Babe of Bethlehem before the realistic crib which he prepared at Greccio on Christmas Eve, 1223. Then at last he was ready for "the final seal" (Dante): the transforming union that God bestowed on him by imprinting the five holy Stigmata on his body on Mount Alverna in September, 1224.

After another two years of increasingly painful illness (eye, stomach, liver, and spleen sickness, with dropsy), during which he composed the beautiful *Canticle of Brother Sun* and wrote an inspiring Testament, St. Francis died peacefully at his beloved Portiuncula on October 3, 1226. His friend Pope Gregory IX canonized him two years later.[1]

Such, in brief outline, was the life of the world's greatest follower of Christ. For one of the most vivid profiles of his personality which has ever been written, we must turn to the *Fioretti.*

## The Garden of "The Little Flowers"

*The Little Flowers of St. Francis* blossomed during the age of Dante in one of the most beautiful gardens on the face of the earth: the Marches (or borderlands) of Ancona and Fermo, a little-known area of central Italy lying between the Apennine Mountains and the Adriatic Sea that has been called a country of unsurpassed, almost terrible beauty . . . the world as a garden—the garden where God walked in the cool of the day."

To this paradise on earth, over a mountain pass, two strangely robed, barefooted young men of Assisi came in the spring of the year 1209. As Francis and Giles strode down the steep winding road in the shadow of rugged, barren peaks, the whole splendor of that gentle, serene, and lovely landscape was spread out before them. Their hearts thrilled as they perceived its waves of long wooded hills extending to the shining curve of the Adriatic seacoast only thirty miles away, its score of small white towns basking in the bright sun on the hilltops —"A city on a hill cannot be hidden"—and its deep warm valleys and sloping meadows rich in wheat and vines.

While the two friars walked through the vast forests of poplar, oak, and beech, and inhaled the soft fragrance of honeysuckle, clover, mountain lilies, and white roses mingling with the fresh sea breezes, it is no wonder that—as an old chronicle noted—"Francis sang aloud in French, praising and blessing the Lord for His goodness. For they felt their hearts overflow with fervent joy, as though they had acquired an immense treasure. And indeed they could rejoice greatly, because they had given up very much." Only a few weeks earlier in Assisi, with Brothers Bernard and Peter, they had begun to live a new life of extreme poverty, for the love of God. Now in return Divine Providence was giving them this treasure, this earthly paradise, as one of the choice fields of their realm-to-be. Francis prophesied then to Giles: "Our Order will be like a fisherman who throws out his net and catches a great mass of fishes. . . ."[2]

For in the garden of the Marches he found a fertile soil in which the seeds of his revolutionary spiritual message were soon destined to bear richer fruit than anywhere else. Psychologically the simple farmers and villagers of the Marches resembled him very much. They too were practical mystics endowed with a rare combination of poetic fancy and shrewd common sense, profound religious insight and sturdy practicality. Abstemious, frank, gay, friendly, warmhearted, loving nature and living close to it in their garden land, they embraced with extraordinary enthusiasm his inspiring message of peace through mystic union with God and good will toward all of God's creatures. In fact, his first biographer reported that when the Saint came to the city of Ascoli on a subsequent journey through the Marches, "in their eagerness to see and hear him they trod on one another. And thirty men (clerics and lay persons) received the holy habit of the Order from him."

Soon the woods and hills of the Marches were dotted with the humble little friaries which the early Franciscans called mere "places" (*loci*). By the year 1282 the small Province of the Marches had the amazing total of eighty-five friaries— twice as many as Tuscany or Umbria; and a century later it had ninety.[3] The majority of those houses were undoubtedly isolated hermitages, for the friars of the Marches were preeminently contemplatives. As evidence of this significant trend, the *Fioretti* contains no less than sixteen passages in which a friar is described as "praying in the woods."

It is therefore obvious that those friars had effectively grasped the essence of the spirituality of St. Francis: the absolute unconditional primacy of the interior life, the life of ceaseless inner union with God, constant humble contemplation of the Savior, and intimate loving communion with Him which the Poverello called "the spirit of prayer." And he repeatedly insisted that the various occupations of his friars should never be allowed to extinguish that holy flame in their hearts. Now it is evident that such a life can be lived in a hermitage in the woods or on a hillside better than anywhere else, as the contemplatives of all ages have found. It is also a little-known but significant fact that St. Francis himself founded and frequently resided in at least twenty-five such hermitages.

However, he also traveled and preached, not only all over Italy but even in France, Spain, Syria, and Egypt. His twenty-year apostolate was a continuous alternation between preaching tours and extended retreats in his beloved hermitages. But in that novel combination of the active with the contemplative life lay the key to the tragic dissension which nearly rent the Order in two during its first hundred years and which directly inspired the writing of *The Little Flowers* by a fervent friar of the Marches about the year 1330.

Owing to a number of factors, such as the extreme loftiness of the Saint's ideal and way of life and the amazingly rapid expansion of the Order—to say nothing of our fallen human nature—three more or less clearly identifiable groups began to evolve among his many followers soon after his death: (1) the moderates who were sincerely convinced that a minimum of adaptation was necessary in order to perform the various apostolic tasks which the Church was increasingly assigning to the friars in towns, universities, and foreign missions; (2) the relaxed who went decidedly too far—in the opinion of such ascetical moderate leaders as St. Bonaventure—and abandoned Franciscan poverty and contemplation in all but name; and (3) opposed to both those groups the so-called *zelanti*, or Spirituals, fanatical Joachimist rigorists and contemplatives who considered the Rule and Testament of St. Francis divinely inspired documents that were equal in rank to the Gospels and were destined to effect in an imminent new age the

complete regeneration of the Church and society along lines
allegedly foretold in writings of the famous twelfth-century
Abbot Joachim of Calabria, who was "gifted with the pro-
phetic spirit" (Dante).


## The Author

A brief outline of the bitter century-long conflict between
those three groups is necessary in order to understand the
historical function, the basic theme, and many of the characters and topical allusions of *The Little Flowers*. But instead
of presenting a dry chronicle of events, we shall try to enable
the reader to relive those momentous decades as they were
experienced by the great writer who is the author of the *Actus*
(the Latin original of the *Fioretti*): Brother Ugolino di Monte
Santa Maria. Unfortunately very little information about his
life and activities is available. Nevertheless, thanks to his book
we know a good deal about his close friends and their associates of the preceding generation. Several of them played
prominent roles in the history of the Order in the Marches,
and their lives and example had a profound influence on his
outlook and hence on his writings.

Hitherto unknown documents of 1294 and 1342 which
were discovered in local archives in 1957 by Father Giacinto
Pagnani, O.F.M.—and generously communicated to me—es-
tablish that his surname was Boniscambi (not Brunforte
of Sarnano) and that members of that family were then
well-to-do citizens of the little town of Monte Santa Maria in
Giorgio, now called Montegiorgio, in the Marches. The years
of his birth and death are not on record, but since he knew
Brother John of Penna who died about 1270, he himself must
have entered the Order at least a few years earlier. And we
know that he was still living in 1342.[4] His active career therefore spans the crucial period 1270–1340 when the dramatic
conflict involving the Spirituals came to a crisis. By 1280 all
of the first companions of St. Francis had probably died.
Ugolino does not claim to have met any of them, but his intimate friend, a lay brother named James of Massa, had known
Brothers Leo, Masseo, Giles, Juniper, and Simon as well as
St. Clare. Moreover, Ugolino was acquainted with at least

three other friars of the second generation who had known the Saint's companions (see the Chart showing the oral tradition of the *Actus-Fioretti*).

Principally from James of Massa the young Ugolino heard many fascinating and inspiring stories about the Poverello that were not included in the incomplete official biographies by Thomas of Celano and St. Bonaventure. At this time only the latter's *Legenda* was approved by the Order. However, in 1276 a General Chapter issued a call for additional material concerning the lives of St. Francis and his companions. Perhaps it was then that Brother Ugolino began to take notes on the unpublished anecdotes that he heard the older friars tell while sitting around the fire on long winter evenings in a hermitage in the Marches.

A talented writer, he could not fail to notice that these new materials added depth and verve and color to the standard portrait of the Poverello. Moreover, they contributed a considerable number of vivid new sketches of his adventures during the early years of the Order with his favorite companions, particularly Brothers Leo, Masseo, Bernard, Giles, and Rufino. Several delightful stories told by Brother James of Massa illustrated the way of life which the Saint led with the first friars in their little hermitages, such as the Carceri on Mount Subasio above Assisi. Above all, Brother Ugolino imbibed from his several informants—and later transmitted to the world in his book—much of the joy-filled spirit of St. Francis and his faithful followers of the first generation.

### The Spirituals

In those evening conversations—or perhaps alone with Brother James in the woods—Ugolino no doubt also learned more about the painful beginnings of dissension among the friars during the Poverello's lifetime. The tribulations of his closest companions after his death were common knowledge.

Brothers Bernard, Masseo, and Riccieri suffered repression. Bernard even had to leave Assisi and did not dare to return until the despotic Brother Elias was deposed as General in 1239 and subsequently excommunicated. While St. Francis was alive, his relations with Elias, according to the earliest documents, were marked by mutual respect and affection. But after the Founder's death, Elias' unmastered pride and ambition apparently became his dominant motives. It was therefore natural that his sensational fall and death-bed repentance resulted in the circulation of all sorts of stories about him, true and false, and that the Spirituals later made him a symbol of their opponents.

It must be emphasized at this point, however, that none of the intimate companions of St. Francis, although they may have sympathized to some extent with the zeal for poverty and self-denial of the Spirituals, was ever accused of the latter's doctrinal errors or rebellious actions. Nevertheless, like the outspoken Blessed Brother Giles, they did not hesitate to manifest their disapproval of the relaxed party in the Order.

Under Elias or his successor some seventy Spirituals in the Marches, including Simon of Assisi, Lucido the Elder, and Matthew of Monte Rubbiano, were severely punished and exiled. But a new Minister General, Blessed John of Parma (1247–57), liberated and pardoned them. Unfortunately, although he was a saintly man, he was apparently tainted with the doctrinal errors of Joachimism, which resulted in his resignation and trial under his successor, St. Bonaventure (1257–74). Only the intervention of a cardinal (later Pope Hadrian V) enabled John to retire to the hermitage of Greccio for the rest of his life. Brother James of Massa's famous Vision of the Tree in Chapter 48 expresses the intense resentment of the Spirituals over the trial of their friend Blessed John of Parma.

Now in 1274—during Ugolino's early years in the Order— a new crisis arose in the Marches. A rumor (later proved unfounded) that the Second Council of Lyons would impose the collective legal ownership of property on all religious orders led the Spirituals to assert that they would never accept such a ruling. Feeling ran high as the friars of the province divided into two factions. Finally the leading Spirituals, including the two later known as Angelo of Clareno and Liberato of Macerata, were condemned by their superiors to life imprisonment for heresy and insubordination.

However, in 1289 a new General visited the province, liberated them, and assigned them to a mission to Armenia. But finding themselves pursued by accusations, they returned to Italy in 1294 and sought the advice of several prominent Spirituals who had remained in the Marches and Umbria: Conrad of Offida, Peter of Montecchio, and the famous Umbrian friar-poet Jacopone da Todi. All agreed that Liberato and Angelo should consult the new Pope Celestine V, a saintly old hermit monk. He gave them permission to live according to the Rule and Testament of St. Francis as a separate Order to be called the Poor Hermits of Pope Celestine.

But within a few months the elderly Pope made what Dante bitterly called "the great refusal": he resigned. When his successor, Boniface VIII, abolished the Poor Hermits, some of them fled to Greece. Henceforth their status with regard to both the Order and the Church was that of rebels. Their followers eventually divided into two groups: the *Clareni*, who were tolerated in some dioceses (e.g., those found later in La Foresta and Sarnano), and who later joined the Observant Franciscans; and the several heretical sects of *Fraticelli*. As Livario Oliger, O.F.M., the leading expert on the Spirituals, has pointed out, their movement failed because its members, despite their idealism, fell into the following grave errors: they stressed the contemplative life at the expense of the mixed life; they equated the Rule with the Gospel; they adopted the divisive Joachimist idea of a carnal Church persecuting a spiritual Church; and above all they erred in thinking that they could withdraw from obedience to the Church in the name of St. Francis who (as even Sabatier admitted)[5] always insisted on humble supernatural submission to the authority of the Church.

### Brother Ugolino and the Spirituals

At this crucial turning point in the history of the Order, Brother Ugolino and every other friar who sympathized in any way with the ascetical ideals of the Spirituals, insofar as they represented the spirit of the first friars, faced a soul-searing decision: should they join the Celestine Hermits or remain in the Order? Just at this time, in the fall of 1295, Conrad of Offida, one of the foremost Spirituals in the Marches, received an important letter from his friend, Jean Pierre Olieu (Olivi), a famous Spiritual leader in southern France with whom he had been closely associated in Florence and Mount Alverna in 1285–89, together with the brilliant Italian Spiritual Ubertino da Casale. In this long letter Olieu fervently urged Conrad and the other Spirituals of the Marches not to leave the Order. "For," he wrote, "did the holy Brother Giles or Brother Leo or Brother Masseo or the other companions of St. Francis who were similar to them in holiness ever leave the Order because of such things?"[6] Now Conrad had known Brother Leo well. In fact, before Leo died in 1270, St. Francis is said to have appeared to Conrad in a vision and told him to visit the elderly Leo in order to gather material about the Saint's life from him.

While it cannot be demonstrated that Olieu's letter prevented Conrad from leaving the Order, it is a fact that he and his intimate friend Peter of Montecchio—another prominent Spiritual—remained loyal Franciscans and apparently broke off relations with the separatist Spirituals under Angelo of Clareno and Ubertino da Casale. The influence which their decision had on Brother Ugolino can hardly be overestimated, since he writes of them as heroes and saints whom he venerated.

The wisdom of the stand taken by Conrad, Peter, and Ugolino received further confirmation during the unedifying verbal battles which raged before the world at the Papal Court in Avignon between 1309 and 1324, when several Popes had to redefine the doctrinal meaning of Christian and Franciscan poverty. This period of political contention between the various factions in the Order culminated in an anti-Spiritual Minister General joining forces with a Prince of Bavaria in electing an anti-Pope!

Now it is of profound significance for our understanding of *The Little Flowers* that at about this time we find the author, Brother Ugolino di Monte Santa Maria, in Naples. For Naples in those years was under the rule of King Robert the Pious and his devout Franciscan Tertiary wife, Queen Sancha, both of whom had a well-known sympathy for the Spirituals, while remaining loyal Catholics enjoying friendly relations with the Popes and the superiors of the Order. We can only surmise that Brother Ugolino went to this favorable center in order to

write his book. All we know is that in 1319 he was a witness
to a peace pact between two towns in the Marches, and in
1331 he testified briefly in Naples against Andrea da Gagliano,
a partisan of the excommunicated Minister General. It is noteworthy that when Brother Ugolino had to take a public stand
he sided with the elements in the Order that remained in union
with the Church. From a chronological note at the end of the
Chapter 41 (found in only two manuscripts), it appears that
he wrote that chapter—and hence perhaps most of his book
—after 1327.[7] In 1342, according to a recently discovered will,
he was back in the Marches. Then he disappears from history, leaving us his masterpiece, the *Actus Beati Francisci et
Sociorum Ejus* (*The Deeds of St. Francis and His Companions*), which became in the later Italian condensation, *I
Fioretti di San Francesco* (*The Little Flowers of St. Francis*).

By writing this most popular of all books on St. Francis, the
fervent and talented friar struck a powerful blow for the true
Franciscan ideal which he shared with James of Massa, Conrad of Offida, John of Alverna, and Queen Sancha: the reform
of the Order from within by the personal holiness of individ-
ual friars living the way of life of St. Francis to the fullest extent of their capacities. Perhaps in his old age, after witnessing
the tragic conflicts which had shaken the Order to its founda-
tions during his lifetime, he felt inclined to agree with the good
friend of his youth in the Marches, Blessed John of Alverna,
who, like all the saints, refusing to judge his brethren, had
declared before he died in 1322: "Sons, you did not come to
raise yourselves up as judges of others, but to offer your wills
to God. . . . When I came into the Order, I received this
grace from God, that for all the things I saw in the Order I
gave praise and thanks to God. And as a result I always lived
in peace."[8]

The effect on Ugolino of this attitude of Blessed John of
Alverna, as well as the example of several other saintly friars
who were not Spirituals, notably James of Falerone and John
of Penna, is the saving element which raises his book far above
the level of a sectarian Spiritual tract to that of a masterly
treatise on the genuine Franciscan spirit. Their influence also
served to infuse into his soul and his writings that humble
supernatural submission to the Church and that crucial bal-

ance between the active and the contemplative lives, which, with strict poverty, formed the essence of the true Franciscan life as it was conceived and lived by the Founder.

Thanks in large part to the many charming stories of James of Massa about St. Francis and his companions, Brother Ugolino's *Actus* became one of the most popular Franciscan documents of the fourteenth and fifteenth centuries. (Over eighty fifteenth-century manuscripts of the Italian translation are extant.) Most of the *Actus* was incorporated into several fifteenth-century compilations of Franciscan history. Thus with other Spiritual works such as the *Speculum Perfectionis* and the writings of Olieu and Ubertino da Casale, it played a major role (that is only now being fully recognized) in the important Observant reform of the early fifteenth century under the three great Saints, Bernardine of Siena, James of the March, and John of Capistrano. Therefore by giving to the world a broader and more vivid portrait of the Poverello and by glorifying his early companions and his later followers in the Marches who, while remaining loyal members of the Order and the Church, had fought and suffered for the pure Franciscan ideal, Brother Ugolino made a major contribution to the regeneration of his Order.

## Historical Value

But the element in his work which is of the greatest value to the world today is the twenty-six incidents (not chapters) dealing with St. Francis which appear first in this book, written perhaps as much as a century after the Poverello's death. The reader has every right to know to what extent this relatively late document is historically reliable. How trustworthy was Brother James of Massa, Ugolino's principal informant? Obviously we should not take literally the statement that all his visions and words were inspired by the Holy Spirit. He was no more infallible than any other chronicler. But it should be recorded to his credit that independent accounts of four of his stories which have come to light in recent decades tend to confirm his reports, at least in their main outlines.[9] True, the alleged meeting of Brother Giles and King Louis was apparently based on a confusion with another Giles. And the tales in the *Actus* concerning the controversial Brother Elias are no doubt highly inaccurate in detail if not in substance, although they were widely accepted at the time. A polemical element is undeniably present, but it is found in only ten of the *Actus'* seventy-five chapters (and several may not have been written by Ugolino).

Nevertheless, even after we admit that the work undoubtedly shows a certain tendency to overstress the marvelous, that a few chapters may border on the legendary, and that some passages betray literary embellishment, the fundamental question remains: what do the foremost modern students of the book have to say regarding the value of its unique additions to our knowledge of St. Francis and his companions? The substance of their verdict is that the *Actus* represents, not folklore, but a direct oral tradition transmitted by several of the Saint's closest friends—Leo, Masseo, and Giles—through a few intermediaries to the author, and that this oral tradition, although occasionally inaccurate in chronology and topography, is in the main reliable, unless disproved by earlier evidence. With all due reservations, the definite historical value of the *Fioretti's* special contribution to our appreciation of St. Francis has been acknowledged by such scholars as Paul Sabatier, the Bollandist François van Ortroy, S.J., Archbishop Paschal Robinson, O.F.M., the Capuchin Father Cuthbert, the Anglican historian John R. H. Moorman, and the great *Fioretti* expert Benvenuto Bughetti, O.F.M., of the Collegio di San Bonaventura at Quaracchi—with Msgr. Michele Faloci-Pulignani, Maurice Beaufreton, and G. M. Bastianini, O.F.M. Conv., dissenting.

How then can we explain the puzzling fact that many of its most interesting stories were not recorded in the first official biographies of the Saint, which were based on the testimony of a number of his companions, including Leo, Angelo, and Rufino? The answer is quite simple. It is really a matter of psychology. The Poverello's best friends would naturally hesitate to mention—and an official biographer would hesitate to describe—a recently canonized Saint of the Church shaking hands with a wolf or eating nothing for forty days or telling his companion to twirl around in a public crossroad or go into a church and preach a sermon while wearing only his

breeches. Such delightful human-interest anecdotes are either
not reported to the first official biographer or (as the subtitle
of the *Actus* specifically states) they are deliberately "omitted," especially in the case of a colorful Saint like the Poverello
about whom innumerable little-known anecdotes were only
gradually recorded in the century after his death—so many in
fact that I have been able to collect well over one hundred
in *The St. Francis Nobody Knows* and *Fifty Animal Stories
of St. Francis*, which are still unknown today.

The same criterion applies with still greater force to the
intimate spiritual experiences which Francis may have revealed to one or two close friends who in turn hesitated to
report them for publication until decades had passed.

## The "Actus"

Unfortunately the monks and friars who copied medieval
manuscripts functioned more nearly like modern newspaper
rewrite men than like photoduplicating machines. They did
not hesitate to edit the text before them by condensing it or by
trying to improve its vocabulary, syntax, and titles. Being
only human, they often misread and miscopied. As a rule, they
concocted new versions of unfamiliar personal and place
names. Most confusing of all, sometimes they freely changed
the order of the chapters, and if the codex on which they
were writing still had some blank space at the end, they
proceeded to fill it with miscellaneous matter, which the next
copyist then included in his manuscript.

As a consequence of these faulty methods of transcription,
we do not know today exactly how many chapters Brother
Ugolino's original *Actus* included, for scholars believe that
about six of the seventy-six that appear in Sabatier's edition
were perhaps added by scribes. But at least four anecdotes
which are not found in any hitherto collated *Actus* codex are
ascribed to Ugolino by the Franciscan annalist Luke Wadding
(d. 1667). The total, therefore, would still be about seventy-
five.

It is quite evident, however, that Ugolino's work comprises
two distinct sections, which are in fact separated by subtitles
in some manuscripts (and in this edition): (1) a series of

chapters dealing with St. Francis and his companions, including contemporaries such as St. Anthony, St. Clare, and Brother Simon of Assisi; and (2) another series dealing with some holy friars who lived in the Province of the Marches two or three generations later, most of whom were contemporaries of the author. However, the strong internal unity of style and theme which links both sections certainly suggests that the *Actus* as a whole was written by one principal author, Ugolino di Monte Santa Maria, who in fact names himself twice and refers to himself twelve times (all but two instances occurring in the second section). There is also one specific reference to a writer or secretary who recorded an anecdote as it was told to him by Ugolino.[10] A few other brief passages may be interpolations.

## The "Fioretti" and "The Considerations on the Holy Stigmata"

Between 1370 and 1385, about fifty years after Brother Ugolino had finished writing the *Actus*, a talented friar with a passion for anonymity decided to translate most of that work into Italian. His identity is still completely unknown. According to philologists, he probably came from the southeastern part of Tuscany, close to Umbria. He must have spent much time on Mount Alverna. Although we do not have the particular Latin manuscript which he used, it is evident that, when not condensing, he translated very faithfully. The humble yet elegant simplicity and charm of his style rank him as one of the great writers of medieval Italian literature, a worthy contemporary of Petrarch and Boccaccio.

He selected fifty-three of the most appealing chapters in both sections of the *Actus* and gathered them in a bouquet which he aptly called *Fioretti* (Little Flowers), a title that was then in vogue. Next he proceeded to compile an entirely new treatise entitled *The Considerations on the Holy Stigmata*, in which he skillfully combined another five *Actus* chapters with texts from Thomas of Celano, St. Bonaventure, various fourteenth-century Franciscan writings, and local traditions to form an inspiring new work which, despite its occasional lapses in chronology or topography, has been described as "the most beautiful piece of Franciscan literature that we possess."

## Additions

Within a century several important additions were made to
the *Fioretti* and *The Considerations on the Holy Stigmata* in
some fifteenth-century manuscripts: (1) *The Life of Brother
Juniper;* (2) *The Life of Brother Giles;* (3) *The Sayings of
Brother Giles;* (4) various *Additional Chapters* taken from the
*Actus* and other fourteenth-century Franciscan writings.

The first three additions, although not written by either
Brother Ugolino di Monte Santa Maria or the anonymous
translator of the *Fioretti,* have an organic affinity with the first
section of Ugolino's work, as they record the lives and sayings
of two of St. Francis' closest companions.

*The Life of Brother Juniper* is a striking illustration of a valuable document, the first extant version of which is found over
a century after the events which it narrates. Only brief references to the hilarious doings of the unpredictable clowning
friar appeared in earlier texts—for quite understandable reasons. Never was there a better example than Brother Juniper
of the need for firm spiritual direction. Our edition uses the
late fourteenth-century Latin text in *The Chronicle of the
Twenty-four Generals* except for Chapter 6, in which we have
included a more extensive Italian version containing an unknown incident that reveals the secret of Juniper's almost
Slavic cult of the Humiliated Christ.

Two early biographies of Brother Giles are available: a relatively short one written by Brother Leo after Giles' death in
1262, and a longer one in *The Chronicle.* Some early manuscript and printed editions of the *Fioretti* contain excerpts from
both. In this edition we have translated the complete Latin
text of Brother Leo's work as found in all published versions
of the best available manuscripts, adopting chapter headings
when necessary from *The Chronicle.*

The incomplete Italian translation of *The Sayings of Brother
Giles,* which is found in most modern editions of the *Fioretti*
and which has served as the basis for all foreign translations,
is extremely free, inaccurate, and unfaithful to the original in
style and spirit. Only the starkly simple Latin conveys all the
pith and pungency and power of the saintly Franciscan lay

brother who had the caustic wit of a Shaw and the love of paradox of a Chesterton. Yet even St. Bonaventure venerated him. We have translated the first twenty-one chapters of the Latin text.

Some medieval and modern editions of the *Fioretti* contain a miscellany of *Additional Chapters* ranging in number from one to twenty, usually including the famous *Canticle of Brother Sun*. Apart from *The Canticle* and two chapters borrowed from the *Actus*, most of them have no direct or indirect connection with Ugolino's work. They are taken from various compilations of anecdotes about the early friars which were made during the fourteenth century and which culminated in the four invaluable Summas of early Franciscan history: *The Conformities* of Bartholomew of Pisa (1399), the *Speculum Vitae* of Fabian of Igal (1440), *La Franceschina* of Giacomo Oddi of Perugia (1470), and the Spanish *Floreto de Sant Francisco* (1492).

The problem of the *Additional Chapters* presents modern editors of *The Little Flowers* with a choice of alternatives: (1) exclude all such materials; (2) include all twenty *Fioretti* additions; (3) include *The Canticle* and the nineteen *Actus* chapters that are not in the *Fioretti* or in *The Considerations on the Holy Stigmata;* or (4) include all thirty-seven additional chapters.

The Italian edition of Benvenuto Bughetti, O.F.M., followed the second course, although he considered the *Additional Chapters* "encumbering." The recent French editions of Alexander Masseron and Omer Englebert were modeled on Bughetti's, but used the ambiguous subtitle "Complete Edition," which a Franciscan critic has stated should rather read "Contaminated Edition." A recent Dutch version adopted the third alternative, i.e., presented a complete translation of the *Actus*. The translator and the publisher of this edition have also decided to follow the third course, thus bringing the complete work of Brother Ugolino to the public for the first time in English.

## The "Fioretti" Becomes a World Classic

The first printed edition of the *Fioretti* was published in 1476 in Vicenza, the first of seventeen editions in that century.

Soon, however, St. Francis himself, along with such works as *The Conformities* and *The Little Flowers*, came under the attacks of the Protestant Reformers. Pier Paolo Vergerio (1498–1565) in particular made the *Fioretti* a target of his zeal, denouncing the book as a shocking collection of blasphemous and ridiculous fables, although he felt obliged to admit that it contained some "golden words" and "jewels." Some critics have even asserted without any evidence that the work was once placed on the Index of Forbidden Books, but it was never listed in any edition of the Index. However, owing in part to these attacks, it was published only half a dozen times in the sixteenth century and almost forgotten in the seventeenth. The rationalistic scholars of the following century, including the Bollandists, looked upon it with disdain, despite its rebirth in popularity with the edition of Filippo Buonarroti in 1718.

The history of modern *Fioretti* studies began in 1822 with the important edition of Antonio Cesari, but did not bear significant fruit until Paul Sabatier and other scholars turned their attention to the original Latin text in a useless search for a nonexistent pre-*Actus Floretum* which they thought Wadding had used. A high point was reached in 1902 with Sabatier's preliminary edition of the *Actus*. However, it was based on only a few of the available manuscripts, and they lacked several *Fioretti* chapters; but the Latin text of those chapters was soon found in the valuable so-called Little Manuscript, which was published in 1914. The 1920s witnessed unproductive controversies concerning the region of origin of the *Fioretti* (Tuscany or the Marches) and regarding its historical value. The interest of scholars in its still unsolved problems unfortunately subsided, only to arise again after 1950 with the important studies of Quaglia, Pagnani, Vicinelli, Abate, Terzi, Petrocchi, Fortini, and others (see Bibliography).

Meanwhile the *Fioretti* had become "the breviary of the Italian people" and one of the favorite books of the reading public of all European and American countries. In 1952 a motion picture based on the book was made in Italy, with Franciscan friars playing all but the leading role. In the United States the Great Books Foundation recently added *The Little Flowers of St. Francis* to its reading and discussion program.

## A New Look at "The Little Flowers"

No less than seven different translations into English have appeared in the last hundred years (all but two by non-Catholics). However, none of those versions—and very few in any language—include certain features which are essential to give the reader a faithful reproduction and a true understanding of Brother Ugolino's work. In preparing this popular new edition, therefore, the translator and the publisher wished to provide it with several useful features embodying the contributions of modern Franciscan research.

This translation, while following the chapter-structure of the *Fioretti*, is based primarily on the original Latin text of the *Actus* as published not only in Sabatier's preliminary edition but in eight other printed versions. Thus it takes advantage of numerous significant variants (often needed to correct corruptions), and it includes the many important phrases, sentences, or entire paragraphs which were omitted either in the *Fioretti* or in the particular Latin manuscript which the Italian translator used. However, the Italian text has also been followed whenever it adds to the clarity or the beauty of the Latin.

This translation deliberately avoids an artificial Victorian imitation of medieval English in favor of modern colloquial English, which (as Michael Bihl, O.F.M., remarked of a German edition based in part on the Latin) may perhaps be less elegant, but has the compensating advantage of being more faithful to the original.

Again adopting a recommendation of the late Father Bihl, the greatest Franciscan scholar of our times, this edition is equipped with a minimum of brief Notes and References designed to supply: (a) correction or confirmation of historical data, (b) identification of all incidents first recorded in the *Actus*, and (c) compact references to relevant sources, parallel texts, or important topical studies. Unfortunately it is still true, as Paschal Robinson, O.F.M., wrote in 1912, that "no critical exhaustive study exists about the historical value of the single parts of the *Actus-Fioretti*." In view of the widespread popularity of the book and of its status as a classic of world literature, it would seem that the scholars of the Franciscan

Order owe to the public a thorough scientific study of each of its chapters. While the Notes of this edition are primarily designed for the average reader, the References may also be of some use to researchers who will prepare those long-overdue studies.

Three brief Appendices supply additional significant texts and comments on two of the work's most famous chapters, "The Perfect Joy" (Ch. 8) and "The Wolf of Gubbio" (Ch. 21), and provide a summary of factual and doctrinal information concerning the puzzling "Mystery of the Stigmata."

In addition, condensed Biographical Sketches outline the careers of all principal characters who are mentioned in more than one chapter, while a Chart shows the transmission of the oral tradition of the *Actus* from the companions of St. Francis to the author.

This edition would of course not be complete without a selective Bibliography of general texts and periodicals, important editions of the *Actus* and the *Fioretti*, and outstanding studies, for no such list of references is available.

Interested readers will no doubt also welcome the Map of the *Fioretti* Country which shows all the towns, villages, and hermitages in Umbria and the Marches that are mentioned in this book.

Lastly, a few technical points: scriptural quotations are adapted from the Douay-Rheims translation of the Vulgate (used in the *Actus-Fioretti*); chapter headings have been selected from various Latin or Italian versions (mostly the former), primarily for conciseness; personal and geographic names have been anglicized whenever that form seemed more natural; the term *Frater* (*Frate*) has been translated as "Brother" when used in the vocative or when accompanying a name (even of a priest) and as "friar" when standing alone; for the Latin *locus* referring to an early Franciscan friary, "Place" has been adopted in preference to "place," "friary," "monastery," or "convent."

The translator wishes to express his cordial thanks to the Florentine publishers Adriano Salani and G. C. Sansoni for their kind permission to make use of the editions of the *Fioretti* prepared, respectively, by Benvenuto Bughetti, O.F.M., and Mario Casella, which are now recognized as the best versions

of the Italian text. It is unfortunately impracticable to list all
the numerous historians and librarians—Franciscan and secular, Italian and American, Catholic and non-Catholic—who
have generously contributed advice, facts, articles, or books to
this work. However, Mr. Zoltan Haraszti, Keeper of Rare Books
at the Boston Public Library, deserves special mention with his
staff for their courtesy in facilitating my research in the valuable Paul Sabatier collection, where I found almost fifty important items in the great Protestant scholar's unpublished marginal notes. I can only record here my intense gratitude to all
who have assisted me—particularly to my wife who typed the
manuscript, and to Mr. John J. Delaney, editor of Image
Books, whose patient guidance improved my work—and ex-
culpate them from the errors and imperfections of this edition.

## Literary and Spiritual Qualities

The remarkable psychological insight and talent of the author of the *Actus* and the charming simplicity and elegance
of the Italian translator's style suffice to explain why the
*Fioretti* has long been considered a masterpiece of early Italian
literature. But to account for the book's rise in recent times to
the status of a classic of world literature, more profound causes
must be sought.

Here we touch on the secret of the popularity of St. Francis
himself and of all his faithful followers through the ages. Two
basic elements, which are not often found together in contemporary writing, probably arouse in modern readers of various
nationalities and cultures a lasting affection for *The Little
Flowers:* its strikingly natural humanness and its soaring spiritual power.

These charming anecdotes about the Poverello and his companions are rich in those human-interest qualities which all
popular entertainment and reading possess: dramatic movement, vivid personalities, and stirring emotion—to say nothing
of delightful humor. Moreover, they are narrated with a child-
like artlessness that is almost akin to that of the Gospels.

Surely it is primarily the fact that the *Fioretti* so faithfully
reflects the magnetic spirituality of St. Francis that has won
for it a permanent place in the hearts of mankind. More than

any other single book, it has brought St. Francis to the world because it has succeeded so well in capturing and communicating the very essence of his spirit and his message.

Today more than ever before, humanity is suffering because it is trying desperately to live without that spirit and that message, which are after all exactly the same as those of Christ, though transmuted by the magic of the Poverello's personal charm. Our unhappy world needs more than ever to learn from him the great lesson that true joy and peace are found only in loving and knowing and serving God as he did, with complete selflessness and dedication and humility. Today millions of spiritually starved souls rightly sense that Francis' pure, generous love for God and man and all created things is the only hidden source of power that will ever unite all men in the peaceable service of their Creator and of their neighbor.

Yet even in this heartless age of guided missiles for mass destruction it is an impressive and an encouraging fact that no less than one and a half million men and women throughout the world are actually serving their God and their neighbor in the various Franciscan religious and lay families.[11] In addition, there are many others, both in and out of the Catholic Church, who look upon the Little Poor Man of Assisi with love and veneration because his beautiful life is to them the most convincing proof on record that Christianity *can* be radiantly lived in this sad world.

Few books beside the New Testament convey that regenerating message so forcefully and so eloquently as *The Little Flowers*, for the simple reason that in its pages throbs the great vibrant heart of the most faithful follower and perfect imitator of Jesus Christ the world has ever seen.

In conclusion, here is a lovely old Franciscan text which strikingly illustrates that unique distinction of St. Francis of Assisi and which also summarizes one of the basic themes of *The Little Flowers*:

> One night when Blessed Peter Pettinaio of the Third Order was praying in the Cathedral of Siena, he saw Our Lord Jesus Christ enter the church, followed by a great throng of saints. And each time Christ raised His foot, the form of his foot remained imprinted on the ground. And all the saints

tried as hard as they could to place their feet in the traces of His footsteps, but none of them was able to do so perfectly. Then St. Francis came in and set his feet right in the footsteps of Jesus Christ.[12]

IN THE NAME OF OUR CRUCIFIED LORD

JESUS CHRIST

AND OF HIS VIRGIN MOTHER MARY

THIS BOOK CONTAINS

CERTAIN LITTLE FLOWERS, MIRACLES, AND INSPIRING STORIES

OF

THE GLORIOUS LITTLE POOR MAN OF CHRIST

SAINT FRANCIS

AND OF SOME OF HIS HOLY COMPANIONS

AS REVEALED BY THEIR SUCCESSORS

WHICH WERE OMITTED IN HIS BIOGRAPHIES

BUT WHICH ARE ALSO VERY USEFUL AND EDIFYING

TO THE PRAISE AND GLORY OF JESUS CHRIST! AMEN.

Part One

# THE LITTLE FLOWERS
# OF ST. FRANCIS

# I SOME MARVELOUS DEEDS OF ST. FRANCIS AND HIS FIRST COMPANIONS

## 1 About the Twelve First Companions of St. Francis

First it should be known that the glorious St. Francis was conformed to Christ in all the acts of his life. For just as the Blessed Christ, when He began His preaching, chose twelve Apostles to despise all things of this world and to follow Him in poverty and in the other virtues, so St. Francis, when he began to found the Order, had twelve chosen companions who were followers of the most complete poverty.

And just as one of the twelve Apostles of Christ, being rejected by God, in the end hanged himself by the neck, so one of the twelve companions of St. Francis, whose name was Brother Giovanni di Capella, left the Order, and in the end hanged himself by the neck with a rope. To the elect this is a great lesson and reason for humility and fear when they reflect that no one is certain of persevering to the end in the grace of God.

And just as those holy Apostles were for the whole world marvels of holiness, filled with the Holy Spirit, so these most holy companions of St. Francis were men of such sanctity that the world has not had such wonderful and holy men from the times of the Apostles until now. For one of them was caught up to the third heaven like St. Paul, and that was Brother Giles. Another—tall Brother Philip—was touched on the lips by an angel with burning coal, like Isaias the Prophet. Another—Brother Silvester, a very pure virginal soul—spoke with God as one friend with another, as Moses did. Another, by the keenness of his mind, soared up to the light of divine wisdom, like the eagle (John the Evangelist)—and this was the very humble Brother Bernard, who used to explain Holy Scripture in a most profound way. Another was sanctified by God and canonized in Heaven while he still was living in this world, as though he had been sanctified in his mother's womb—and he was Brother Rufino, a nobleman of Assisi and a man most loyal to Christ.

And thus all of them were favored with evident marks of sanctity, as will be reported hereafter.[1]

## 2 About the Perfect Conversion of Brother Bernard

Among them the first and the first-born, both by priority in time and by privilege of sanctity, was Brother Bernard of Assisi, whose conversion took place in the following way.

St. Francis was still dressed as a layman, although he had already renounced the world, and for a long time he had been going around Assisi looking contemptible and so mortified by penance that many people thought he was simple-minded, and he was laughed at as a lunatic and driven away with many insults and stones and mud by his relatives and by strangers. Yet being nourished by the divine salt and firmly established in peace of soul by the Holy Spirit, he bore all the insults and scorn with great patience and with a joyful expression on his face, as if he were deaf and dumb.

Now the Lord Bernard of Assisi, who was one of the richest and wisest noblemen in the whole city, whose judgment everyone respected, wisely began to think over St. Francis' utter contempt for the world and his great patience when he was insulted and the fact that although he had been scorned and despised by everybody for two years, he always appeared more serene and patient. He began to think and to say to himself: "This Francis certainly must have great graces from God."

So inspired by the Lord, he invited St. Francis to have supper with him one evening. The Saint humbly accepted and ate supper with him that evening.

But the Lord Bernard secretly wished and planned to put St. Francis' holiness to a test, so he invited him to sleep in his house that night. And when St. Francis humbly agreed, the

Lord Bernard had a bed prepared in his own room, in which a lamp was always kept burning at night.

Now St. Francis, as soon as he entered the room, in order to conceal the divine graces which he had, immediately threw himself down on the bed, showing that he wished to sleep. But the Lord Bernard planned to watch him secretly during the night. And he too soon lay down, and he used such cunning that after he had rested in bed a while, he pretended to be sleeping soundly, and he began to snore loudly.

Therefore St. Francis, who faithfully concealed the secrets of God, when he thought that the Lord Bernard was fast asleep, during the first part of the night, got out of bed and began to pray. Looking up to Heaven and raising his hands, he prayed with intense fervor and devotion, saying: "My God and my all!" And he sobbed out those words with so many tears and kept repeating them with such devout persistence that until matins he said nothing but "My God and my all!"[1]

St. Francis said this while contemplating and marveling at the goodness of Almighty God who seemed to take compassion on the imperiled world and was preparing to provide a remedy for its salvation through the little poor man Francis himself. For being enlightened by the spirit of prophecy, when he foresaw the great things which God was to accomplish through his Order, and when under the guidance of that same spirit he considered his own incapacity and small degree of virtue, he called upon the Lord in order that God, without whom human weakness can achieve nothing, should by His compassion and almighty power supply, assist, and accomplish what he himself would not be capable of doing. And that is why he said: "My God and my all!"[2]

Now the Lord Bernard saw the very inspiring actions of St. Francis by the light of the lamp burning there. And while he was attentively meditating on the words which the Saint was saying and carefully observing his devotion, he was touched by the Holy Spirit in the depths of his heart and felt inspired to change his life.

Therefore when morning came, he called St. Francis and said to him: "Brother Francis, I have definitively resolved in my heart to leave the world and to follow you in whatever you order me to do."

When St. Francis heard this, he rejoiced in spirit and said: "Lord Bernard, what you say is so great and difficult an undertaking that we must seek the advice of Our Lord Jesus Christ concerning it, so that He Himself may deign to show us His will regarding it and teach us how we should carry it out. So let us go together to the Bishop's Church where there is a good priest, and we will have him say Mass, and after hearing it, we will pray there until tierce. And in our prayer we will ask the Lord Jesus Christ to deign to show us in three openings of the missal the way which He wants us to choose." And the Lord Bernard replied that this pleased him a great deal.

They therefore went to the Bishop's Church.[8] And after they had heard Mass and had prolonged their prayers until tierce, the above-mentioned priest took up the missal at the request of St. Francis and the Lord Bernard. And having made the Sign of the Cross, he opened it three times in the name of Our Lord Jesus Christ.

At the first opening there appeared the words that Christ said in the Gospel to the young man who asked Him about the way of perfection: "If you wish to be perfect, go, sell all you have, and give to the poor, and come, follow Me."

At the second opening there appeared those words which Christ said to the Apostles, when He sent them out to preach: "Take nothing for your journey, neither staff, nor wallet, nor bread, nor money," wishing thereby to teach them that they should place all their hope for support in God and concentrate entirely on preaching the Holy Gospel.

At the third opening of the missal there appeared those words which Christ said: "If anyone wishes to come after Me, let him deny himself, and take up his cross, and follow Me."

And when they had seen these words, St. Francis said to the Lord Bernard: "That is the counsel which Christ gives us. So go and do perfectly what you have heard. And blessed be Our Lord Jesus Christ who has deigned to show us His Gospel way of life!"

On hearing this, the Lord Bernard immediately went and brought out all his possessions and sold all that he owned—and he was very rich. And with great joy he distributed it all to the poor. Carrying the money in a pocket in his bosom, he gave it out plentifully and generously to widows and orphans and pilgrims and monasteries and hospitals. And in all this St. Francis accompanied him and faithfully assisted him.

Now when a man named Lord Silvester saw St. Francis giving away so much money to the poor and causing it to be given away, he was seized with greed and said to St. Francis: "You did not pay me all you owe me for those stones you bought from me to repair the churches." Then St. Francis, marveling at his greed and not wishing to argue with him, as a true observer of the Gospel—giving to everyone who asked—put his hands in the Lord Bernard's bosom and then placed them, filled with money, in the Lord Silvester's bosom. And he said: "If you ask for more, I will give you still more." But he was satisfied and went home.

Later that evening, when he thought over what he had done during the day, he reproached himself for his greed and reflected on the fervor of the Lord Bernard and the holiness of St. Francis. And on the first and the second and the third night he was given this vision from God: from the mouth of St. Francis came forth a cross of gold, the top of which reached to Heaven, while its arms seemed to extend from east to west, to the end of the world. As a result of this vision he was touched by the Lord, and for God's sake he disposed of all his property and gave it away to the poor. And later he became a Friar Minor, and in the Order he was so holy and filled with grace that he spoke with God as one friend to another, as St. Francis several times experienced and as will be narrated hereafter.

Similarly the Lord Bernard, after he had given all his property away for God, received so much grace from God that he was often rapt in contemplation by the Lord. And St. Francis used to say of him that he was worthy of all reverence, and that it was he who had founded this Order, because he was the first who had begun to live the poverty of the Gospel by distributing all he had to the poor, retaining nothing whatever for himself, but offering himself naked to the arms of the Crucified. May He be blessed by us forever and ever! Amen.[4]

### 3   *About the Humility and Obedience of St. Francis and Brother Bernard*

Francis, the very devout servant of Christ Crucified, had become almost blind, so that he could see very little, as a result of his severe penances and continual crying.

One day he left the Place where he was and went to a Place where Brother Bernard was staying, in order to speak about God with him. And when he came to the Place, he found that Bernard was praying in the woods, completely absorbed in holy contemplation and united with God.[1]

Then St. Francis went into the woods and called him, saying: "Come and talk to this blind man!"

But Brother Bernard did not answer St. Francis and did not go to him because, as he was a great contemplative, his consciousness was at that moment suspended and uplifted in God.

Brother Bernard had a remarkable ability to speak about God, as St. Francis had already experienced many times, and that was why he wanted very much to talk to him. So after a while he called him again a second and a third time, repeating the same words: "Come and talk to this blind man." But Brother Bernard did not hear him at all and so he did not answer him or go to him. Therefore St. Francis went away, feeling rather disappointed, wondering and almost complaining within himself that Brother Bernard, though called by him three times, had not wanted to come to him.

While St. Francis was thinking that way as he returned along the path, he said to his companion when he had gone a short distance: "Wait here for me a moment!" And he went to a solitary spot nearby and began to pray, begging God to reveal to him why Brother Bernard had not answered him. And as he was praying, a Voice came to him from God that said: "And why are you troubled, you poor little man? Should a man leave God because of any creature? Brother Bernard, when you called him, was united with Me, and so he could not go to you or answer you. Therefore do not be surprised if he could not talk to you, because he was so unconscious of his surroundings that he did not hear you at all."

As soon as St. Francis had received this answer from God, he immediately went back toward Brother Bernard in a great hurry, in order humbly to accuse himself of the thoughts he had just had against him.

But the holy Brother Bernard, seeing him coming, ran to meet him and threw himself down at his feet. And the humility of St. Francis and the charity and reverence of Brother Bernard came together. Then St. Francis made him get up and told him very humbly about the thoughts and anxiety which he had regarding him, and how God had reproved him for it. And he ended thus: "Under holy obedience I order you to do whatever I command you."

Brother Bernard was afraid that St. Francis might order something excessive, as he often did, and he wanted to escape from that obedience as best he could. So he replied: "Father, I am ready to obey you, if you also promise me to do what I command you."

St. Francis replied: "I agree."

Then Brother Bernard said: "Say what you want me to do, Father."

And St. Francis said: "In order to punish my presumption and the insolence of my heart, I command you under holy obedience, while I lie on my back on the ground, to put one of your feet on my throat and the other on my mouth, and thus to step over me three times from one side to the other. And while stepping on me that way, you are to insult and mock me, and especially you are to say: 'Lie there, you country lout, son of Pietro di Bernardone!' And you must inflict still greater insults on me, saying: 'How is it that you have so much pride, since you are such an extremely worthless creature?'"

When Brother Bernard heard this, it was hard for him to do it. However, because of holy obedience, he performed as courteously as he could what St. Francis had commanded him to do.[2]

And when it was done, St. Francis said: "Now, Brother Bernard, order me to do what you want me to do, because I have promised to obey you."

Brother Bernard said: "Under holy obedience I command you that whenever we are together you scold and correct me harshly for my faults."

When St. Francis heard this, he was very much surprised, because Brother Bernard was so holy that St. Francis had great reverence for him and did not think that he should be corrected at all.

And henceforth St. Francis avoided staying too long with him, so that on account of that obedience he should not have to speak a word of correction to him whom he knew to be so saintly. But though he longed to see Brother Bernard or to hear him speak of God, he would leave him and go away as soon as he could. And it was wonderful to see how certain conflicts took place in the revered Father and in his first-born son, Brother Bernard, especially how the obedience and charity and the patience and humility of each came into conflict. But it was also very inspiring to see the affection and awe and humility with which St. Francis treated and spoke to Brother Bernard.

To the praise and glory of Christ. Amen.

## 4    How St. Francis Went to St. James, and about the Question That the Angel Asked Brother Elias

In the beginning of the Order, when there were few friars and the Places had not yet been occupied, St. Francis, to satisfy his devotion, went to visit St. James in Galicia, and he took with him some companions, one of whom was Brother Bernard.[1]

And while they were traveling along the road, they found in a certain land a poor sick man for whom St. Francis felt compassion, and he said to Brother Bernard: "Son, I want you to stay here and take care of this sick man."

And Brother Bernard quickly and humbly genuflected and bowed his head, thus accepting the command of the holy Father, and he stayed in that place while St. Francis went on to St. James with his other companions.

When they arrived there and were spending the night in prayer and adoration in the Church of St. James, God revealed to St. Francis in that church that he should found many Places throughout the world, because his Order was destined to spread and grow to a large number of friars. Consequently, as a result of this divine command, he henceforth began to accept Places in various lands.

When he returned along the same road, St. Francis found Brother Bernard. Now the sick man whom he had entrusted to his care had fully recovered. So the following year St. Francis gave Brother Bernard permission to go to St. James. Meanwhile St. Francis went back to the Valley of Spoleto.

And when he was staying in a certain isolated Place[2]—he and Brother Masseo and Brother Elias and several others—one day St. Francis went into the woods to pray. Now his companions had great reverence for him and they were afraid to disturb his prayers in any way because of the great graces which God gave him in prayer.

And it happened that a very handsome young man, dressed as though prepared to go on a journey, came to the gate of the Place and knocked so urgently and loudly and long that the friars were amazed at such an unusual way of knocking. Brother Masseo went to the gate and opened it and said to the young man: "Son, I think you have never yet come to a gate of the friars because you don't know how to knock gently."

The young man answered: "And how should I knock?"

Brother Masseo said to him: "Knock three times, one knock after another. Then wait until the friar has said one Our Father and comes to you. And if he does not come by that time, knock again."

But the young man replied: "I am in a great hurry because I have to make a long journey—that is why I knock so loudly. I have come here to talk to Brother Francis, but he is now in contemplation in the woods, and therefore I don't want to disturb him. So go and send Brother Elias to me, for I have heard that he is very wise, and I want to ask him a question."

Brother Masseo went and told Brother Elias to go to the young man, but as he was proud and irritable he became angry and refused to go. Then Brother Masseo did not know what to do or what to say to the young man, because if he said, "Brother Elias cannot come," he would be lying, but if he said that Brother Elias was angry and did not want to come, he was afraid of giving the young man a bad example.

Meanwhile, as Brother Masseo delayed in coming, the young man knocked again as before. Then the friar went back to the gate and said to the young man: "You did not knock the way I told you to do."

Now the young man was an angel of God, and foreseeing Brother Masseo's answer, he said: "Brother Elias does not want to come to me, so go to Brother Francis and tell him that I have come to speak to him, but as I do not want to disturb him in his prayers, tell him to send Brother Elias to me."

Then Brother Masseo went to Brother Francis, who was praying in the woods with his face turned toward Heaven. And he told him all the young man's message and Brother Elias' answer.

Without moving or lowering his face, St. Francis said: "Go and tell Brother Elias to go to the young man immediately, under obedience."

When Brother Elias heard St. Francis' order, he was so angry that when he went to the gate, he opened it violently, making a great noise and disturbance, and said to the young man: "What do you want?"

And the young man replied: "Take care, Brother, not to be angry, as you appear to be, because anger darkens the mind and prevents it from discerning the truth."

Then Brother Elias said: "Tell me what you want!"

And the young man answered: "I ask you whether it is lawful for observers of the holy Gospel to eat whatever is set before them, as Christ said to His Disciples. And I also ask you whether it is lawful for any man to impose on observers of the holy Gospel anything that is contrary to the liberty of the Gospel?"

Brother Elias replied arrogantly: "I know the answer very well, but I won't tell you. Go on your way."

The young man said: "I know the answer to that question better than you do."

Then Brother Elias angrily slammed the gate shut and went away. And he began to think over the question and to be puzzled, and he could not find the answer. For when he was Vicar of the Order, he had dared to make a regulation, beyond the Gospel and beyond the Rule of St. Francis, that no friar in the Order could eat meat, so that question was aimed directly at him. Not knowing how to solve the problem, and reflecting that the young man was humble and that he had said he could answer that question better than Brother Elias could, he went back to the gate and opened it in order to ask the young man about the question. But when he opened the gate, no one was there, and he could not find the young man, though he searched round about. For that young man was an angel of God, and he had not waited because Brother Elias in his pride was not worthy to speak with an angel.[3]

When this had happened, St. Francis, to whom all had been revealed by God, came back from the woods and strongly scolded Brother Elias in a loud voice, saying: "You do wrong, proud Brother Elias, for you drive away the holy angels who come to visit and instruct us. And I tell you, I strongly fear that your pride will make you end your days outside this Order." And so it happened to him later, as St. Francis had prophesied to him, for he died outside the Order.

On the same day and at the same hour as that angel went away, he appeared in the same form to Brother Bernard, who was returning from St. James and was standing on the bank of a broad river which he could not cross. And he greeted Brother Bernard in his own language, saying: "God give you peace, good Brother."

Brother Bernard marveled at the young man's good looks and the language of his own native land, and also at his peaceful greeting and joyful features, and he asked him: "Where are you from, good young man?"

The angel replied: "I have come from the Place where St. Francis is staying, and I went to speak with him, but I was unable to do so because he was contemplating God in the woods, and I did not want to disturb him. And Brother Masseo and Brother Giles and Brother Elias were staying with him in that Place. And Brother Masseo taught me how to knock at your gate the way the friars do. But Brother Elias, because he did not want to answer the question which I asked him, later regretted it and wanted to hear and see me, but could not do so."

And after saying these words, the angel said to Brother Bernard: "Dear friend, why are you hesitating to cross the river?"

He replied: "Because I am afraid of the deep water I see."

And the angel said: "Let us cross over together—don't be afraid!"

And taking his hand, in an instant he deposited Brother Bernard safely on the other side of the river.

Then Brother Bernard realized that he was one of God's angels, and with great devotion and reverence and joy he said in a loud voice: "O blessed angel of God, tell me your name!"

The angel replied: "Why do you ask my name, which is wonderful?"

And having said that, he disappeared and left Brother Bernard very happy, so that he was filled with joy during all the rest of his journey. And he noted the day and hour when the angel had appeared to him. And when he came to the Place where St. Francis was staying with his above-mentioned companions, he told them the whole story in detail. Therefore, they knew for sure that that same angel had appeared to them and to him on the same day and at the same hour. And they gave thanks to God. Amen.

## 5  *How Brother Bernard Went to Bologna*

Because St. Francis and his companions had been called by God and chosen to bear the Cross of Christ in their hearts and in their actions and to preach it by their words, they appeared to be and they were crucified men, both as to their habit and their austere life and their deeds and their actions. Therefore they had a greater desire to receive shame and insults for the love of Christ than the vain honors or respect or praise of the world. On the contrary, they rejoiced in being insulted, and they were made sad by being honored. And so they went through the world as pilgrims and strangers, taking with them nothing but Christ Crucified. And because they were living branches of the True Vine, that is Christ, they produced great and good fruit in the souls that they won for God.

Once in the beginning of the Order it happened that St. Francis sent Brother Bernard to Bologna, in order that he might produce fruit for God according to the grace which God had given him. And Brother Bernard, arming himself with the Cross of Christ and taking holy obedience as his companion, made the Sign of the Cross and left and came to Bologna.[1]

When the children saw him in his unusual and contemptible

habit, they began to make fun of him and insult him, as they would do with a lunatic. But the truly holy Brother Bernard endured all their insults not just patiently but with intense joy, for the love of Christ. Moreover, in order to follow and be truly conformed to Christ, who made Himself "the reproach of men and the outcast of the people," he deliberately went to the public square of the city and sat down there so that people would have a better opportunity to make fun of him. While he was sitting there, many boys and men gathered around him, and some of them pulled him back and others forward, and some threw dust at him and others stones, and some pushed him heavily this way and others that way. At all these insults Brother Bernard remained patient and rejoicing, with a happy expression on his face, and he did not resist or complain at all. Furthermore, he deliberately went back to that same square for several days in order to endure the same mistreatment. And no matter how much they insulted him, his joyful features always showed that his soul was not troubled.

And because patience is a work of perfection and a proof of virtue, a certain learned doctor of laws, seeing and reflecting on Brother Bernard's constancy and virtue in not being at all disturbed by any injury or insult for so many days, said to himself: "That man certainly must be a saint." And going up to Brother Bernard he asked him: "Who are you, and why have you come here?"

As his reply Brother Bernard put his hand in his bosom and brought out the Rule of St. Francis, which he bore in his heart and practiced in his deeds, and gave it to him to read.[2]

And when that judge had read it through, reflecting on its lofty state of perfection, he was utterly amazed, for he was an intelligent man. And turning to his companions, he said with the greatest surprise and admiration: "This certainly is the highest form of religious life I have ever heard of! And therefore this man and his companions are some of the holiest men in the world. So those who insult him are committing a very great sin, for he should be given the highest honors rather than insults, as he is a great and true friend of God!"

And he said to Brother Bernard: "My dear man, if I were to show you a place where you could serve God in a suitable way, and you wished to accept it, I would be very glad to give it to you for the salvation of my soul."

Brother Bernard answered: "Dear Sir, I believe that Our Lord Jesus Christ has inspired you to do this. And so I willingly accept your offer, for the honor of Christ."

Then the judge led Brother Bernard with great joy and affection to his home. And later he showed him the place which he had promised him and gave it to him, and arranged and prepared it all at his own expense. And henceforth he became a father and a special protector to Brother Bernard and his companions.[3]

And Brother Bernard began to be greatly honored by the people because of his holy conversation, to such a point that those who were able to touch or hear or see him considered themselves blessed. But Brother Bernard, like a true and humble disciple of Christ and the humble Francis, fearing that the worldly honor which was being shown him there might interfere with the peace and salvation of his soul, left and went back to St. Francis.

And he said to St. Francis: "Father, the Place has been founded in the city of Bologna, so send some friars to maintain it and stay there, because I am no longer doing any good there. Rather because of the great honor that is shown me, I am afraid of losing more than I would gain there."

Then St. Francis, on hearing in detail all that God had performed through Brother Bernard, rejoiced and exulted and began to praise and thank God, who was thus beginning to spread the poor little followers of the Cross for the salvation of the people. And then he chose some of his companions and sent them to Bologna and Lombardy. And as the devotion of the people toward them increased, they began to accept many Places in various districts.

To the praise and reverence of the good Jesus. Amen.

### 6 *About the Beautiful Death of Brother Bernard*

Brother Bernard was so holy that St. Francis, as long as he lived, had a very affectionate reverence for him, honored him by often talking with him, and in his absence often praised him highly.

One day while St. Francis was praying devoutly, God revealed to him that Divine Providence was to allow Brother Bernard to endure many fierce attacks by devils. For many days, therefore, St. Francis, having great compassion for Brother Bernard, whom he loved as a son, prayed to God for him and wept, committing him to the Lord Jesus Christ, so that He might give him victory over so many trials of the devil. And while St. Francis was thus praying and watching anxiously and fervently, one day God gave him this answer: "Francis, do not fear, because all the temptations by which Brother Bernard is to be assailed are given to him and permitted by God so that he may practice virtues and earn a crown of merit. And in the end he will win a joy-filled victory over all the enemies that attack him. For this Brother Bernard is one of the great ones of the Kingdom of God."

St. Francis was made exceedingly happy by this answer, and he gave fervent thanks to the Lord Jesus Christ. And henceforth he no longer had any doubts or fears regarding Brother Bernard, but loved him with ever increasing joy and treated him with still greater affection and reverence.[1]

He showed this affection for him not only during his life but also at the hour of his death. For when St. Francis was dying, like the holy Patriarch Jacob, with his devoted sons standing around him, grieving and weeping over the departure of their beloved father, he asked: "Where is my first-born son? Come to me, dear son, so that my soul may bless you before I die."

Then Brother Bernard whispered to Brother Elias, who was at that time the Vicar of the Order: "Father, go to the Saint's right hand, so that he may give you his blessing."

And when Brother Elias had placed himself on the right side, St. Francis, who had lost his sight from too much weeping, put his right hand on Brother Elias' head and said: "This is not the head of my first-born, Brother Bernard."

Then Brother Bernard went to his left hand, and St. Francis crossed his arms, and changing the position of his hands, put his left hand on the head of Brother Elias and his right hand on Brother Bernard's head, and he said to him: "May the Father of my Lord Jesus Christ bless you with every spiritual and heavenly blessing in Christ. And as you were the first one in this holy Order who was chosen to give the example of the Gospel life and to imitate Christ in the poverty of the Gospel —for not only did you generously give up your belongings and distribute them entirely among the poor for the love of Christ, but you also offered yourself up to God as a sweet sacrifice in this Order—so may you be blessed by Our Lord Jesus Christ and by me, His poor little servant, with everlasting blessings, going and coming, watching and sleeping, living and dying. Whoever blesses you shall be filled with blessings, and whoever curses you shall not remain unpunished. Be the head of all your Brothers, and let all the friars obey your orders. You have permission to receive into the Order and to send away from it whomever you wish. And no friar has any power over you. And you are free to go and to stay wherever you wish."[2]

After the death of St. Francis the friars loved and revered Brother Bernard as a venerable father. And when he was dying, many friars came to him from different parts of the world. Among them was that angelic and godlike Brother Giles. When he saw Brother Bernard, he said with great joy: "*Sursum corda,* Brother Bernard, *sursum corda!*"

And the saintly Brother Bernard secretly told one of the friars to prepare for Brother Giles a place suitable for contemplation.

And when Brother Bernard came to the last hour of his life, he had them raise him up, and he said to the friars who were standing around him: "My very dear Brothers, I do not want to say much to you. But you must reflect that I have been in the state in which you are now, and that you will be in the state in which I am now. And I find this in my soul: not for a thousand worlds equal to this one would I want not to have served Our Lord Jesus Christ. And I accuse myself to my Lord and Savior Jesus Christ and to you of all my offenses. My dearest Brothers, I beg you to love one another."

And after he had said those words and given some other good advice, as he lay back on his bed, his features became very radiant and joyful, to the great amazement of all the friars present. And in that same joy his blessed and most holy soul, crowned with glory, passed from this life to the life of the angels and the blessed in the victory which had previously been promised to him.

To the praise and glory of Christ. Amen.

### 7 About the Wonderful Forty Days' Fast of St. Francis

Because St. Francis, the true servant of Christ, was in certain things like another Christ, given to the world for the salvation of people, God the Father willed to make him in many acts conformed and similar to His Son Jesus Christ, as is shown in the venerable group of the twelve companions, in the wonderful mystery of the holy Stigmata, and in the continuous fast of the holy Lent which he kept in this way.

Once when St. Francis was near the Lake of Perugia on Carnival Day, in the home of a devoted friend with whom he had spent the night, he was inspired by God to go and spend Lent on an island of that lake. St. Francis therefore asked his friend, for the love of Christ, to take him in his little boat to an island in the lake where no one lived, and to do this on the night of Ash Wednesday, so that nobody should perceive it.

And that man, because of the great devotion which he had for St. Francis, thoughtfully carried out his wish. He arose during the night and made his little boat ready and rowed him to that island on Ash Wednesday. And St. Francis took along nothing but two small loaves of bread.

When they reached the island and the friend was leaving to return home, St. Francis earnestly asked him not to reveal to anyone that he was there, and not to come for him before Holy Thursday. And so the man left the island, and St. Francis remained there alone.

As there was no building where he could take shelter, he went into a very dense thicket in which many thorn bushes and small trees had made a sort of little cabin or den. And he began to pray and contemplate heavenly things in that place.

And he stayed there all through Lent without eating and without drinking, except for half of one of those little loaves of bread. His devoted friend came for him on Holy Thursday, as they had agreed. And of the two loaves, he found one whole and half of the other. It is believed that St. Francis ate the other half out of reverence for the fast of the Blessed Christ, who fasted forty days and forty nights without taking any material food. And so with that half loaf he drove from himself the poison of pride, while according to Christ's example he fasted forty days and forty nights.

Later through his merits, God performed many miracles in that place where St. Francis had practiced such marvelous abstinence. From that time men began to build houses on that island and to live there; and in a short while a fine and large walled village was made. And there also is the Place of the Friars Minor which is called the Island. And the men and women of that village still have great reverence and devotion for the place where St. Francis kept that Lent.[1]

To the glory of Christ. Amen.

## 8   *How St. Francis Taught Brother Leo That Perfect Joy Is Only in the Cross*

One winter day St. Francis was coming to St. Mary of the Angels from Perugia with Brother Leo, and the bitter cold made them suffer keenly. St. Francis called to Brother Leo, who was walking a bit ahead of him,[1] and he said: "Brother Leo, even if the Friars Minor in every country give a great example of holiness and integrity and good edification, nevertheless write down and note carefully that perfect joy is not in that."

And when he had walked on a bit, St. Francis called him again, saying: "Brother Leo, even if a Friar Minor gives sight to the blind, heals the paralyzed, drives out devils, gives hearing back to the deaf, makes the lame walk, and restores speech to the dumb, and what is still more, brings back to life a man who has been dead four days, write that perfect joy is not in that."

And going on a bit, St. Francis cried out again in a strong voice: "Brother Leo, if a Friar Minor knew all languages and all sciences and Scripture, if he also knew how to prophesy and to reveal not only the future but also the secrets of the consciences and minds of others, write down and note carefully that perfect joy is not in that."

And as they walked on, after a while St. Francis called again forcefully: "Brother Leo, Little Lamb of God, even if a Friar Minor could speak with the voice of an angel, and knew the courses of the stars and the powers of herbs, and knew all about the treasures in the earth, and if he knew the qualities of birds and fishes, animals, humans, roots, trees, rocks, and waters, write down and note carefully that true joy is not in that."

And going on a bit farther, St. Francis called again strongly: "Brother Leo, even if a Friar Minor could preach so well that he should convert all infidels to the faith of Christ, write that perfect joy is not there."

Now when he had been talking this way for a distance of two miles, Brother Leo in great amazement asked him: "Father, I beg you in God's name to tell me where perfect joy is."

And St. Francis replied: "When we come to St. Mary of the Angels, soaked by the rain and frozen by the cold, all soiled with mud and suffering from hunger, and we ring at the gate of the Place and the brother porter comes and says angrily: 'Who are you?' And we say: 'We are two of your brothers.' And he contradicts us, saying: 'You are not telling the truth. Rather you are two rascals who go around deceiving people and stealing what they give to the poor. Go away!' And he does not open for us, but makes us stand outside in the snow and rain, cold and hungry, until night falls—then if we endure all those insults and cruel rebuffs patiently, without being troubled and without complaining, and if we reflect humbly and charitably that that porter really knows us and that God makes him speak against us, oh, Brother Leo, write that perfect joy is there!

"And if we continue to knock, and the porter comes out in anger, and drives us away with curses and hard blows like bothersome scoundrels, saying: 'Get away from here, you dirty thieves—go to the hospital! Who do you think you are? You certainly won't eat or sleep here!'—and if we bear it patiently and take the insults with joy and love in our hearts, oh, Brother Leo, write that that is perfect joy!

"And if later, suffering intensely from hunger and the painful cold, with night falling, we still knock and call, and crying loudly beg them to open for us and let us come in for the love of God, and he grows still more angry and says: 'Those fellows are bold and shameless ruffians. I'll give them what they deserve!' And he comes out with a knotty club, and grasping us by the cowl throws us onto the ground, rolling us in the mud and snow, and beats us with that club so much that he covers our bodies with wounds—if we endure all those evils and insults and blows with joy and patience, reflecting that we must accept and bear the sufferings of the Blessed Christ patiently for love of Him, oh, Brother Leo, write: that is perfect joy!

"And now hear the conclusion, Brother Leo. Above all the graces and gifts of the Holy Spirit which Christ gives to His friends is that of conquering oneself and willingly enduring sufferings, insults, humiliations, and hardships for the love of Christ. For we cannot glory in all those other marvelous gifts of God, as they are not ours but God's, as the Apostle says: 'What have you that you have not received?'

"But we can glory in the cross of tribulations and afflictions, because that is ours, and so the Apostle says: 'I will not glory save in the Cross of Our Lord Jesus Christ!' "[2]

To whom be honor and glory forever and ever. Amen.

### 9    *How God Spoke to St. Francis Through Brother Leo*

Once in the beginning of the Order St. Francis was with Brother Leo in a little Place where they did not have any books to use in saying the Divine Office. One night when they got up to recite matins, St. Francis said to Brother Leo: "Dear Brother, we have no breviary with which to say matins, but so as to spend the time in praising God, I will say something and you must answer what I tell you, and be careful not to change my words. I will say this: 'Oh, Brother Francis, you have done so much evil and sin in the world that you deserve hell'—and you, Brother Leo, shall answer: 'It is true that you deserve the depths of hell.' "

And the very pure-hearted Brother Leo replied with the simplicity of a dove: "All right, Father. Begin in the name of the Lord."

Then St. Francis began to say: "Oh, Brother Francis, you have done so many evil deeds and sins in the world that you deserve hell."

And Brother Leo answered: "God will perform so much good through you that you will go to Paradise."

And St. Francis said: "Don't say that, Brother Leo! But when I say: 'Oh, Brother Francis, you have done so many wicked things against God that you deserve to be cursed by God,' then you answer this way: 'You certainly deserve to be placed among the damned.'"

And Brother Leo replied: "All right, Father."

Then St. Francis said aloud, crying and sighing and beating his breast: "Oh, my Lord God of Heaven and earth, I have committed so many evil deeds and sins against You that I deserve to be utterly damned by You."

And Brother Leo answered: "Oh, Brother Francis, God will make you such that you will be remarkably blessed among the blessed."

St. Francis wondered why Brother Leo always answered just the opposite of what he told him to say, and he scolded him, saying: "Why don't you answer as I tell you, Brother Leo? I command you under holy obedience to answer what I tell you. I will say: 'Oh, wicked little Brother Francis, do you think God will have pity on you, for you have committed too many sins against the Father of mercy and the God of all consolation for you to deserve any mercy?' And you, Brother Leo, Little Lamb, answer: 'You certainly are not worthy of finding mercy.'"

And then Brother Leo answered: "Go ahead, Father, because I will say just what you tell me."

And St. Francis, kneeling down and lifting his hands toward the Lord and looking up to Heaven with a joyful expression, said very sadly: "Oh, Brother Francis, you great sinner—oh, you wicked Brother Francis, do you think God will have mercy on you, for you have committed so many sins?"

But Brother Leo answered: "God the Father, whose mercy is infinitely greater than your sins, will be very merciful to you and moreover will give you many graces."

At this reply St. Francis was gently angry and patiently troubled, and he said to Brother Leo: "Brother, why have you dared to go against obedience and to have already answered so many times the opposite of what I told you?"

And then Brother Leo exclaimed very humbly and reverently: "God knows, dear Father, that each time I have resolved in my heart to answer as you told me, but God makes me speak as pleases Him and not as pleases me."

St. Francis was amazed at this and said to him: "Brother, I beg you to answer me this time as I tell you."

Brother Leo replied: "Go ahead, in God's name, for this time I will answer as you wish."

And St. Francis cried out, weeping: "Oh, wicked little Brother Francis, do you think God will have mercy on you?"

Brother Leo answered: "Yes, Father, God will have mercy on you. Besides, you will receive a great grace from God for your salvation, and He will exalt and glorify you for all eternity, because 'whoever humbles himself shall be exalted'—and I cannot say anything else because God is speaking through my mouth!"

And they stayed up until dawn in this humble contest, with many tears and great spiritual consolations.[1]

To the praise and glory of Our Lord Jesus Christ. Amen.

### 10    *How Brother Masseo Tested St. Francis' Humility*

Once St. Francis was staying at the Place of Portiuncula with Brother Masseo of Marignano, a man of great holiness and discernment and grace in speaking about God, because of which St. Francis loved him very much.

One day when St. Francis was coming back from the woods, where he had been praying, and was at the edge of the forest, Brother Masseo went to meet him, as he wanted to find out how humble he was, and he said to St. Francis, half jokingly: "Why after you? Why after you? Why after you?"

St. Francis replied: "What do you mean, Brother Masseo?"

"I mean, why does all the world seem to be running after you, and everyone seems to want to see you and hear you and obey you? You are not a handsome man. You do not have great learning or wisdom. You are not a nobleman. So why is all the world running after you?"

On hearing this, St. Francis rejoiced greatly in spirit, and he raised his face toward Heaven and stood for a long time with his mind absorbed in God.

Coming back to himself, he genuflected and praised and gave thanks to God. Then with great fervor of spirit he turned to Brother Masseo and said: "You want to know why after me? You want to know why after me? You really want to know why everyone is running after me? I have this from the all-holy eyes of God that see the good and the evil everywhere. For those blessed and all-holy eyes have not seen among sinners anyone more vile or insufficient than I am. And so in order to do that wonderful work which He intends to do, He did not find on earth a viler creature, and therefore He chose me, for God has chosen the foolish things of the world to put to shame the wise, and God has chosen the base things of the world and the despised, to bring to naught the noble and great and strong, so that all excellence in virtue may be from God and not from the creature, in order that no creature should glory before Him, but 'let him who takes pride, take pride in the Lord,' that honor and glory may be only God's forever."

Then Brother Masseo, at such a humble answer spoken with such fervor, was deeply moved and knew for sure that St. Francis was grounded in true humility, as a true and humble disciple of Christ.[1]

To the glory of Christ. Amen.

### 11 *How St. Francis Made Brother Masseo Twirl Around*

Once St. Francis was traveling in Tuscany with Brother Masseo, whom he most willingly used to take along as his companion because of his pleasant conversation and unusual discretion and because of the help which he gave him in his raptures by dealing with people and hiding him from them, so that they should not disturb him.

One day they were walking along a road together, with

Brother Masseo going a bit ahead of St. Francis. But when they came to a crossroad where three roads met, where they could go to Siena or Florence or Arezzo, Brother Masseo said: "Father, which road should we take?"

St. Francis replied: "We will take the road God wants us to take."

Brother Masseo said: "How will we be able to know God's will?"

St. Francis answered: "By the sign I will show you. Now under the merit of holy obedience I command you to twirl around in this crossroad, right where you are standing, just as children do, and not to stop turning until I tell you."

So Brother Masseo obediently began to turn around, and he twirled around so long that he fell down several times from dizziness in his head, which usually results from such turning. But as St. Francis did not tell him to stop, and he wanted to obey faithfully, he got up again and resumed his gyrations.

Finally, after he had been twirling around bravely for a long time, St. Francis said: "Stand still! Don't move!"

And he stood still. And St. Francis asked him: "What direction are you facing?"

Brother Masseo replied: "Toward Siena."

And St. Francis said: "That is the road God wants us to take."

While they were going along that road, Brother Masseo marveled very much over St. Francis' having made him twirl around in such a childish way before all the lay people who were passing by. However, because of his reverence for the Saint, he did not dare say anything to him about it.

When they drew near to Siena and the people of the city heard that St. Francis was arriving, they came out to meet him. And out of devotion they carried him and his companion under the arms to the Bishop's mansion, so that their feet hardly touched the ground all the way.

Now at that same hour some citizens of Siena were fighting together, and two of them had already been killed. So St. Francis went there and stood up and preached to those men in such a beautiful and holy way that he brought all of them back to peace and great unity and harmony.

And when the Bishop of Siena heard about the wonderful

deed which St. Francis had performed, he invited him into his house and made him welcome that day and also overnight. The next morning the truly humble St. Francis, who sought nothing but the glory of God in his actions, got up early with his companion and left without the Bishop's knowing it.

Brother Masseo murmured at this as they went along the road, saying to himself: "What has this good man done? Yesterday he made me twirl around like a child, and today he did not say one good word or express his thanks to the Bishop who honored him so much!"

And it seemed to Brother Masseo that St. Francis had acted indiscreetly. But then, by an inspiration from God, he came back to his senses and reproached himself severely in his heart: "Brother Masseo, you are too proud, passing judgment on the work of divine grace, and you deserve hell for revolting against God with your indiscreet pride! For yesterday on this journey Brother Francis performed such holy deeds that they would not be more marvelous if an angel had done them. So if he should order you to throw stones, you should obey him. For all that he did on this journey was the work of God, as is shown by the good results that followed. Because if he had not made peace between those men who were fighting, not only would the sword have slain many bodies, as it had already begun to do, but—what is still worse—many souls would have been thrown into hell by the devil. And so you are very stupid and proud for murmuring against what was clearly the will of God."

Now all these things which Brother Masseo was pondering in his heart as he walked along a bit ahead of St. Francis were revealed to the latter by the Holy Spirit, to whom all things are bare and open. And calling Brother Masseo, the Saint came up to him and disclosed the secret thoughts of Masseo's heart by saying to him: "Hold to the thoughts which you are thinking now, for they are good and helpful to you and inspired by God. But the complaining that you did before was blind and evil and proud and was planted in your soul by the devil."

On hearing this, Brother Masseo was astounded, and he clearly realized that St. Francis knew the secrets of his heart, and he understood with certainty that the Spirit of divine wisdom and grace guided St. Francis in all his actions.[1]

To the praise and glory of Our Lord Jesus Christ. Amen.

### 12   *How St. Francis Tested Brother Masseo's Humility*

St. Francis wished to humble Brother Masseo, in order that pride should not lift him up because of the many gifts and graces which God gave him, but that he should advance from virtue to virtue by means of humility. And one day when he was staying at a solitary Place with those truly saintly first companions of his, among whom was Brother Masseo, he said to him before all the others: "Brother Masseo, all these companions of yours have the grace of prayer and contemplation, but you have the grace of preaching the word of God to satisfy the people who come here. Therefore, so that the friars may give themselves better to prayer and contemplation, I want you to take care of opening the gate, giving out alms, and cooking the meals. And when the friars are eating, you are to eat outside the gate of the Place, so that you may satisfy with a few good devout words the people who come to the Place before they knock at the gate. Thus no one else need go out to them except you. And you are to do this by merit of holy obedience."

Then Brother Masseo immediately bowed his head, lowering his cowl, and humbly accepted and faithfully obeyed this order. For several days he served as gatekeeper, almsgiver, and cook.

But his companions, as men enlightened by God, began to feel intense remorse in their hearts, reflecting that Brother Masseo was a man of great perfection and prayer, like themselves or even more so, and yet the whole burden of the Place was put on him and not on them. Consequently they agreed among themselves, and they went to ask their holy Father that he should kindly distribute the duties among them, because their consciences simply could not bear having Brother Masseo burdened with so much work. Furthermore, they felt that they would be cold in their prayers and troubled in their consciences if Brother Masseo were not relieved of those duties.

On hearing this, St. Francis agreed to their charitable suggestion. And calling Brother Masseo, he said to him: "Brother Masseo, these companions of yours want to share in the duties I gave you, and so I want those duties to be divided among them."

And Brother Masseo said very humbly and patiently: "Whatever you impose on me—either in part or in whole—I consider it done by God."

Then St. Francis, seeing their charity and Brother Masseo's humility, gave them a wonderful sermon on holy humility, teaching them that the greater the gifts and graces which God gives us, the greater is our obligation to be more humble, because without humility no virtue is acceptable to God. And after he had finished preaching, he distributed the duties among them with great affection and gave all of them a blessing by the grace of the Holy Spirit.[1]

To the glory of God. Amen.

13  *How St. Francis Lifted Brother Masseo in the Air, and How St. Peter and St. Paul Appeared to St. Francis*

Just as Christ, according to the Gospels, sent His disciples, two by two, to all the towns and places where He was to go Himself, so St. Francis, the wonderful servant of God and true follower of Christ, in order to conform himself perfectly to Christ in all things, after he had gathered twelve companions, following Christ's example sent them out in groups of two to preach to the world. And to give them an example of true obedience, he himself was the first to go, following the precedent of Christ who first practiced what He taught. Therefore, after he had assigned various other parts of the world to his friars, taking Brother Masseo as his companion, he set out on the road toward the Province of France.

And one day when they came to a village and they were quite hungry, they went begging for bread for the love of God, according to the Rule. And St. Francis went along one street and Brother Masseo along another. But because St. Francis was a very small and insignificant-looking man, and therefore was considered a common little pauper by nearly all who did not know him—for human foolishness judges not what is inside but only externals—he received nothing but a few mouthfuls of food and some small pieces of dry bread. But to Brother Masseo, because he was a tall handsome man, people gave plenty of good large pieces and some whole loaves.

When they had finished begging, the two came together to eat somewhere outside the village. They found nothing but the dry ground to put their begged food on, because that region was quite bare of stones. However, with God's help they came to a spring, and beside it there was a fine broad stone, which made them very happy. And each of them placed on the stone all the pieces of bread he had acquired. And when St. Francis saw that Brother Masseo's pieces of bread were more numerous and better and bigger than his, he was filled with intense joy because of his longing for poverty, and he said: "Oh, Brother Masseo, we do not deserve such a great treasure as this!" And he repeated those words several times, raising his voice each time.

Brother Masseo replied: "Dear Father, how can this be called a treasure when there is such poverty and such a lack of things that are necessary? For here we have no cloth, no knife, no dish, no bowl, no house, no table, no waiter, no waitress."

St. Francis answered: "That is what I consider a great treasure—where nothing has been prepared by human labor. But everything here has been supplied by Divine Providence, as is evident in the begged bread, the fine stone table, and the clear spring. Therefore, I want us to pray to God that He may make us love with all our hearts the very noble treasure of holy poverty, which has God as provider."

And after he had said those words and they had prayed and eaten the pieces of bread and drunk the spring-water, they arose to travel on toward France, rejoicing and praising the Lord in song.

And when they came to a certain church, St. Francis said to his companion: "Let's go in and hear Mass and pray there." And they entered, but as the priest was absent, St. Francis went and hid himself behind the altar to pray. And while he was praying there, he was given a divine vision and visitation which wholly inflamed his soul with such an intense longing and love for holy poverty that flames of love seemed to issue from his face and mouth.

And going out to his companion, all afire with love, he said forcefully: "Ah! Ah! Ah! Brother Masseo, give yourself to me!"

And he said it three times. And Brother Masseo, greatly amazed at his fervor, threw himself into the holy Father's arms when he said for the third time: "Give yourself to me!"

Then St. Francis, with his mouth wide open and repeating very loudly "Ah! Ah! Ah!", by the power of the Holy Spirit lifted Brother Masseo up in the air with his breath and projected him forward the length of a long spear.

Brother Masseo was completely astounded. And later he told his companions that he had experienced such spiritual consolation and sweetness in being raised up and projected by the breath of St. Francis that he did not recall ever having had such a great consolation in all his life.

Afterward, St. Francis said to Brother Masseo: "My dear companion, let us go to Rome, to St. Peter and St. Paul, and let us pray to them to teach us and help us to possess the infinite treasure of holy poverty."

And St. Francis added: "My dear and beloved Brother, the treasure of blessed poverty is so very precious and divine that we are not worthy to possess it in our vile bodies. For poverty is that heavenly virtue by which all earthly and transitory things are trodden under foot, and by which every obstacle is removed from the soul so that it may freely enter into union with the eternal Lord God. It is also the virtue which makes the soul, while still here on earth, converse with the angels in Heaven. It is she who accompanied Christ on the Cross, was buried with Christ in the Tomb, and with Christ was raised and ascended into Heaven, for even in this life she gives to souls who love her the ability to fly to Heaven, and she alone guards the armor of true humility and charity. So let us pray to the very holy Apostles of Christ, who were perfect lovers of the pearl of the Gospel, that they may procure this grace for us from Our Lord Jesus Christ: that He who was an observer and teacher of holy poverty may by His most holy mercy grant that we may be worthy to be true lovers and observers and humble followers of the most precious and beloved poverty of the Gospel."

When they arrived in Rome, conversing like that, they entered St. Peter's Church. And St. Francis went into one corner of the church and Brother Masseo to another, to pray to God and His holy Apostles that they might instruct and help them to possess the treasure of holy poverty. And they prayed for it a long time with great devotion and many tears. And while they were persisting humbly in prayer, the holy Apostles Peter and Paul appeared in great splendor to St. Francis. And embracing and kissing him, they said: "Brother Francis, because you request and desire to observe what Christ and the holy Apostles observed, Our Lord Jesus Christ Himself has sent us to announce to you that your desire is fulfilled and your prayer is answered, and that the treasure of very holy poverty is perfectly granted to you and your followers. And on behalf of Christ we say to you that whoever by your example perfectly follows this desire shall be assured of the happiness of everlasting life. And you and all your followers shall be blessed by God." And after saying those words they disappeared, leaving St. Francis full of consolation.

Rising from prayer, he went to his companion and asked him whether God had revealed anything to him. And he answered: "No." Then St. Francis told him how the holy Apostles had appeared to him and what they had revealed to him. And both of them were so overwhelmed with joy and happiness that they forgot to go to France, as they had first intended, but they hastened to return to the Valley of Spoleto, where this heavenly and angelical way of life was to begin.[1]

To the glory of Christ. Amen.


14  *How While St. Francis Was Talking about*
*God with His Companions, Christ Appeared*
*among Them*


Our very holy Father Francis plunged all his thoughts into the Blessed Christ and directed all his efforts and desire and way of praying and speaking and conversing toward His pleasure, both for himself and his other companions. Once he wanted to talk about God and the salvation of souls when he was with those holy and apostolic companions of his, who had come together in one Place to converse about God, at the beginning of the Order when they were still few. The devout Father was sitting with his very blessed sons, and in fervor of spirit he commanded one of them in the name of the Lord to open his mouth and say about God whatever the Holy Spirit suggested to him.

But after that friar had at once obediently begun and uttered marvelous words under the guidance of the Holy Spirit, St. Francis told him to be quiet. And he ordered another to speak similarly about God according to the grace which the Holy Spirit gave him. And as he obeyed and was speaking very profoundly about the Lord by the grace of God, St. Francis imposed silence on him as he had on the first. And he ordered a third to say something without preparation in praise of Our Lord Jesus Christ. And this third one, following the example of the others and humbly obeying, likewise began to speak so profoundly about the hidden mysteries of the Divinity that there was no doubt the Holy Spirit was speaking through him and the others, and that St. Francis certainly knew it.

And this was also proved by a specific sign, for while those holy simple men were thus, at their Father's command, one after another speaking sweetly about God and spreading the perfume of divine grace, Our Lord Jesus Christ appeared among them in the form of a very handsome young man. And giving His blessing to all of them, He filled them with such sweet grace that St. Francis as well as all the others were rapt out of themselves, and they lay on the ground like dead men, completely unconscious.

Later when they regained consciousness, St. Francis said to them: "My dear Brothers, give thanks to Our Lord Jesus Christ who has deigned to reveal the treasures of divine wisdom through the mouths of simple ones. For God is He who opens the mouths of infants and the dumb, and when He wishes, He makes the tongues of the simple speak very wisely."[1]

To the glory of God. Amen.

### 15   *How St. Clare Ate a Meal with St. Francis and His Friars*

When St. Francis was staying in Assisi, he often visited St. Clare and consoled her with holy advice. And as she had a very great desire to eat a meal with him once, she asked him several times to give her that consolation. But St. Francis always refused to grant her that favor.

So it happened that his companions, perceiving St. Clare's desire, said to St. Francis: "Father, it seems to us that this strictness is not according to divine charity—that you do not grant the request of Sister Clare, a virgin so holy and dear to God, in such a little thing as eating with you, especially considering that she gave up the riches and pomp of the world as a result of your preaching. So you should not only let her eat a meal with you once, but if she were to ask an even greater favor of you, you should grant it to your little spiritual plant."

St. Francis answered: "So you think I should grant this wish of hers?"

And the companions said: "Yes, Father, for she deserves this favor and consolation."

Then St. Francis replied: "Since it seems so to you, I agree. But in order to give her greater pleasure, I want this meal to be at St. Mary of the Angels, for she has been cloistered at San Damiano for a long time and she will enjoy seeing once more for a while the Place of St. Mary where she was shorn and made a spouse of the Lord Jesus Christ. So we will eat there together, in the name of the Lord."

He therefore set a day when St. Clare would go out of the monastery with one sister companion, escorted also by his companions.

And she came to St. Mary of the Angels. And first she reverently and humbly greeted the Blessed Virgin Mary before her altar, where she had been shorn and received the veil. And then they devoutly showed her around the Place until it was mealtime. Meanwhile St. Francis had the table prepared on the bare ground, as was his custom.

And when it was time to eat, St. Francis and St. Clare sat down together, and one of his companions with St. Clare's companion, and all his other companions were grouped around that humble table. But at the first course St. Francis began to speak about God in such a sweet and holy and profound and divine and marvelous way that he himself and St. Clare and her companion and all the others who were at that poor little table were rapt in God by the overabundance of divine grace that descended upon them.

And while they were sitting there, in a rapture, with their eyes and hands raised to Heaven, it seemed to the men of Assisi and Bettona and the entire district that the Church of St. Mary of the Angels and the whole Place and the forest which was at that time around the Place were all aflame and that an immense fire was burning over all of them. Consequently the men of Assisi ran down there in great haste to save the Place and put out the fire, as they firmly believed that everything was burning up.

But when they reached the Place, they saw that nothing was on fire. Entering the Place, they found St. Francis with St. Clare and all the companions sitting around that very humble table, rapt in God by contemplation and invested with power from on high. Then they knew for sure that it had been a heavenly and not a material fire that God had miraculously shown them to symbolize the fire of divine love which was burning in the souls of those holy friars and nuns. So they withdrew, with great consolation in their hearts and with holy edification.

Later, after a long while, when St. Francis and St. Clare and the others came back to themselves, they felt so refreshed by spiritual food that they paid little or no attention to the material food. And when that blessed meal was over, St. Clare, well accompanied, returned to San Damiano.

The sisters were very glad to see her, for they had feared that St. Francis might send her to direct some other monastery, as he had already sent her holy sister Agnes to be Abbess of the Monastery of Monticelli in Florence. For at that time St. Francis was sending Sisters out to rule other monasteries. And he had once said to St. Clare: "Be prepared, in case I have to send you somewhere else." And she had replied like a truly

obedient daughter: "Father, I am always ready to go wherever
you send me." And so the sisters rejoiced greatly when they
had her back. And henceforth St. Clare was much consoled
in the Lord.[1]

To the glory of Christ. Amen.

### 16   *How God Revealed to St. Clare and Brother*
### *Silvester That St. Francis Should Go and Preach*

The humble servant of Christ, St. Francis, at the beginning
of his conversion, when he had already gathered many companions and received them in the Order, was placed in a great
agony of doubt as to what he should do: whether to give himself only to continual prayer or to preach sometimes. He
wanted very much to know which of these would please Our
Lord Jesus Christ most. And as the holy humility that was in
him did not allow him to trust in himself or in his own prayers,
he humbly turned to others in order to know God's will in
this matter.

So he called Brother Masseo and said to him: "Dear Brother,
go to Sister Clare and tell her on my behalf to pray devoutly
to God, with one of her purer and more spiritual companions,
that He may deign to show me what is best: either that I
preach sometimes or that I devote myself only to prayer. And
then go also to Brother Silvester, who is staying on Mount
Subasio, and tell him the same thing."

This was that Lord Silvester who had seen a cross of gold
issuing from the mouth of St. Francis which extended in length
to Heaven and in width to the ends of the world. And this
Brother Silvester was so devout and holy that God immediately
granted or revealed to him whatever he asked in prayer. The
Holy Spirit had made him remarkably deserving of divine com-
munications, and he conversed with God many times. And
therefore St. Francis was very devoted to him and had great
faith in him. This holy Brother Silvester often stayed alone in
the above-mentioned Place.

Brother Masseo went, and as St. Francis had ordered him,
gave the message first to St. Clare and then to Brother Silvester. When the latter received it, he immediately set himself

to praying. And while praying he quickly had God's answer. And he went out at once to Brother Masseo and said: "The Lord says you are to tell Brother Francis this: that God has not called him to this state only on his own account, but that he may reap a harvest of souls and that many may be saved through him."

After this Brother Masseo went back to St. Clare to know what she had received from God. And she answered that both she and her companion had had the very same answer from God as Brother Silvester.

Brother Masseo therefore returned to St. Francis. And the Saint received him with great charity: he washed his feet and prepared a meal for him. And after he had eaten, St. Francis called Brother Masseo into the woods. And there he knelt down before Brother Masseo, and baring his head and crossing his arms, St. Francis asked him: "What does my Lord Jesus Christ order me to do?"

Brother Masseo replied that Christ had answered both Brother Silvester and Sister Clare and her companion and revealed that "He wants you to go about the world preaching, because God did not call you for yourself alone but also for the salvation of others."

And then the hand of the Lord came over St. Francis. As soon as he heard this answer and thereby knew the will of Christ, he got to his feet, all aflame with divine power, and said to Brother Masseo with great fervor: "So let's go—in the name of the Lord!"[1]

And he took as companions Brother Masseo and Brother Angelo, holy men. And he set out like a bolt of lightning in his spiritual ardor, not paying any attention to the road or path.

They arrived at a village called Cannara. And St. Francis began to preach, first ordering the swallows who were twittering to keep quiet until he had finished preaching. And the swallows obeyed him. He preached there so fervently that all the men and women of that village, as a result of his sermon and of the miracle of the swallows, in their great devotion wanted to follow him and abandon the village. But St. Francis did not let them, saying to them: "Don't be in a hurry and don't leave, for I will arrange what you should do for the salvation of your souls." And from that time he planned to organize the Third Order of the Continent for the salvation of all people everywhere.[2]

And leaving them much consoled and disposed to do penance, he left there and came between Cannara and Bevagna. And while going with the same fervor through that district with his companions, he looked up and saw near the road some trees on which there was such a countless throng of different birds as had never been seen before in that area. And also a very great crowd of birds was in a field near those trees. While he gazed and marveled at the multitude of birds, the Spirit of God came over him and he said to his companions: "Wait for me here on the road. I am going to preach to our sisters, the birds."

And he went into the field toward the birds that were on the ground. And as soon as he began to preach, all the birds that were on the trees came down toward him. And all of them stayed motionless with the others in the field, even though he went among them, touching many of them with his habit. But not a single one of them made the slightest move, and later they did not leave until he had given them his blessing, as Brother James of Massa, a holy man, said, and he had all the above facts from Brother Masseo, who was one of those who were the companions of the holy Father at that time.

The substance of St. Francis' sermon to those birds was this: "My little bird sisters, you owe much to God your Creator, and you must always and everywhere praise Him, because He has given you freedom to fly anywhere—also He has given you a double and triple covering, and your colorful and pretty clothing, and your food is ready without your working for it, and your singing that was taught to you by the Creator, and your numbers that have been multiplied by the blessing of God—and because He preserved your species in Noah's ark so that your race should not disappear from the earth. And you are also indebted to Him for the realm of the air which He assigned to you. Moreover, you neither sow nor reap, yet God nourishes you, and He gives you the rivers and springs to drink from. He gives you high mountains and hills, rocks and crags as refuges, and lofty trees in which to make your nests. And although you do not know how to spin or sew, God gives you and your little ones the clothing which you need. So the Creator loves you very much, since He gives you so many good things. Therefore, my little bird sisters, be careful not to be ungrateful, but strive always to praise God."

Now at these words of St. Francis, all those birds began to open their beaks, stretch out their necks, spread their wings, and reverently bow their heads to the ground, showing by their movements and their songs that the words which St. Francis was saying gave them great pleasure. And when St. Francis noticed this, he likewise rejoiced greatly in spirit with them, and he marveled at such a great throng of birds and at their very beautiful variety and also at their attention and familiarity and affection. And therefore he devoutly praised the wonderful Creator in them and gently urged them to praise the Creator.

Finally, when he had finished preaching to them and urging them to praise God, St. Francis made the Sign of the Cross over all those birds and gave them permission to leave. Then all the birds rose up into the air simultaneously, and in the air they sang a wonderful song. And when they had finished singing, according to the form of the Cross which St. Francis had made over them, they separated in an orderly way and formed four groups. And each group rose high into the air and flew off in a different direction: one toward the east, another toward the west, the third toward the south, and the fourth toward the north. And each group sang marvelously as it flew away.

Thereby they signified that, just as St. Francis—who was to bear the marks of Christ's Cross—had preached to them and made the Sign of the Cross over them, so they had separated in the form of a cross and had flown away, singing, toward the four quarters of the world, thus suggesting that the preaching of the Cross of Christ, which had been renewed by St. Francis, was to be carried throughout the world by him and by his friars, who, like birds, possess nothing of their own in this world and commit themselves entirely to the Providence of God.

And so they were called eagles by Christ when He said, "Wherever the body shall be, there the eagles will gather." For the saints who place their hope in the Lord will take on

wings like eagles and will fly up to the Lord and will not die
for all eternity.[3]

To the praise of Christ. Amen.

### 17   *How a Young Friar Fainted When He Saw St. Francis Speaking with Christ*

A young boy who was pure as a dove and innocent as an angel
was received into the Order while St. Francis was living. And
he stayed in a certain small Place where the Brothers did not
have cells and because of poverty slept on the ground without
beds.

One day St. Francis came to that little Place. And in the
evening, after saying compline, he went to rest somewhat before the others, so that later in the night, while the others were
sleeping, he could get up and pray, as he usually did.

That boy decided carefully to observe where St. Francis
went, so as to know how holy he was, and especially what he
did when he got up during the night. In order that sleep
should not prevent him, the boy lay down to sleep beside St.
Francis and tied his cord to that of St. Francis, so that he
would feel it when the Saint got up. And St. Francis was not
aware that he had tied the cords together.

During the first part of the night, when all the friars were
fast asleep, St. Francis got up, and finding his cord attached,
he untied it so carefully that the boy did not feel anything.
And St. Francis went out to a hill near the Place where there
was a very beautiful forest in order to pray alone in a small
hut that was there.

A little while later the boy awoke and found that his cord
was untied and that St. Francis was gone. So he immediately
got up in order to observe the holy Father, as he had planned.
Finding the gate leading to the forest open, he thought the
Saint had gone out that way, and he quickly went after him
into the woods and reached the top of the hill where St. Francis had gone to pray.

And when he came to the place where St. Francis was praying, he stopped at a certain distance, for he began to hear a
number of persons talking. Going nearer in order to see and

hear more clearly what they were saying, he perceived a marvelous light completely surrounding St. Francis, and in that light he saw Christ and the Blessed Virgin Mary and St. John the Baptist and St. John the Evangelist and a great throng of angels, who were talking with St. Francis.

On seeing and hearing all this, the boy began to tremble, and he fainted and fell like a corpse onto the path that led back to the monastery.

Later, when that very wonderful conversation was over and the mystery of that holy apparition was ended, St. Francis, while returning to the Place in the dark of the night, stumbled on the boy lying on the path as though he were dead. And he had compassion on the boy, and taking him up in his arms St. Francis carried him back to his bed, like the good shepherd carrying his little lamb.

And later, hearing from the boy how he had seen that vision, the Saint commanded him not to tell it to anyone during his lifetime.

The boy did indeed keep the secret. He grew up in great grace of God and devotion to St. Francis, and he lived as a worthy member of the Order until he died. And only after the death of St. Francis did he reveal all that vision to the friars.[1]

To the glory of Our Lord Jesus Christ. Amen.


## 18 *About the Marvelous Chapter That St. Francis Held at St. Mary of the Angels*

Once the most faithful servant of Christ, St. Francis, held a General Chapter on the plain at St. Mary of the Angels, where more than five thousand friars gathered together. And St. Dominic, the head and founder of the Order of Friars Preachers, was also there with seven friars of his Order. He was at that time going from Bologna to Rome, and on hearing about the Chapter which St. Francis was holding on the plain at St. Mary of the Angels, he went to see it.

There was also present at that Chapter the Lord Hugolin, Cardinal of Ostia, who was very devoted to St. Francis and his friars. St. Francis prophesied that he would be Pope, and so it happened: he was later the Pope called Gregory the Ninth. As the Court of the Lord Pope was then in Perugia, that Cardinal deliberately came to Assisi, and he used to come every day to see St. Francis and his friars, and sometimes he sang the Mass, and sometimes he gave a sermon to the friars at the Chapter.

The Cardinal felt the greatest delight and inspiration when he came to visit that holy assembly and saw the friars sitting about on the plain around St. Mary in groups of sixty or a hundred or two or three hundred, all occupied only in talking about God or in praying, weeping, or doing deeds of charity. And they were so quiet and meek that there was no sound or noise. And marveling at such a great crowd organized as an army camp, he would say with tears and great devotion: "Truly this is the camp and the army of the knights of God!"

Indeed in all that throng no one was heard telling stories or jokes, but wherever a group of friars gathered, either they prayed or recited the office, or they wept over their own sins or those of their benefactors, or they talked about the salvation of souls.

And in that camp each group had made tents covered on top and round about with rushes and mats; accordingly this Chapter was called the Chapter of Rushes or Mats. They slept on the bare ground or on some straw, and their pillows were stones or pieces of wood.

As a result, everyone who saw or heard them had such devotion for them, and the fame of their holiness was so great, that many people came to see them from the Pope's Court, which was then nearby at Perugia, and from other parts of the Valley of Spoleto. Many counts and barons and knights and other noblemen and many plain people, and cardinals and bishops and abbots with other members of the clergy, flocked to see this very holy and large and humble gathering of so many saintly men, such as the world has never seen. And they came especially to see the venerable leader and very saintly Father of all that company, who had stolen such beautiful prey from the world and had gathered such a fine and devout flock to follow in the footsteps of the true shepherd Jesus Christ.

When the entire General Chapter had assembled, St. Francis, the holy Father of all and Minister General, stood up and with fervor of spirit explained the word of God and of life to that holy flock, and—in a loud voice, as clear as a bugle, which divine unction gave him—preached to them whatever the Holy Spirit made him utter. And he took these words as the theme of his sermon: "My little sons, we have promised great things, but far greater things have been promised to us by God. Let us keep those promises which we have made, and let us aspire with confidence to those things that have been promised to us. Brief is the world's pleasure, but the punishment that follows it lasts forever. Small is the suffering of this life, but the glory of the next life is infinite." And preaching very devoutly on these words, he consoled and encouraged all the friars to reverence and obedience to Holy Mother Church and to sweet brotherly love, to pray for all the people of God, to have patience in the adversities of the world and temperance in prosperity, to maintain an angelic purity and chastity, to remain in peace and harmony with God and with men and with their own conscience, to humility and meekness toward all, to the contempt of the world and a love and fervent practice of holy poverty, to care and attention in holy prayer and the praise of God, to place all their hope and anxiety for soul and body in the Good Shepherd who nourishes our bodies and souls: Our Blessed Lord Jesus Christ.

And then he said: "In order that you may better observe this, by merit of holy obedience I command all you friars who are gathered here that none of you is to have any care or anxiety concerning anything to eat or drink or the other things necessary for the body, but to concentrate only on praying and praising God. And leave all your worries about your body to Christ, because He takes special care of you."

And all of them received this order with joy in their hearts and on their faces. And when St. Francis ended his sermon, they all ran and gave themselves to prayer.

But St. Dominic, who was present, was greatly surprised at St. Francis' command and thought that he was proceeding in an imprudent way in ordering that not a single friar in such a large gathering should take any thought regarding things that are necessary for the body, and he thought that such a great crowd would suffer as a result. But the Lord Jesus Christ wanted to show that He takes special care of His sheep and His poor, for by God's Providence it soon happened that He inspired the people of Perugia, Spoleto, Foligno, Spello, Assisi, and all the surrounding country to bring food and drink to that holy assembly. And all of a sudden men came from those places with many donkeys, mules, and wagons loaded with bread and wine, beans and cheese, and all other good things to eat which they thought those blessed poor men of Christ would need and could use. Moreover, they brought large and small pitchers and glasses and tablecloths and other things which such a crowd would need.

And whoever among them could bring the most supplies or serve most thoughtfully considered himself fortunate to provide for the needs of all in that holy gathering. And you could see the knights and noblemen who came to the meeting gladly and humbly and devoutly serving that assembly of saints. You could see members of the clergy faithfully and eagerly running around everywhere like servants. You could see young men serving with so much reverence that it seemed as though they were serving, not the poor friars, but the Apostles of Our Lord Jesus Christ.

Therefore, when St. Dominic saw all this and realized that Divine Providence was acting through them, he humbly reproached himself for having misjudged St. Francis regarding the imprudent order, and he meekly knelt before him and accused himself of his fault, adding: "God is truly taking care of these holy little poor men, and I did not realize it. Therefore I promise henceforth to observe the holy poverty of the Gospel. And in the name of God I lay a curse upon all the friars of my Order who shall presume to have private property."

Thus St. Dominic was greatly edified by St. Francis' faith and the obedience and poverty of such a great and orderly assembly and by Divine Providence and the abundant supply of all good things. For as a truly saintly and wise man he acknowledged in all he said the perfectly faithful Lord who, just as He makes the lilies and plants of the fields grow and He nourishes the birds of the air, also furnishes everything that His devoted poor men need.

During that same Chapter St. Francis was told that many

friars were wearing breastplates and iron rings on their flesh, and as a result some had become ill and some were dying, and others were hindered in praying. So St. Francis as a very wise Father commanded under holy obedience that whoever had a breastplate or an iron ring should take it off and deposit it before him. And they did so. And at least five hundred breastplates and many more iron rings worn on the arm or the torso were found, and they formed a large pile. And St. Francis made the friars leave them there.

Later when the Chapter was over, St. Francis instructed and encouraged all of them to do good, and he taught them how to escape without sin from this evil world. And he sent them all back to their provinces comforted and filled with spiritual joy, with God's blessing and his own.[1]

To the glory of Our Lord Jesus Christ—may He be blessed! Amen.

### 19  *How God Spoke to St. Francis, and How St. Francis Made the Wine Increase in a Poor Priest's Vineyard*

Once when St. Francis was suffering grievously in his eyes, the Lord Cardinal Hugolin, the Protector of the Order, because he loved him dearly, wrote to him, ordering St. Francis to come to him in Rieti, where there were some very good eye doctors. And when St. Francis received the letter of the Lord Cardinal, he went first to San Damiano, where the very devout spouse of Christ St. Clare was. For he intended to visit her and console her before he left, and then go to Rieti.

And the first night after he went to San Damiano, his eyes became so much worse that he could not see any light. Since he was unable to leave, St. Clare had a little cell made for him out of reeds and straw, in which he might stay in seclusion and get more rest.

And St. Francis stayed there for fifty days with such pain in his eyes and so greatly disturbed by a large number of mice instigated by the devil that he was unable to obtain any rest at all, either by day or night. And after he had been enduring that trial and tribulation for many days, he began to reflect and to realize that it was a punishment from the Lord for his sins. And he began to thank God with all his heart and to praise him, crying in a loud voice: "My Lord, I deserve this and much more." And he prayed to the Lord, saying: "My Lord Jesus Christ, Good Shepherd, who have shown Your very gentle mercy to us unworthy sinners in various physical pains and sufferings, give grace and strength to me, Your little lamb, that in no tribulation or anguish or pain I may turn away from You!"

And when he had uttered this prayer, a Voice came to him from Heaven that said: "Francis, answer Me. If the whole earth were made of gold, and all the oceans and rivers and springs were balsam, and all the mountains and hills and rocks were precious stones, and you found another treasure that was as much more valuable than all those things as gold is than earth, and balsam than water, and gems than mountains and rocks, and if that most valuable treasure were given to you for this illness of yours, should you not be very happy and rejoice greatly?"

St. Francis answered: "Lord, I am not worthy of so precious a treasure."

And the Voice of God said to him: "Rejoice therefore, Brother Francis, because that is the treasure of eternal life which I am keeping for you. And right now I invest you with it. And this illness and affliction are a pledge of that blessed treasure."

Then St. Francis, thrilled with joy by that glorious promise, called his companion and said: "Let's go to Rieti—to the Lord Cardinal!"

And after first consoling St. Clare with holy and honey-sweet words and saying good-by to her humbly, as he usually did, he set out for Rieti.[1]

But when he arrived near Rieti, such a great crowd of people came out to meet him that he therefore did not want to go into the city, but turned aside and went to a certain church that was about two miles away from the town. But the people, knowing that he was staying at that church, flocked out to see him in such throngs that the vineyard of the priest of that church—for it was vintage time—was completely ruined and all the grapes were taken and eaten. When the priest saw the damage, he was bitterly sorry and he regretted that he had allowed St. Francis to go into his church.

The priest's thoughts were revealed to the Saint by the Holy Spirit, and he summoned the priest and said to him: "My dear Father, how many measures of wine does this vineyard produce in a year when it produces well?"

The priest answered: "Twelve."

And St. Francis said: "Then I beg you, Father, to bear patiently my staying here in this church of yours for some days, because of the rest and quiet that I find here. And let everyone take the grapes from this vineyard of yours, for the love of God and my poor little self. And I promise you on behalf of my Lord Jesus Christ that this year you will get twenty measures."

St. Francis did this—staying on there—because of the great good which he saw the Lord was performing in the souls of the people who came there, for he saw that many of them, when they went away, were inebriated with the love of God and converted to heavenly longings, forgetting the world. Therefore it seemed to him better that the material vineyard should be damaged than that the vineyard of the Lord of Hosts should be sterile in heavenly wine.

So the priest trusted in the promise of St. Francis and freely let the people who came there take and eat the grapes. It certainly is a wonderful thing that the vineyard was completely stripped and ruined by them, so that only a few little bunches of grapes remained. But when the vintage came, the priest, trusting in the Saint's promise, gathered those little bunches of grapes and put them in the wine press and pressed them. And as St. Francis had promised, he obtained twenty measures of the very best wine that year.

By that miracle it was clearly shown that, just as through the merits of St. Francis the vineyard with its ruined grapes had produced an abundance of wine, so the Christian people, who were sterile in virtue because of sin, through the merits and teaching of St. Francis frequently brought forth good fruits of penance.[2]

To the glory of Our Lord Jesus Christ. Amen.

### 20  *How St. Francis Appeared in Glory to a Novice Who Was Tempted to Leave the Order*

A very delicate young man of noble birth entered the Order of St. Francis. A few days after he took the habit, through the instigation of the devil, he began to hate the habit he was wearing so much that he felt as though he was wearing a very coarse sack. The sleeves got on his nerves, he disliked the cowl, and the length and roughness of the habit seemed an unbearable burden to him. And so it happened that as his distaste for the Order increased, he firmly resolved to throw the habit away and return to the world.

Now the novicemaster of this young man, to whom he had been assigned in the beginning, had taught him that when he passed in front of the altar of the friary in which the Blessed Sacrament of the Body of Christ was kept, he should kneel down very reverently and bow very devoutly with his head uncovered and his hands crossed on his chest. And this young man always carefully did so.

And it happened on the night when he had decided to put aside the habit and leave the Order that he had to pass before the altar of the friary, and there, as usual, he knelt and bowed. And all of a sudden he was rapt in spirit and was shown a marvelous vision by God.

For he saw passing before him an almost countless throng of saints, two by two, in procession, and they were dressed in very ornate and precious vestments, and their faces and hands and the visible parts of their bodies were shining more radiantly than the sun. And they marched by, singing hymns, while angels were solemnly and beautifully chanting their joy.

Among those saints there were two who were more splendidly dressed and adorned and who were surrounded by such brilliance that they dazzled anyone who looked at them. And almost at the end of that procession he saw one who was adorned with such glory that he seemed like a new knight being especially honored by the others.

When that young man saw this vision, he was greatly amazed, and he did not know what the procession meant. Yet he did not question those who were passing by—nor could he as he was overwhelmed with bliss. But when the whole procession had passed and he saw only the last ones, he gained courage and ran to them, asking them very timidly: "Dear friends, I beg you to tell me who are those very wonderful persons who are in this venerable procession?"

They turned their radiant faces toward him and answered: "Son, all of us are Friars Minor who have just come from the glory of Paradise."

And he asked again: "Who are those two who shine more brightly than the others?"

And they replied: "Those two who are brighter than the others are St. Francis and St. Anthony. And that last one whom you saw being so honored is a holy friar who recently died. Because he fought valiantly against temptations and persevered in his holy undertaking until the end, we are now conducting him in triumph and glory to the joy of Paradise, with the Saints as companions, while the angels rejoice. And these very beautiful garments which we are wearing were given to us by God in exchange for the rough habits which we wore with patience as religious. And the glorious radiance which you see in us was given to us by God for the humble penance and holy poverty and obedience and pure chastity which we observed to the end with joyful minds and faces. Therefore, son, it should not be hard for you to wear the 'sack' of such a fruitful Order because if, with the 'sack' of St. Francis, for the love of Our Lord Jesus Christ, you despise the world and mortify your body and fight valiantly against the devil, you will likewise have a similar garment and will shine with us in glory."

And when they had said those words, the young man came back to himself. And encouraged by that vision, he rejected all temptation and acknowledged his fault before the guardian and the other friars.

Henceforth, moreover, he longed for the roughness of penance and of the habit as for wealth. And thus converted into a better man, he lived a very holy life and died in the Order.[1]

To the glory of Our Lord Jesus Christ. Amen.

### 21  How St. Francis Tamed the Very Fierce Wolf of Gubbio

At a time when St. Francis was staying in the town of Gubbio, something wonderful and worthy of lasting fame happened.

For there appeared in the territory of that city a fearfully large and fierce wolf which was so rabid with hunger that it devoured not only animals but even human beings. All the people in the town considered it such a great scourge and terror—because it often came near the town—that they took weapons with them when they went into the country, as if they were going to war. But even with their weapons they were not able to escape the sharp teeth and raging hunger of the wolf when they were so unfortunate as to meet it. Consequently everyone in the town was so terrified that hardly anyone dared go outside the city gate.

But God wished to bring the holiness of St. Francis to the attention of those people.

For while the Saint was there at that time, he had pity on the people and decided to go out and meet the wolf. But on hearing this the citizens said to him: "Look out, Brother Francis. Don't go outside the gate, because the wolf which has already devoured many people will certainly attack you and kill you!"

But St. Francis placed his hope in the Lord Jesus Christ who is master of all creatures. Protected not by a shield or a helmet, but arming himself with the Sign of the Cross, he bravely went out of the town with his companion, putting all his faith in the Lord who makes those who believe in Him walk without any injury on an asp and a basilisk and trample not merely on a wolf but even on a lion and a dragon. So with his very great faith St. Francis bravely went out to meet the wolf.

Some peasants accompanied him a little way, but soon they said to him: "We don't want to go any farther because that wolf is very fierce and we might get hurt."

When he heard them say this, St. Francis answered: "Just stay here. But I am going on to where the wolf lives."

Then, in the sight of many people who had come out and

climbed onto places to see this wonderful event, the fierce wolf came running with its mouth open toward St. Francis and his companion.

The Saint made the Sign of the Cross toward it. And the power of God, proceeding as much from himself as from his companion, checked the wolf and made it slow down and close its cruel mouth.

Then, calling to it, St. Francis said: "Come to me, Brother Wolf. In the name of Christ, I order you not to hurt me or anyone."

It is marvelous to relate that as soon as he had made the Sign of the Cross, the wolf closed its terrible jaws and stopped running, and as soon as he gave it that order, it lowered its head and lay down at the Saint's feet, as though it had become a lamb.

And St. Francis said to it as it lay in front of him: "Brother Wolf, you have done great harm in this region, and you have committed horrible crimes by destroying God's creatures without any mercy. You have been destroying not only irrational animals, but you even have the more detestable brazenness to kill and devour human beings made in the image of God. You therefore deserve to be put to death just like the worst robber and murderer. Consequently everyone is right in crying out against you and complaining, and this whole town is your enemy. But, Brother Wolf, I want to make peace between you and them, so that they will not be harmed by you any more, and after they have forgiven you all your past crimes, neither men nor dogs will pursue you any more."

The wolf showed by moving its body and tail and ears and by nodding its head that it willingly accepted what the Saint had said and would observe it.

So St. Francis spoke again: "Brother Wolf, since you are willing to make and keep this peace pact, I promise you that I will have the people of this town give you food every day as long as you live, so that you will never again suffer from hunger, for I know that whatever evil you have been doing was done because of the urge of hunger. But, my Brother Wolf, since I am obtaining such a favor for you, I want you to promise me that you will never hurt any animal or man. Will you promise me that?"

The wolf gave a clear sign, by nodding its head, that it promised to do what the Saint asked.

And St. Francis said: "Brother Wolf, I want you to give me a pledge so that I can confidently believe what you promise."

And as St. Francis held out his hand to receive the pledge, the wolf also raised its front paw and meekly and gently put it in St. Francis' hand as a sign that it was giving its pledge.

Then St. Francis said: "Brother Wolf, I order you, in the name of the Lord Jesus Christ, to come with me now, without fear, into the town to make this peace pact in the name of the Lord."

And the wolf immediately began to walk along beside St. Francis, just like a very gentle lamb. When the people saw this, they were greatly amazed, and the news spread quickly throughout the whole town, so that all of them, men as well as women, great and small, assembled on the market place, because St. Francis was there with the wolf.

So when a very large crowd had gathered, St. Francis gave them a wonderful sermon, saying among other things that such calamities were permitted by God because of their sins, and how the consuming fire of hell by which the damned have to be devoured for all eternity is much more dangerous than the raging of a wolf which can kill nothing but the body, and how much more they should fear to be plunged into hell, since one little animal could keep so great a crowd in such a state of terror and trembling.

"So, dear people," he said, "come back to the Lord, and do fitting penance, and God will free you from the wolf in this world and from the devouring fire of hell in the next world."

And having said that, he added: "Listen, dear people. Brother Wolf, who is standing here before you, has promised me and has given me a pledge that he will make peace with you and will never hurt you if you promise also to feed him every day. And I pledge myself as bondsman for Brother Wolf that he will faithfully keep this peace pact."

Then all the people who were assembled there promised in a loud voice to feed the wolf regularly.

And St. Francis said to the wolf before them all: "And you, Brother Wolf, do you promise to keep this pact, that is, not to hurt any animal or human being?"

The wolf knelt down and bowed its head, and by twisting its body and wagging its tail and ears it clearly showed to everyone that it would keep the pact as it had promised.

And St. Francis said: "Brother Wolf, just as you gave me a pledge of this when we were outside the city gate, I want you to give me a pledge here before all these people that you will keep the pact and will never betray me for having pledged myself as your bondsman."

Then in the presence of all the people the wolf raised its right paw and put it in St. Francis' hand as a pledge.

And the crowd was so filled with amazement and joy, out of devotion for the Saint as well as over the novelty of the miracle and over the peace pact between the wolf and the people, that they all shouted to the sky, praising and blessing the Lord Jesus Christ who had sent St. Francis to them, by whose merits they had been freed from such a fierce wolf and saved from such a terrible scourge and had recovered peace and quiet.

From that day, the wolf and the people kept the pact which St. Francis made. The wolf lived two years more, and it went from door to door for food. It hurt no one, and no one hurt it. The people fed it courteously. And it is a striking fact that not a single dog ever barked at it.

Then the wolf grew old and died. And the people were sorry, because whenever it went through the town, its peaceful kindness and patience reminded them of the virtues and the holiness of St. Francis.[1]

Praised be Our Lord Jesus Christ. Amen.

## 22   *How St. Francis Freed Some Doves and Made Nests for Them*

A boy of the town of Siena caught a number of turtle doves in a snare, and he was carrying them all alive to the market to sell them.

But St. Francis, who was always very kind and wonderfully compassionate, especially toward gentle animals and little birds, was stirred by love and pity on seeing the doves. And he said to the boy who was carrying the doves: "Good boy, please give me those doves so that such innocent birds, which in Holy Scripture are symbols of pure, humble, and faithful souls, will not fall into the hands of cruel men who will kill them."

The boy was then inspired by God to give all the doves to St. Francis.

When the kind Father had gathered them to his bosom, he began to talk to them in a very gentle way, saying: "My simple, chaste, and innocent Sister Doves, why did you let yourselves be caught? I want to rescue you from death and make nests for you where you can lay your eggs and fulfill the Creator's commandment to multiply."

And St. Francis took them with him and made a nest for all of them.

And the doves settled in the nests made by St. Francis, and laid their eggs and reared their young right among the friars, and they increased in numbers. They were so tame and familiar with St. Francis and the other friars that they seemed to be like chickens that had always been raised by the friars. And they did not leave until St. Francis gave them permission, with his blessing.

The Saint had said to the boy who gave him the doves: "My son, one day you will become a Friar Minor in this Order, and you will serve Our Lord Jesus Christ well."

And it happened as the Saint foretold, because later the boy entered the Order and, through the merits of St. Francis, he led a praiseworthy and very exemplary life until he died.

So St. Francis not only obtained comfort for those little birds in this life but also the joys of eternal life for that youth.[1]

May Our Lord Jesus Christ be praised! Amen.

### 23   *How St. Francis Saw the Place of the Portiuncula Besieged by Devils*

Once at the Place of the Portiuncula, when St. Francis was praying devoutly, as was his custom, by divine revelation he saw the whole Place surrounded and besieged by devils, as by a great army. But not one of them was able to enter into the

Place because the friars were so holy that the devils could find no one to whom they could gain admittance.

However, while they were thus persevering, one of the friars was stirred to anger and impatience against one of his companions, and he thought how he could accuse him and take revenge on him. As a result, the gate of virtue being abandoned and the door of wickedness being open, he gave the devil a way to come in. And immediately, while St. Francis was watching, one of those devils entered into the Place and attacked that brother as a winner attacks a loser, and he crouched on the friar's neck.

When the compassionate Father and shepherd, who always watched over his flock very faithfully, saw that a wolf had entered to devour one of his little lambs, and knew that his sheep were in great danger, he had that friar called to him.

And when the friar obediently came running to his anxious shepherd, St. Francis ordered him to reveal at once the poison of hatred against his neighbor that he had conceived and kept in his heart, as a result of which he had given himself over to the enemy.

And he, seeing that the holy Father had read his thoughts, was afraid and revealed his wound—all his poison and rancor—and acknowledged his fault and humbly asked for forgiveness and a penance. And when he had done that, he was absolved from his sin and received the penance, and all of a sudden St. Francis saw the devil fly away.

And the friar, having thus been freed from the hands of the cruel beast, gave thanks to God and to St. Francis, and he persevered to the end in great holiness of life, through the merits of his shepherd.[1]

To the praise of the Lord Jesus Christ and of the holy Father. Amen.

### 24   How St. Francis Converted the Sultan and the Prostitute Who Solicited Him to Sin

Spurred on by zeal for the faith of Christ and incited by a desire for martyrdom, St. Francis at one time went beyond the seas with twelve of his very holy companions, planning to travel right to the Sultan of Babylonia.

Now when he arrived in a certain country of the Saracens, where such cruel men guarded the roads that no Christian passing through there could escape being killed, by the grace of God they were not killed, but were taken prisoners, beaten in various ways and very roughly bound and then led before the Sultan.

In his presence St. Francis preached under the guidance of the Holy Spirit in such a divine way about the holy Catholic faith that he offered to enter the fire for it. As a result, the Sultan began to feel great devotion for him, both because of the unshakable conviction of his faith and because of his contempt of the world—for though he was utterly poor he would not accept any gifts—and also because of his fervent longing for martyrdom. And thereafter the Sultan willingly listened to him and asked him to come back to see him many times. Moreover, he generously granted permission to him and to his companions to go anywhere and freely preach wherever they wished in all his empire. And he gave them a certain little token so that no one who saw it should harm them.[1]

After receiving that generous permission, St. Francis sent those chosen companions of his, two by two, into various lands of the Saracens to preach the faith of Christ. And with one companion he chose a certain district, and he went into an inn where he had to rest overnight. And there he found a certain woman who was very beautiful in face and body but very foul in mind and soul. That cursed woman solicited St. Francis to commit a most shameful act with her.

St. Francis answered her: "If you wish me to do what you want, you must also do what I want."

"I agree," she said. "So let's go and prepare a bed." And she led him toward a room.

But St. Francis said to her: "Come with me, and I will show you a very beautiful bed." And he led her to a very large fire that was burning in that house at that time. And in fervor of spirit he stripped himself naked and threw himself down on the fire in the fireplace as on a bed. And he called to her, saying: "Undress and come quickly and enjoy this splendid, flowery, and wonderful bed, because you must be here if you wish to obey me!" And he remained there for a long time with a joyful face, resting on the fireplace as though on flowers, but the fire did not burn or singe him.

On seeing such a miracle that woman was terrified and felt remorse in her heart. And she not only repented her sin and evil intention but was also perfectly converted to the faith of Christ, and through the merits of the holy Father she became so holy in grace that she won many souls for the Lord in that region.[2]

At last, seeing that he was unable to gather the fruit which he desired in that country, St. Francis, as a result of a revelation from God, prepared to return to the lands of the faithful with all his companions, and he assembled them together again. Then he went back to the Sultan and told him that he planned to leave.

The Sultan said to him: "Brother Francis, I would willingly be converted to the faith of Christ, but I am afraid to do it now, because these Saracens, if they heard about it, would immediately kill me and you, with all your companions. And since you can still do a great deal of good, and I have to do many important things for the salvation of my soul, I do not want to bring about your premature death and mine. But show me how I can achieve salvation, and I am ready to obey you in everything."

Then St. Francis said to him: "My Lord, I am leaving you now, but after I have returned to my country and at the call of God, gone to Heaven, after my death, through Divine Providence, I will send you two of my friars from whom you will receive the baptism of Christ and you will be saved, as my Lord Jesus Christ has revealed to me. And meanwhile free yourself from all that may hinder you, so that when the grace of Christ comes to you, He may find you well disposed in faith and devotion."

The Sultan gladly agreed and promised to do so, and he faithfully obeyed.

After saying good-by to him, St. Francis went back to the lands of the faithful with that venerable group of his holy companions. And after some years St. Francis gave up his soul to God by the death of the body.

And the Sultan grew ill. But awaiting the fulfillment of the dead Saint's promise, he stationed guards at the gates with orders to bring quickly to him two friars in the habit of St. Francis if they should show up.

At that time St. Francis appeared to two of his friars and ordered them to travel without delay to the Sultan and to obtain for him the salvation which the Saint had promised him. Those friars set out immediately and devoutly to fulfill his command. And after going over the sea, they were led to the Sultan by his guards.

When he saw them, the Sultan was filled with intense joy and he said: "Now I know indeed that the Lord has sent His servants to me for my salvation, as St. Francis promised me through a divine revelation."

And after receiving instructions in the faith of Christ and holy Baptism from those friars, he died reborn in that illness, and his soul was saved through the merits of St. Francis.[3]

To the glory of Christ the Blessed. Amen.

### 25    How St. Francis Miraculously Healed a Man with Leprosy in Soul and Body

That true disciple of Christ, St. Francis, while he was still living in this miserable and pitiable world, being enlightened by the Holy Spirit, always strove with all his strength to follow in the footsteps of Our Lord Jesus Christ, the perfect Master.

Thus as Christ Himself condescended to become a pilgrim, so St. Francis showed himself and his friars as true pilgrims, and he also had it written in the Rule that all his friars should serve the Lord in this world as pilgrims and strangers.

Moreover, as Christ came not only to serve people with leprosy, healing and cleansing them in body, but He also wished to die for them, sanctifying and cleansing them in their soul, so St. Francis, longing to be entirely conformed to Christ, used to serve victims of leprosy with very great affection, giving them food, washing their sore limbs, cleaning and washing their clothes, and, moreover, frequently and fervently giving them kisses. And so it happened many times that God by His power simultaneously healed the soul of one whose body the Saint healed, as we read of Christ.

And therefore St. Francis not only served victims of leprosy willingly, but, in addition, he ordered that the friars of his Order should serve them with care wherever they might be going or staying in the world, for the love of Christ who for our sake wished to be considered like a man with leprosy. And the friars used to do this in many places very gladly, as truly obedient sons.[1]

Now it happened once, in a Place near the one where St. Francis was then living, that the friars were taking care of leprosy patients and sick people in a hospital. And a certain man was there who was so seriously ill with leprosy and so impatient and irritable that everyone was sure he was possessed by an evil spirit—and such was the case. For he not only attacked any of the friars who nursed him with horribly foul language and shot insults at them like arrows, but what was worse, he would also whip and wound them in various ways. Yet the most fearful and worst of all was that he would curse and blaspheme the Blessed Christ and His most holy Mother and the other Saints, so that no one could be found who could or would take care of him.

And although the friars tried to endure the insults and injuries meekly in order to increase the merit of their patience, their consciences could not tolerate his blasphemous insults to Christ and His holy Mother, lest they should seem to be participating in such a great sin. Therefore they decided to abandon that man completely in order not to become blasphemers of God and supporters of an instrument of the devil.

But they did not want to do this until they had duly told the whole story to St. Francis, who was then living in another Place nearby.

After hearing them, St. Francis went to that perverse man with leprosy, and entering, he greeted him: "God give you peace, my dear brother."

The man answered reproachfully: "What peace can I have from God, who has taken from me all peace and everything that is good, and has made me all rotten and stinking?"

And St. Francis said: "My dear son, be patient, because the weaknesses of the body are given to us in this world by God for the salvation of soul. So they are of great merit when they are borne patiently."

And the sick man replied: "How can I bear patiently this constant pain that is afflicting me day and night? For not only am I burned and crucified by my sickness, but I am sorely wronged by the friars whom you gave me to take care of me, because there is not one who serves me the way he should."

Then St. Francis, knowing by the Holy Ghost that he was troubled by an evil spirit, went and began to pray devoutly to God for him.

And having prayed, St. Francis came back to him and said: "Dear son, I want to take care of you, since you are not satisfied with the others."

And the sick man replied: "All right. But what more can you do for me than the others?"

And St. Francis said: "I will do whatever you want."

And the leprosy patient said: "I want you to wash me all over, because I smell so bad that I cannot stand it myself."

Then St. Francis immediately had water boiled with many sweet-scented herbs. Next, he undressed the man with leprosy and began to wash him with his holy hands, while another friar poured the water over him.

And by a divine miracle, wherever St. Francis touched him with his holy hands, the leprosy disappeared, and the flesh remained completely healed.

And as externally the water washed his body and the flesh began to heal and be wholly cleansed from leprosy, so too interiorly his soul began to be healed and cleansed. And when the man with leprosy saw himself being healed externally, he immediately began to have great compunction and remorse for his sins. And he began to cry very bitterly. Just as his body was washed with water and cleansed from leprosy, so his conscience was baptized by tears and contrition and cleansed from all evil and sin.

When he was completely washed and healed physically, he was perfectly anointed and healed spiritually. And he was overcome with such compunction and weeping that he humbly accused himself and cried out in a loud voice: "Woe to me, for I deserve hell for the insults and injuries I have given to the friars and for my impatience and blasphemies against God!"

So for a good fifteen days he kept bitterly lamenting his

sins with a remarkable wailing that burst from the inner depths of his soul. And he constantly sought nothing but the mercy of God. And with that compunction and weeping he confessed all his sins to a priest.

St. Francis, seeing such a clear miracle which God had performed through his hands, gave thanks to God and left there for a distant region, so that when that miracle became known to the people they should not all run to him, because through humility he wanted to flee any worldly glory, and in all that he did, as a faithful and prudent servant, he sought to procure the honor and glory of God and not his own, and to receive humiliation and disgrace among men for himself.

Later, as it pleased God, the man who had had leprosy and whose body and soul had been healed, soon after the fifteen days of his marvelous penance, fell sick with another illness. And well armed with the Sacraments of the Church, he died a holy death.

While St. Francis was praying in a certain remote Place in a forest, the dead man's soul, brighter than the sun, appeared to him in the air going to Paradise, and said to him: "Do you recognize me?"

St. Francis said to him: "Who are you?"

And he answered: "I am the man with leprosy whom the Blessed Christ healed through your merits. And today I am going to Paradise and to eternal life—for which I give thanks to God and to you. Blessed be your soul and your body, and blessed be your words and your deeds, because many souls are being saved and will be saved by you in the world. And know that there is not one day when the holy angels and all the other saints do not give fervent thanks to God for the holy fruits which are produced through you and your Order in different parts of the world. Therefore be comforted, and give thanks to God. And abide with the blessing of God!"

And having said those words, he disappeared on his way to Heaven.

And St. Francis remained much consoled.[2]

Praised be Christ. Amen.

### 26    *How St. Francis Converted Three Murderous Robbers, and How the Pains of Hell and the Glory of Paradise Were Revealed to One of Them*

Wishing to lead all men to salvation, the blessed Father Francis traveled through various provinces. And wherever he went, he always acquired a new family for the Lord because he was guided by the Spirit of God. As a vessel chosen by God, it was his mission to spread the balsam of grace. Therefore, he went to Slavonia, the Marches of Trevisi, the Marches of Ancona, Apulia, the Saracen country, and many other provinces, multiplying everywhere the servants of Our Lord Jesus Christ.

Once when St. Francis was going through Monte Casale, a village in the district of Borgo Sansepolcro, he was visited by a young nobleman of that town who was very delicate.

When he came to St. Francis, he said to him: "Father, I would like very much to become one of your friars."

But St. Francis answered him: "Son, you are young, delicate, and noble. Perhaps you could not endure our poverty and our hard life."

But he said: "Father, are you not men, as I am? So since you who are like me endure it, I too, with the help of Christ, will be able to bear it."

This answer pleased St. Francis very much, and he received him into the Order at once and gave him his blessing and named him Brother Angelo.

And that young man's conduct was so good that soon afterward St. Francis appointed him guardian of the Place of Monte Casale.

At this time there were in that area three famous robbers who committed many crimes thereabouts. One day those robbers came to the Place of the friars, and they asked Brother Angelo, the guardian, to give them something to eat. And the guardian answered, scolding them severely: "You robbers and cruel murderers—not only are you not ashamed of stealing from others the fruit of their labor, but in your audacity you even dare to eat up the offerings which have been given to the servants of God! You do not deserve that the earth should bear you up, for you respect no man and you scorn God who created you! So go about your business—and don't you ever come back here!"

They were angry at this, and they went away highly indignant.

That same day St. Francis came back to the Place, carrying a sack of bread and a little jug of wine which he had begged with his companions. And when the guardian told how he had driven the robbers away, St. Francis scolded him severely, saying: "You acted in a cruel way, because sinners are led back to God by holy meekness better than by cruel scolding. For our Master Jesus Christ, whose Gospel we have promised to observe, says that the doctor is not needed by those who are well but by the sick, and 'I have come to call not the just but sinners to penance,' and therefore He often ate with them. So, since you acted against charity and against the example of Jesus Christ, I order you under holy obedience to take right now this sack of bread and jug of wine which I begged. Go and look carefully for those robbers over the mountains and valleys until you find them. And offer them all this bread and this wine for me. And then kneel down before them and humbly accuse yourself of your sin of cruelty. And then ask them in my name not to do those evil things any more, but to fear God, and not to offend their neighbors. And if they do so, I promise them that I will supply them with provisions for their needs and I will give them food and drink all the time. And when you have humbly told them that, come back here."

While the guardian went to carry out St. Francis' order, the Saint began to pray and begged the Lord to soften the hearts of those robbers and convert them to repentance.

The obedient guardian found them and gave them the bread and wine, and did and said what St. Francis had commanded. And it pleased God that while those robbers were eating the gifts which St. Francis had sent them, they began to say to one another: "What terrible tortures are waiting in hell for us who are such miserable and unhappy men! For we go around not merely robbing and beating and wounding our neighbors but also killing them! And yet we feel no fear of God or remorse of conscience over those horrible crimes and murders that we commit. But here is this holy friar who just came to

us because of a few words which he said to us quite rightly
on account of our wickedness, and he very humbly accused
himself of his fault before us. And, besides, he brought us a
very generous promise of the holy Father and charitably gave
us the bread and wine. Those friars really are saints of God,
and they deserve Paradise. But we are sons of eternal damnation who deserve the pains of hell, and every day we increase
the vengeful flames by our horrible crimes. And we do not
know whether we will be able to obtain mercy from God for
the crimes and misdeeds which we have committed so far."

When one of them had said those and similar words, the
other two said: "What you say certainly is the truth. But what
should we do?"

And he said: "Let's go to St. Francis, and if he gives us
hope that we can obtain mercy from God for our great sins,
let's do whatever he commands us, so that we may free our
souls from the punishment of hell."

All three agreed to follow this advice. And so they went in
haste to St. Francis and said to him: "Father, because of our
many great sins we do not believe we can obtain mercy from
God, but if you have confidence that God will have mercy on
us, we are ready to do penance with you and to obey you
in whatever you command us."

Then St. Francis made them welcome with kindness and
holy affection, and he consoled them by telling them many inspiring true stories, and he gave them back assurance that
they would win God's mercy. Moreover he promised them that
he would obtain mercy and grace for them from the Lord
Jesus. He also taught them how the infinite greatness of divine
mercy surpasses all our sins, even if they are boundless, and
how, according to the Gospels and St. Paul the Apostle, Christ
came into this world in order to redeem sinners.

As a result of these wholesome instructions, the three robbers renounced the world and the devil and his works, and
St. Francis received them into the Order, and they remained
faithful to him in mind and deed. And they began to do great
penance.

Two of them lived only a short time after their praiseworthy
conversion and at God's call went from this world to Paradise.[1]

But the third lived on, and thinking over the many great

sins which he had committed, he began to do such penance that for fifteen successive years, except for the regular forty-day fasts which he made as the others did, on three days a week he always ate only a little bread and drank water. And he was satisfied with only one habit, and he always walked around barefoot, and he never slept after matins.

During that fifteen-year period St. Francis passed from this sad world to our home in Heaven.

Now when this friar had persevered in that strict penance for many years, one night after matins such a temptation to fall asleep came over him that he simply could not resist it and stay awake as he usually did. Finally, being unable to overcome his drowsiness or to pray, he yielded to the temptation and went and lay down on his bed to sleep.

The moment he rested his head on the bed, he fell into a rapture and was led in spirit up a very high mountain on which there was a very deep ravine. And on each side there were broken and splintered rocks and uneven ledges jutting out from the rocks, so that this ravine was a frightening thing to look at.

And the angel who was leading the friar held him over and then pushed him down from the top of that ravine. He fell down headlong, striking and bouncing off from rock to rock and ledge to ledge, until he reached the bottom of the ravine, where it seemed to him as though all his bones and limbs were shattered and broken.

And while he was lying wounded on the ground like that, his guide called to him: "Get up, because you still have a long journey to make."

The friar answered: "You seem to me a very unreasonable and cruel man, for although you see me dying from the fall that has broken me to pieces, yet you say to me, 'Get up!'"

And the angel went to him and by touching him instantaneously healed all his limbs and made him perfectly well.

And then the angel showed him a great plain full of sharp and cutting stones and thorns and briars and muddy and watery swamps, and told the friar that he had to walk barefoot across it until he came to the end of that plain, where there was a blazing furnace that could be seen from a distance, which he had to enter.

When the friar had crossed all the plain with great anguish

and pain and had reached the furnace, the angel said to him: "Go into that furnace, because you must."

The friar answered: "Oh, what a cruel guide you are to me! You see me nearly dead because of that frightful plain and so exhausted that I need a real rest—and now as rest you say to me, 'Go into that blazing furnace!'"

And while he looked at the furnace, he saw all around it many devils with red-hot iron pitchforks in their hands, with which they suddenly drove him in as he hesitated to enter.

When he had gone into the fire, he looked and saw a man who had been his godfather and who was all on fire. And he exclaimed: "Oh, unhappy godfather, how did you come here?"

And he replied: "Go a little farther into this fire and you will find my wife, your godmother, who will tell you the reason for our damnation."

When the friar had gone somewhat farther through the fire, the godmother appeared, all on fire, sitting enclosed in a measure of burning corn. And he asked her: "Oh, unfortunate and unhappy godmother, why have you fallen into such a cruel torment?"

And she replied: "Because during the great famine, which St. Francis prophesied would come, when my husband and I sold grain, we falsified the measure, and consequently I am burning in this narrow measure."[2]

After she had said those words and he had stood there for a while, the angel who was leading the friar thrust him out of the furnace, and then said to him: "Get ready to go on, because you still have a horrible peril to go through."

And he said, complaining: "Oh, you very cruel guide—you have no pity on me! You see that I have been nearly burned alive in that furnace—yet you say, 'Come on a dangerous and horrible journey!'"

But then the angel touched him and made him feel perfectly well and strong.

Next the angel led him to a bridge which he could not pass over without great danger because it was very small and narrow and very slippery and without any railing on the side. And underneath it flowed a terrible river filled with serpents and dragons and scorpions and toads, and it gave out a fearful stench. And the angel said to him: "Go across that bridge, because you must."

But he answered: "How can I go across it without falling into that dangerous river?"

The angel said: "Come after me, and put your foot where you see me put mine, and that way you will cross it all right."

The friar walked after the angel, as he had told him, and he safely reached the middle of the bridge.

And when he was there in the middle, the angel flew away, up to a very marvelous mansion on top of a very high mountain, a long way off on the far side of the bridge. And he noticed that the angel had flown away. But when he remained on the bridge without a guide, and he looked down and saw the heads of those horrible beasts rising out of the river with mouths open, ready to devour him if he fell, he was so terrified that he simply did not know what to do or say, because he could not go forward or backward.

So, finding himself in such trouble and danger, and seeing that he had no one to turn to except God, he bowed down and embraced the bridge and began to call on the Lord Jesus Christ with all his heart, sobbing, that He might deign to save him by His most holy mercy. And after he had prayed, it seemed to him that wings were growing on him. And with great joy he waited until they had grown, hoping that he would be able to fly to the far side of the river where the angel had flown.

But after some time, owing to his great desire to cross that bridge and his haste, he began to fly, and because his wings were not yet fully grown, he fell onto the bridge, and all the feathers also fell out. So in his fright he again clung to the bridge and begged with tears for Christ's mercy, as before.

And after he had prayed, again it seemed to him that his wings were growing. But like the first time he hastened to fly without waiting for them to grow perfectly, and again he fell down onto the bridge, and his wings dropped off as before.

Realizing that he fell that way because of the haste he had to fly before he was ready, he began to say to himself: "If the wings grow a third time, I certainly will wait until they are big enough so that I can fly without falling again."

And while he was thinking this, he saw the wings growing

for the third time, and he waited a long time until they were quite large. And it seemed to him that between the first and second and third growth of wings he had to wait for a hundred and fifty years or more. But finally, when he believed that the wings had grown to perfection, for the third time he raised himself in the air with all his strength and flew up to the palace to which the angel had flown.

When he reached the gate of that marvelous palace, he knocked, and the gatekeeper asked him: "Who are you who have come here?"

He answered: "I am a Friar Minor."

The gatekeeper said: "Wait for me, because I am going to bring St. Francis to see whether he acknowledges you."

While he went for St. Francis, the friar began to look at the wonderful walls of that marvelous palace. And those walls seemed so transparent with brightness that he could clearly see all that was going on inside and the choirs of saints who were inside. And while he was gazing at them in amazement, St. Francis and the holy Brother Bernard and Brother Giles appeared, and after St. Francis such a great multitude of men and women saints of God who had followed in his footsteps that they seemed to be countless.

And when St. Francis came to him, he said to the gatekeeper: "Let him come in, because he is one of my friars."

Then St. Francis led him in. As soon as the friar entered, he felt such consolation and sweetness that he forgot all the tribulations he had had before, as if they had never happened.

Then St. Francis showed him many wonderful things there, and later said to him: "Son, you have to go back to the world and stay there for seven days. During that time prepare yourself carefully and with all devotion, as well as you can, because after the seven days I will come for you, and then you will accompany me to this marvelous place of the blessed."

St. Francis was dressed in a wonderful robe adorned with very beautiful stars, and his five Stigmata were like five very bright stars which radiated such brilliance that they lit up the whole palace with their rays. And Brother Bernard had on his head a very beautiful crown of stars. And Brother Giles was radiant with bright light. And he recognized many other holy

Friars Minor in glory with St. Francis whom he had never seen in the world.

Having taken leave of St. Francis, he returned to the world, though quite unwillingly. When he awoke and came back to himself and recovered consciousness, the friars were ringing for prime, so that although it seemed to him like many years, the time in which he had had that vision was not more than from matins until the dawn of the same night.

And the friar told his guardian the vision and also about the period of seven days. And soon he began to have a fever.

And on the seventh day St. Francis came for him with a great throng of glorious saints, as he had promised. And he led to the joys of the blessed in the Kingdom of Eternal Life the soul of that friar that had been purified in the vision under the guidance of the angel.[8]

To the praise and glory of Our Lord Jesus Christ. Amen.

### 27   How St. Francis Converted Two Students in Bologna

At one time while St. Francis was traveling, he came to the city of Bologna. When the people heard about his arrival, they ran to see him, and there was such a crowd that he could hardly walk. For they all wanted to see him, as a new flower of the world and an angel of the Lord, so that he had a hard time to reach the city square.

And when the entire square was filled with men and women and students, St. Francis stood up on a high place in the center and began to preach what the Holy Spirit dictated to him. And he preached such marvelous and astounding things that he seemed to be not a man but an angel. And his heavenly words seemed like sharp arrows which were shot from the bow of divine wisdom and pierced the hearts of everyone so effectively that by this sermon he converted a very great multitude of men and women from a state of sin to remorse and penance.[1]

Among them were two noble students from the Marches of Ancona. One was called Pellegrino, whose home was in Falerone, and the other's name was Riccieri from Muccia.

Among others whose hearts had been touched interiorly by divine inspiration through the sermon, they came to St. Francis, saying that they had an intense desire to leave the world and receive the habit of his friars.

Then St. Francis, considering their fervor, knew by a revelation of the Holy Spirit that they were sent by God, and moreover he understood what way of life each of them would find most suitable. Therefore he received them with joy, saying to them: "You, Pellegrino, keep to the path of humility in the Order. And you, Riccieri, serve the friars."

And so it happened. For Brother Pellegrino never wanted to become a cleric but remained a lay brother, although he was a very learned scholar and an expert in Roman law. By means of that humility he attained to very great perfection in virtue and especially to the grace of compunction and love for Our Lord Jesus Christ.

For inflamed by the love of Christ and burning with the desire for martyrdom, he went to Jerusalem in order to visit the Holy Places of the Savior, carrying with him the Book of the Gospels. And when he read about the sacred places where the God-man had walked, and he touched them with his feet and saw them with his eyes, he bowed down to pray to God and confidently embraced those very holy spots with his arms and lovingly kissed them with his lips and moistened them with tears of devotion, so that he inspired great devotion in all who saw him.

As Divine Providence ordained, he returned to Italy. And like a true pilgrim and citizen of the heavenly Kingdom, he very rarely visited his noble relatives. He would encourage them to despise the world, and by his serious conversation he would urge them to love God, and then, quickly and hurriedly, he would leave them, saying that Christ Jesus who makes the soul noble is not found among relatives and familiar friends.

Brother Bernard, the first-born son of our very holy Father Francis, used to say something truly wonderful about this Brother Pellegrino, namely, that he was one of the most perfect friars in this world.

And he really was a pilgrim. For the love of Christ, which he always had in his heart, did not allow him to find peace in any creature or to attach his affections to any temporal thing, but he always strove for his heavenly home and looked to his heavenly home, and he climbed from virtue to virtue until he transformed the lover into the loved one. Finally Brother Pellegrino passed, full of virtue, from this life to Christ whom he loved with all his heart, and rested in peace, with many miracles before and after his death.[2]

Brother Riccieri, the companion of Brother Pellegrino on earth and now his fellow citizen in Heaven, led an active life, living in great sanctity and humility, traveling on foot, and devoutly and faithfully serving his neighbors, the friars. And he became very intimate and popular with St. Francis, so that he learned many things from the Saint and under his instruction clearly grasped the truth concerning many doubtful points, and he perceived the will of the Lord in matters with which he had to deal. And as the holy Father prophesied, he served the friars. He was appointed Minister in the Province of the March of Ancona. And owing to the zeal for God which always burned in his heart, he governed the province for a long time in great peace and wisdom, following the example of Christ who preferred action to teaching.

Now after some time, for the good of his soul, Divine Providence permitted a very great temptation to come over him, so that in his intense anxiety and trouble he afflicted himself severely with abstinence and disciplines and tears and prayers day and night. But he could not free himself from that temptation. And many times he was led into intense despair, because owing to the power of the temptation he believed himself abandoned by God.

But while he was plunged into extreme desolation and desperation, he reflected in his heart and said to himself: "I will get up and go to my Father Francis. And if he welcomes me and shows himself friendly to me, as he usually does, I believe that God will still be merciful to me. But if not, it will be a sign that I have been abandoned by God. . . ."

So he set out and went to St. Francis. The Saint was then lying seriously ill in the palace of the Bishop of Assisi. And while he was meditating about God, the whole matter of that friar's temptation and desperation and plan and coming was revealed to him by God.

St. Francis immediately called his companions, Brother

Masseo and Brother Leo, and said to them: "Go out quickly to meet my dear son Riccieri, and embrace and welcome him for me, and tell him that of all the friars who are in the world, I have a special love for him."

Now like obedient sons they went right out to meet Brother Riccieri. And finding him on the road, as St. Francis had said, they embraced him and told him the Father's loving words, which so filled his soul with sweet consolation that he was almost beside himself with joy. How happy he showed himself, and how he expressed his joy, and how he praised and thanked God with all his heart because God had made his journey successful, can hardly be put in words. O good Jesus, You never abandon those who hope in You, but always give us strength with a temptation so that we can sustain it!

He went to the place where that angelic and godlike man Francis was lying. And although St. Francis was gravely‾sick, he got to his feet and went to meet Brother Riccieri. And embracing him affectionately, he said to him: "My very dear son, Brother Riccieri, among all the friars who are in the world I have a special love for you."

And after saying that, he made the Sign of the Cross on his forehead and lovingly kissed him on the same spot and then said to him: "My beloved son, God gave you that temptation in order that you might gain very great merit. But if you do not want any more of that merit, you will not have it."

It is wonderful to relate that as soon as St. Francis had said those words, all that diabolical temptation suddenly left the friar, as though he had never in his life felt it. And he remained utterly consoled in God.[8]

To the glory of Our Lord Jesus Christ. Amen.

### 28    *About Brother Bernard's Gift of Contemplation*

How much grace God often gave to the poor men who followed the Gospel and who voluntarily gave up all things for the love of God was manifested in Brother Bernard of Quintavalle who, after he had taken the habit of St. Francis, was very frequently rapt in God by the contemplation of heavenly things.

Thus one time it happened that while he was attending Mass in a church and his whole mind was on God, he became so absorbed and rapt in contemplation that during the Elevation of the Body of Christ he was not at all aware of it and did not kneel down when the others knelt, and he did not draw his cowl back as did the others who were there, but he stayed motionless, without blinking his eyes, gazing straight ahead, from morning until none.

But after none he came back to himself and went through the Place shouting in a voice filled with wonder: "Oh, Brothers! Oh, Brothers! Oh, Brothers! There is no man in all this country, no matter how great and noble he is, who, if he were promised a very beautiful palace full of gold, would not willingly carry a sack full of the most filthy manure in order to obtain that very noble treasure!"

Now the mind of this Brother Bernard was so uplifted to that heavenly treasure which is promised to those who love God that for fifteen continuous years he always went about with both his mind and his face raised toward Heaven. And during those fifteen years, because his mind was raised to the light of Heaven and his feelings were utterly absorbed by divine graces, he never satisfied his hunger at meals. He used to eat a little of everything that was set before him, for he used to say that to abstain from what a man does not enjoy cannot be called perfect abstinence, because true abstinence is to resist things that taste good.

He also attained to such clarity of understanding that even great scholars of the Church consulted him for solutions of difficult questions, and he unraveled obscure problems in whatever passage of the Bible they requested.

And because his mind was utterly freed and detached from earthly matters, he used to soar to the heights of contemplation as a swallow flies high up into the sky. And sometimes for twenty days, sometimes for thirty days, he used to stay alone on the tops of mountains, contemplating heavenly things. Therefore Brother Giles used to say of him that this gift which was given to Brother Bernard of Quintavalle was not given by

God to everyone, namely, that he should feed while flying, like swallows.[1]

And because of that outstanding grace which had been given him by the Lord, St. Francis used to talk with him willingly and frequently both day and night. So that sometimes they were found to have spent an entire night together rapt in God in the woods, where they had met to talk about Our Lord Jesus Christ, who is blessed forever and ever. Amen.

### 29    *How St. Francis Freed Brother Rufino from a Temptation of the Devil*

Brother Rufino, one of the great noblemen of Assisi, a companion of St. Francis and a man of great sanctity, was once, while St. Francis was alive, very fiercely attacked and tempted in his soul by the devil on the subject of predestination. For the ancient enemy injected the suggestion into his heart that he was damned and was not among those who were predestined to eternal life, and that whatever he did in the service of the Order was wasted. As a result of this temptation, which lasted many days, he became very sad and depressed, and he was ashamed to tell St. Francis about his conflict. Nevertheless, he did not stop performing his usual prayers and fasts.

Therefore the ancient enemy, wishing to heap sorrow onto sorrow, which sorely wounds the servants of God, also added to his inner struggle an outer one by attacking him outwardly by false apparitions.

So one day he appeared to him in the form of the Crucified One and said to him: "Oh, Brother Rufino, why do you afflict yourself with prayers and penances since you are not among those who are predestined to eternal life? And you should believe me, because I know whom I have chosen and predestined. And do not believe the son of Peter Bernardone if he tells you the contrary. And also do not ask him about this matter, because neither he nor anyone else knows it—no one but I who am the Son of God knows it. Therefore believe me for sure that you are among the damned. And Brother Francis himself, your Father, is also damned. And whoever follows him is deceived."

Brother Rufino on hearing these words became so darkened by the Prince of Darkness that he lost all the faith and love which he had had for St. Francis, and did not want to tell him anything about himself.

But the Holy Spirit revealed what Brother Rufino did not tell the holy Father. Therefore, when St. Francis perceived spiritually the great peril of Brother Rufino, he sent Brother Masseo to him to tell him to come to him. For Brother Rufino and St. Francis and Brother Masseo were staying at the Place of Mount Subasio near Assisi.

Brother Rufino answered sharply: "What have I to do with Brother Francis?"

Then Brother Masseo, who was filled with divine wisdom, clearly recognizing the deceit of the evil enemy, said: "Oh, Brother Rufino, don't you know that Brother Francis is like an angel of God who has brought light to so many souls in the world and from whom we too have so many gifts of God's grace? Therefore, by all means I urge you to come to him, because I clearly see that you are deceived by the devil."

On hearing this, Brother Rufino set out at once and went to St. Francis. And when St. Francis saw him coming in the distance, he began to cry: "Oh, Brother Rufino, you naughty boy, whom have you believed?"

And when Brother Rufino came to him, the Saint told him in detail all about the temptation, exterior and interior, which he had had from the devil. And he showed Brother Rufino clearly that the one who had appeared to him and had suggested the above-mentioned things to him was the devil and not Christ, and therefore he should in no way consent to his suggestions.

"But when the devil says to you again, 'You are damned,'" St. Francis said, "you answer him confidently, 'Open your mouth—and I will [empty my bowels] in it!'[1] And let it be a sign to you that he is the devil that when you say those words, he will immediately go away. You should also have known that he was the devil because he hardened your heart to everything that is good, for that is exactly his job. But the Blessed Christ never hardens the heart of the faithful man but rather softens it, as He says through the Prophet: 'I will take away your heart of stone and will give you a heart of flesh.'"

Then Brother Rufino, seeing that St. Francis had told him in detail all about his interior and exterior temptation, and being moved to remorse by his words, began to weep bitterly and knelt before him and humbly acknowledged his fault in having concealed his temptation from him. And he remained greatly consoled and comforted by the advice of the holy Father and completely changed for the better.

Finally St. Francis said to him: "Go to confession, son. And do not stop devoting yourself to your usual prayers. And know for sure that this temptation will be very helpful and consoling to you, as you will find out in a short while."

So Brother Rufino went back to his cell to pray in the woods. And while he was praying with many tears, the ancient enemy came in the appearance of Christ, as in the previous apparitions, and said to him: "Brother Rufino, didn't I tell you not to believe the son of Peter Bernardone and not to exhaust yourself with weeping and praying, because you are damned? What good does it do you to afflict yourself while you are alive, since when you die you will be damned?"

Brother Rufino quickly answered: "Open your mouth—and I will [empty my bowels] in it!"[2]

Then the devil angrily went away with such a commotion and fall of rocks on Mount Subasio (which was nearby) that a great mass of stones hurtled down for a long while, where the fearful ravine filled with rocks is still to be seen. And the collisions of the falling rocks caused horrible flashes of fire through the ravine of that mountain. The noise of the stones was so frightful that St. Francis and his companions were amazed and came out of the Place in order to see what was happening.

Then Brother Rufino clearly realized that it had been the devil who had deceived him. So he went back to St. Francis and prostrated himself on the ground and accused himself again of his fault.

And St. Francis comforted him once more with kind words and sent him back to his cell deeply consoled.

Later while he was praying in it very devoutly, the Blessed Christ appeared to him and made his whole soul burn with divine love, saying: "Son, you did well to believe Brother Francis, because he who made you depressed was the devil. But

I am Christ, your Master, and to make you perfectly sure of it I give you this sign: as long as you live, you will never again be sad or depressed."

And after saying that, Christ gave Brother Rufino His blessing and left him in such joy and peace of soul and inspiration of mind that he was absorbed in God day and night.

Thereafter he was so confirmed in grace and in the assurance of his eternal salvation that he became completely changed into a new man. And his mind was so concentrated on Heaven and he persevered so much in prayer that he would spend days and nights in praying and in contemplating divine things, if others would let him.

Therefore St. Francis used to say of him that Brother Rufino had been canonized in Heaven by the Lord Jesus Christ while he was still alive and that he would not hesitate to say "St. Rufino" (except in his presence), though he was still living on earth.[8]

To the glory of Our Lord Jesus Christ. Amen.

## 30  *How St. Francis Sent Brother Rufino to Preach in Assisi without His Habit*

Brother Rufino was so absorbed in God as a result of continual contemplation that he became almost mute and insensible to external things. He used to speak very rarely, and, besides, he had neither the gift nor courage nor ability to preach the word of God.

Nevertheless, one day St. Francis told Brother Rufino to go to Assisi and preach to the people whatever God would inspire him to say.

But Brother Rufino answered: "Reverend Father, please excuse me and don't send me on that assignment because, as you well know, I do not have the grace of preaching, and also I am just a simple ignorant fellow."

Then St. Francis said: "Because you did not obey me at once, I also command you under holy obedience to go to Assisi naked—wearing only your breeches—and to go into some church and preach to the people naked like that!"

At this command Brother Rufino obediently undressed and

went to Assisi naked and entered into a church. And after he had knelt in reverence before the altar, he went up into the pulpit and began to preach.

At this, the children and men began to laugh and to say: "Look—they are doing so much penance they have gone crazy!"

Meanwhile, St. Francis, thinking over the prompt obedience of Brother Rufino, who was one of the foremost gentlemen of Assisi, and the very difficult command he had given him, began to reproach himself very severely, saying: "How can you, the son of Peter Bernardone—you vile little wretch—order Brother Rufino, who is one of the noblest citizens of Assisi, to go naked and preach to the people like a madman? By God, I am going to see to it that you yourself experience what you order others to do!"

And having said that, in the fervor of the Holy Spirit he too immediately took off his habit and went to Assisi naked, accompanied by Brother Leo, who very discreetly carried along the Saint's habit and Brother Rufino's.

And when the people of Assisi saw him naked too, they laughed at him as at a lunatic, thinking that both he and Brother Rufino had gone mad from doing too much penance.

But St. Francis found and entered the church where Brother Rufino had already begun to preach. And he was saying these words devoutly and severely: "Oh, dear people, flee the world. Give up sin. Restore to others what belongs to them if you want to escape hell. But keep God's commandments and love God and your neighbor if you want to go to Heaven. And do penance, because the Kingdom of Heaven is drawing near!"

Then St. Francis went up naked into the pulpit, and he began to preach so marvelously about contempt for the world, holy penance, holy voluntary poverty, the desire for the Kingdom of Heaven, and about the nakedness and humiliations and most holy Passion of Our Lord Jesus Christ Crucified that the whole crowd of men and women who had gathered there for the sermon in great numbers began to weep very bitterly. And with unbelievable devotion and compunction of heart they cried out aloud to God for mercy, so that nearly all of them were converted to a new state of mind.

And not only there, but throughout all Assisi on that day

there was such mourning among the people over the Passion of Our Lord Jesus Christ that so much weeping had never been heard in that town.

And after the people had thus been edified and Christ's sheep had been consoled by the deed of St. Francis and Brother Rufino, and after they had received a blessing in the name of Our Lord Jesus Christ, St. Francis put Brother Rufino's habit on him again, and he himself got dressed with him.

And so wearing their habits once more, they went back to the Place of the Portiuncula, glorifying and praising the Lord for having given them the grace to overcome themselves by self-contempt and for having edified the little sheep of Christ by their good example and for having shown how the world is to be despised.

And on that day the devotion of the people toward them increased so much that those who could touch the hem of their clothes considered themselves blessed.[1]

To the glory of Our Lord Jesus Christ, who is blessed! Amen.

### 31  *How Brother Rufino Was One of Three Chosen Souls*

Just as Our Lord Jesus Christ says in the Gospel, "I know my sheep, and Mine know Me," so our blessed Father Francis, like a good shepherd, knew by divine revelation all the merits and virtues of his companions. And furthermore he knew their faults and failings. Consequently he knew how to provide the best remedy for all by humbling the proud and exalting the humble and by blaming vices and praising virtues, as we read in the wonderful revelations which he had concerning that first family of his.

For once—to record only one instance among many—St. Francis was sitting in a certain little Place with his companions and he was talking with them about God. But Brother Rufino, a man who was very remarkable for his holiness, was not with them then in that conversation because he had not yet come out of the woods, where he had gone to pray and contemplate. And while St. Francis was continuing his holy exhortations and holy conversation with those companions, Brother

Rufino—a noble citizen of Assisi but a still more noble servant of God, who was of virginal purity and uplifted by the noble grace of divine contemplation and adorned by the sweet-smelling flowers of virtue before God and men—came out of the forest where he had been contemplating heavenly things and passed by not far from St. Francis.

When the Saint perceived him in the distance, he turned to his companions and asked them: "Tell me, dear Brothers, who do you think is the holiest soul that God has in the world now?"

And they humbly answered that they thought he himself was honored with that privilege.

But St. Francis said to them: "I am of myself the most unworthy and the vilest man that God has in the world. But do you see Brother Rufino there coming out of the woods? God has revealed to me that his soul is one of the three holiest souls that God has in this world now. And I frankly tell you that I would not hesitate to call him St. Rufino while he is still living his life in the body, since his soul has been confirmed in grace and sanctified and canonized in Heaven by Our Lord Jesus Christ."

But St. Francis never said those words in the presence of Brother Rufino.

In such incidents it was shown that like a good shepherd, the holy Father knew his sheep in their failings also, as he clearly showed with Brother Elias, whom he scolded several times for his pride; and with Brother Giovanni di Capella, to whom he prophesied that because of his malice he would hang himself by the throat; and with that friar whose throat the devil held fast when he was corrected for disobedience; and with the friars who were coming from Terra di Lavoro, when he reproved one of them for the offense he gave his companion on the way. Moreover, he knew those sheep of his in whom grace abounded, as is evident with Brother Bernard and Brother Rufino and many other friars, whose secret faults and virtues he clearly knew by revelation from the Blessed Christ. Amen.[1]

### 32 *How Christ Appeared to Brother Masseo*

Those first companions of our blessed Father Francis who were poor in material things but rich in God did not hope or strive to become rich in gold or silver but tried with all their strength to enrich themselves with holy virtues, by which we attain the true everlasting riches of Heaven.

It happened one day that Brother Masseo, one of the holy Father's chosen companions, was with them while they were talking about God. And one of them told this story: "There was a man who was a great friend of God and who had much grace in the active and the contemplative life, and at the same time he had such extreme and profound humility that he considered himself a very great sinner. That humility sanctified and confirmed him in grace and made him constantly grow in virtues and gifts of God, and what is still better, it never let him fall away from God in sin."

When Brother Masseo heard these marvelous things about humility and realized that it was the treasure of salvation and eternal life, he began to be inflamed with such love and desire for that virtue of humility, which was most worthy of divine favor, that, looking up toward Heaven, with great fervor he made a vow and a very powerful resolve never to consent to rejoice in this world until he should feel that most excellent humility perfectly present in his soul.

And after he had made that vow with a holy motive, he remained shut up in his cell almost all the time every day, afflicting himself with fasts, vigils, prayers, and a very bitter weeping before God in order to obtain that virtue without which he considered himself worthy of hell and with which, as he had heard, that friend of God had been so richly endowed.

And while Brother Masseo remained sad in that desire for many days, it happened that he went into the forest one day. And he was going through it in fervor of spirit, uttering mournful cries and tearful sighs, ardently begging the Lord to give him that divine virtue.

And because the Lord heals those who are contrite in heart and willingly hears the prayers of the humble, while Brother Masseo was standing there, a Voice came from Heaven that called him twice: "Brother Masseo! Brother Masseo!"

And he knew by the Holy Spirit that it was the Voice of Christ, and he answered: "My Lord!"

And Christ said to him: "What do you want to give—what do you want to give in order to possess that grace you are asking for?"

And Brother Masseo replied: "Lord, the eyes out of my head!"

And Christ said to him: "But I want you to have your eyes and the grace too."

And after saying that, the Voice vanished. And Brother Masseo remained so filled with the grace of the desired virtue of humility and with the light of God that from then on he rejoiced all the time. And often when he was praying, he would express his joy in a soft constant cooing sound like a gentle dove: "Ooo-Ooo." And he would remain in contemplation that way, with a joyful expression on his face and a happy heart. Moreover, he became extremely humble and considered himself the least of all the men in the world.

Brother James of Falerone, of holy memory, asked him why he never changed tone in his rejoicing. And he replied very joyfully: "Because when we have found all that is good in one thing, it is not necessary to change tone."[1]

To the glory of Our Lord Jesus Christ. Amen.

### 33  How St. Clare Miraculously Imprinted the Cross on Some Loaves of Bread

St. Clare, a most devout disciple of the Cross of Christ and a noble little plant of St. Francis, was so holy that not only bishops and cardinals but also the Pope strongly desired to see and hear her, and often visited her in person.

At one time among others the Pope went to St. Clare's monastery in order to listen to her heavenly and divine conversation, for she was a shrine of the Holy Spirit. And as both of them conversed for a long time about the salvation of the soul and the praise of God, St. Clare meanwhile ordered loaves of bread to be set out on the tables for all the Sisters, for she wished to keep those loaves after they had been blessed by the Vicar of Christ.

So when their very holy conversation was over, the Saint knelt with great reverence and asked the Supreme Pontiff whether he would deign to bless the loaves of bread which had been placed on the tables.

The Pope answered: "Very faithful Sister Clare, I want you to bless those loaves of bread and to make over them the Sign of the Cross of Christ to whom you have offered yourself completely as a spotless sacrifice."

But St. Clare replied: "Most Holy Father, please excuse me, but I would deserve to be severely blamed if a vile little woman like myself should presume to give such a blessing in the presence of the Vicar of Christ."

And the Pope answered: "So that it should not be attributed to presumption, but that you may also earn merit by doing it, I command you under holy obedience to make the Sign of the Cross over these loaves of bread and to bless them in the name of Our Lord Jesus Christ."

Then St. Clare, as a truly obedient daughter, very devoutly made the Sign of the Cross over those loaves of bread and blessed them. And a marvelous thing happened: all of a sudden a very beautiful and clearly marked cross appeared on all the loaves.

Afterwards some of those loaves were eaten with great devotion, and some were set aside as evidence of the miracle for the future.

And when the Holy Father saw the miraculous cross that had been made by the spouse of Christ, he first gave thanks to God and then, after granting to St. Clare the consolation of his blessing, he took some of the bread and left.

At that time there were living in that monastery Sister Ortolana, St. Clare's mother, and Sister Agnes, her sister, all of whom, with many other holy nuns and spouses of Christ, were full of virtue and of the Holy Spirit. St. Francis used to send many sick persons to them. And by the power of their prayers and of the Cross, which they loved with all their hearts, they would restore to health everyone over whom they made the Sign of the Cross.[1]

To the glory of Christ. Amen.

### 34    *How St. Louis, the King of France,*
### *Visited Brother Giles*

When St. Louis, the King of France, decided to go on a pilgrimage and visit the shrines throughout the world, he heard reliable reports about the wonderful holiness of the saintly Brother Giles, who had been one of the first companions of St. Francis, and he resolved and set his heart on paying him a personal visit. Therefore in that journey he made a detour to Perugia, where he had heard that Brother Giles was staying at that time.

And upon arriving at the gate of the friars' Place as a poor and unknown pilgrim with only a few companions, he asked very earnestly for Brother Giles, without telling the brother porter who it was who was asking for him. So the brother porter went and told Brother Giles that some pilgrim was asking for him at the gate.

Now Brother Giles immediately perceived spiritually that it was the King of France. So in great fervor he came out of his cell and quickly ran to the gate. And without asking any questions, though neither had ever seen the other, both of them hastened to embrace each other, kneeling together very devoutly and exchanging an affectionate kiss, as though they had been intimate friends for a long time. Despite all this, they did not say anything to each other, but remained in that embrace, with those gestures of loving friendship, in silence. And after they had stayed that way for a long time without saying a word, they separated. And St. Louis continued on his journey, and Brother Giles went back to his cell.

But while King Louis was leaving, a friar asked one of his companions who was the man who had hastened to embrace Brother Giles so affectionately, and the other answered that he was King Louis of France who had wanted to see Brother

Giles during his pilgrimage. And after saying this, he and the King's companions rode rapidly away.

Now the friars were very sorry that Brother Giles had not said a single good word to the King, and they complained to him very much, saying: "Oh, Brother Giles, how is it that you were unwilling to say anything to such a great King who came from France in order to see you and hear some good words from you?"

Brother Giles answered: "Dear Brothers, do not be surprised that neither he nor I was able to say anything to each other, because in the moment when we embraced, the light of divine wisdom revealed his heart to me and mine to him. And so by God's grace we looked into each other's hearts, and whatever he thought of saying to me or I to him, we heard without sound made by lips and tongue even better than if we had spoken with our lips—and with greater consolation. For if we had wanted to explain with the help of our voices what we felt in our hearts, because of the defect of human language, which cannot clearly express the secret mysteries of God except by mystic symbols, that conversation would have saddened rather than consoled us. And so you should know for sure that the King departed marvelously consoled."[1]

To the glory of Our Lord Jesus Christ. Amen.

### 35   *How St. Clare Was Miraculously Carried on Christmas Eve to the Church of St. Francis*

At one time the most devout spouse of Christ, St. Clare, while staying at San Damiano, was seriously ill, so that she was unable to go and say the office in church with the other nuns.

Now the Feast of the Nativity of Our Blessed Lord Jesus Christ came, when the Sisters used to recite matins and devoutly receive Holy Communion at the Mass of the Nativity. While all the others went to matins, St. Clare remained alone in bed, seriously ill and very sad because she could not go with the others to attend such a holy ceremony and have that spiritual consolation.

But Our Lord Jesus Christ wished to give this most faithful spouse of His a consolation, and He miraculously let her attend in spirit both the matins and the Mass as well as the whole celebration of the Feast by the friars in the Church of St. Francis, so that she clearly heard the organ and the friars' chanting to the end of the Mass. Moreover, she received Holy Communion and was fully consoled. Then He had her carried back to bed.

Now when the Sisters had finished the office in San Damiano, they came back to St. Clare and said to her: "Oh, dear Mother, Sister Clare, what great consolations we have had in this holy Feast of the Savior's Nativity—if only you could have been with us!"

But she answered: "My dear little sisters and daughters, I give thanks and praise to God, my Blessed Lord Jesus Christ, because my soul had the consolation of attending all the ceremonies of this most holy night—but still greater and more solemn and beautiful ones than yours. For by the grace of my Lord Jesus Christ and through the intercession of my most blessed Father St. Francis, I was present in the Church of my Father St. Francis, and with my bodily and spiritual ears I heard all the chanting and the organ, and moreover I received Holy Communion there. So rejoice and praise Our Blessed Jesus Christ with all your hearts for such a great grace which He gave me, since while I was lying here sick, as I said, I was present at the whole ceremony in the Church of St. Francis— whether in the body or outside the body, I don't know; my God who took me there to attend His ceremony knows."[1]

To the glory of Our Lord Jesus Christ. Amen.

## 36  *How St. Francis Explained to Brother Leo a Vision Which He Had Seen*

At a certain time when St. Francis was seriously ill, Brother Leo was taking care of him with great devotion and zeal. And once while Brother Leo was near St. Francis and gave himself to prayer, he was rapt in an ecstasy and was led in spirit to a very great, broad, and rapid river.

And as he was watching those who were crossing it, he saw several friars with loads on their backs go into the river. Suddenly the powerful current swept them away, and the depth of the water sucked them under. Some others went as far as one third of the way across, and others got halfway across, and others almost all the way to the other bank. But all of them, in various ways according to their burdens, were submerged by the rushing waters and finally fell and died a cruel death, without any chance of being saved, because of their heavy burdens which they were carrying on their backs.

And Brother Leo felt very sorry for them when he saw such a tragedy.

Then all of a sudden, while he was standing there, some friars appeared without any load or burden of any kind. Only holy poverty shone forth in them. And they went into the river and crossed over without any trouble. And after he had seen that, Brother Leo came to himself again.

Now St. Francis, sensing in spirit that Brother Leo had seen a vision, called him and said: "Tell me what you saw."

And after he told him everything he had seen, St. Francis said to him: "What you saw is true, for the great river is this world. The friars who were swallowed by the river are those who do not want to follow the teachings of the Gospel and do not keep voluntary poverty. But those who went across without danger are the friars who, having the spirit of God, neither love nor desire nor possess any carnal or earthly thing in this world, but 'having food and sufficient clothing' they are 'content,' following Christ naked on the Cross. And joyfully and willingly they embrace, take up, and carry every day the very light and sweet burden of His Cross and the yoke of His very holy obedience. And consequently they pass easily and without danger—indeed with joy—from this world to God, who is blessed forever and ever. Amen."[1]

## 37 How St. Francis Was Very Kindly Received in a Home

Late one evening, when the venerable and admirable Father St. Francis arrived at the house of an important and noble gentleman, he and his companion were welcomed and given lodging with so much reverence and courtesy that it seemed as though that nobleman was welcoming angels from Paradise.

Because of this courtesy, St. Francis conceived a great affection for him. For that nobleman received St. Francis when he entered the house with a friendly embrace and the kiss of peace. And after he entered, the nobleman washed and wiped St. Francis' feet and humbly kissed them. And he lit a great fire and prepared the table with an abundance of good food. And while they were eating, he served them with a joyful expression on his face.

After they had eaten, the nobleman said to St. Francis and his companion: "Father, I offer you myself and my belongings. Whenever you need habits and cloaks or anything, buy it and I will pay for it. And know that I am ready to provide for all your needs, because the good Lord has given me an abundance of worldly property, and so for love of Him I willingly give to those who are poor and in need."

Consequently St. Francis, when he saw his great courtesy and affection and when he heard his generous offer, felt such love in his heart for him that later when he was going away with his companion, he said: "That gentleman certainly would make a good member of our Order: he is so grateful to God, so kind to his neighbor, so generous to the poor, and so cheerful and courteous to guests. For, dear Brother, courtesy is one of the qualities of God, who courteously gives His sun and His rain and everything to the just and to the unjust. And courtesy is a sister of charity. It extinguishes hatred and keeps love alive. And because I have observed so much divine virtue in this good man, I would be glad to have him as a companion. Therefore I wish that we go back to him some day, in case God might perhaps touch his heart so that he should want to join us in serving the Almighty. Let us pray the Lord God to infuse that desire into his heart and to give him the grace to put it into effect."

It certainly is wonderful that a few days later, after the Saint had prayed, the Lord granted the desire of his heart and did not deprive him of what he had prayed for. For a few days after he had uttered his prayer, St. Francis said to his companion: "Dear Brother, let's go to the courteous nobleman, because I have a sure confidence in God that with his generosity in temporal things he will give himself to our Order as a companion."

And taking that road they approached the house of the above-mentioned man. But before they came to him, St. Francis said to his companion: "Wait a while for me, as first I want to ask God to make our journey successful, so that Christ may deign, through the merits of His most holy Passion, to grant to us poor little weak ones the noble prey whom we are thinking of snatching from the world."

And after saying that, St. Francis began to pray very fervently in a certain place where he could clearly be seen by that courteous nobleman. And as Christ arranged matters, while that nobleman was looking here and there, he saw St. Francis praying very devoutly and standing before Christ, and the Blessed Christ standing before St. Francis in a very bright light and looking very beautiful. And in that bright light he saw that St. Francis was raised a great distance above the ground in a physical and spiritual uplifting.

When that nobleman clearly perceived all these things, the hand of the saving Lord quickly came over him, and he was so touched at heart by God and inspired to scorn and leave the world that he immediately went out of his mansion and ran in fervor of spirit toward St. Francis. And when he came to him, he found St. Francis standing on the ground, praying very devoutly. So that nobleman likewise began to pray, and he knelt down and very fervently and eagerly begged him to deign to let him do penance and stay with him.

Then St. Francis, seeing and hearing that the nobleman was urgently asking what he himself had wished, and realizing that this very wonderful conversion had been accomplished by the power of the Lord, rose to his feet in joy and fervor of spirit and devoutly embraced and kissed him, thanking and praising God for having added such a knight to his army.

Meanwhile, that man said to St. Francis: "My holy Father, what do you command me to do? At your order I am ready to give everything I have to the poor and to run after Christ with you, unburdened by all temporal things."

And so it came about that through the merits and prayers of St. Francis, and following his advice, he distributed all his property to the poor and became a Friar Minor. And he lived all the rest of his life in great penance and sanctity and purity.[1]

To the glory of Christ. Amen.


### 38  *How It Was Revealed to St. Francis That Brother Elias Was to Leave the Order*

At one time when St. Francis and Brother Elias were staying together as members of the community in a certain small Place, it was revealed to St. Francis by God that Brother Elias was damned and would leave the Order and finally die outside the Order. Consequently St. Francis conceived such a distaste for him that he did not want to speak to him or converse with him or see him or eat with him. And if it sometimes happened that Brother Elias was coming toward him, St. Francis would turn aside and go in another direction in order not to meet him.

When this had happened several times, Brother Elias began to notice and realize that St. Francis was displeased with him. So wishing to know the reason, one day he went up to St. Francis to speak to him, and when St. Francis tried to avoid him, he respectfully detained him by force and began to beg him earnestly to explain to him the reason why he was avoiding his company and conversation that way.

And St. Francis answered him: "Because it has been revealed to me by God that as a result of your sins you will leave the Order and die outside the Order. Moreover, it has been revealed to me by the Lord that you are damned."

On hearing this, Brother Elias burst into tears and threw himself at St. Francis' feet, saying: "My reverend Father, I beg you by the love of Christ not to avoid me and drive me away from you because of that, but—like a good shepherd who, following the example of Christ, goes to seek the sheep that has wandered—seek and find and accept this sheep that will perish without your help. And I beg you to pray your holy prayers to God for me, your sheep, so that He may, if it be possible, revoke the sentence of my damnation. For it is written that God can remit the sentence if the sinner makes amends for his fault. And I have so much faith in your prayers that if I were lying in the depths of hell and you prayed to God for me, I would feel some relief. So I beg you again to recommend me, a sinner, to God who came to save sinners, that He may not forget me at the end, but that when the end of my life comes, He may deign to have mercy on me."

And Brother Elias said this with great devotion and weeping, so that St. Francis was moved with fatherly pity and promised him that he would pray to God for him. And while he was very fervently praying to God for him, he understood by a revelation that his prayer had been granted by the Lord as to revoking the sentence—that is, that in the end the soul of Brother Elias would not be damned, but that he surely would leave the Order and die outside the Order.

And that is what happened. For when Frederick the King of Sicily revolted against the Church and consequently the Pope excommunicated him with all those who gave him aid and advice, Brother Elias, who was considered one of the wisest men in the world, at the invitation of King Frederick went over to his side and became a rebel against the Church and an apostate from the Order. For that he was excommunicated by the Pope and deprived of the habit of St. Francis.

And while he was thus excommunicated, he became seriously ill. When his own brother—a lay brother who had remained in the Order and a man of good life and pure and praiseworthy conversation—heard about his illness, he went to visit him. And among other things he said to him: "My dear brother, I am very sorry that you are excommunicated and that you will die without a habit outside your Order. But if you can see any way by which I could deliver you from that great danger, I would be glad to go to any trouble for you."

Now Brother Elias answered: "Dear brother, I see no other way but for you to go to the Pope and ask him, for the love of Christ and His servant and standard-bearer St. Francis, through whose teaching I left the world, to absolve me from the excommunication and restore to me the habit of the Order."

The brother replied: "I will gladly labor for your salvation, if I can obtain that grace."

And leaving him, he went to the Pope and very humbly asked him to have mercy on his brother for the love of Christ and of St. Francis. And through the grace of God and the help of St. Francis' prayers it happened that the Lord Pope granted to the brother that if he went back and found Brother Elias alive, he might absolve him of the excommunication and restore the habit to him.

So the brother joyfully hurried away from the Papal Court and hastened back to Brother Elias in order to bring him that absolution. And by Divine Providence and the prayers of St. Francis, he found Brother Elias alive but very close to death, and he absolved him from the excommunication. And after putting on the habit again and receiving the last Sacraments of the Church, Brother Elias ended his life in peace and went to the Lord. And it is believed that he obtained this grace at the end and that his soul was saved through the merits and prayers of St. Francis, in which Brother Elias had placed so much faith.[1]

To the glory of Christ. Amen.

### 39  *How St. Anthony Preached and Was Heard by Men of Different Languages*

At one time that wonderful vessel of the Holy Spirit, St. Anthony of Padua, one of the chosen followers and companions of St. Francis, whom St. Francis used to call his bishop,[1] was preaching before the Pope and Cardinals in a consistory where there were men from different countries—Greeks and Latins, French and Germans, Slavs and English—and men of many other different languages and idioms. And being inflamed by the Holy Spirit and inspired with apostolic eloquence, he preached and explained the word of God so effectively, devoutly, subtly, clearly, and understandably that all who were assembled at that consistory, although they spoke different languages, clearly and distinctly heard and understood every one of his words as if he had spoken in each of their languages. Therefore they were all astounded and filled with devotion, for it seemed to them that the former miracle of the Apostles at the time of Pentecost had been renewed, when by the power of the Holy Spirit they spoke in different languages.

And in amazement they said to one another: "Is he not a

Spaniard? How then are we all hearing him in the language of the country where we were born—we Greeks and Latins, French and Germans, Slavs and English, Lombards and foreigners?"

The Pope also was astonished at St. Anthony's profound knowledge of Holy Scripture and said: "He is truly the Ark of the Covenant and the Treasury of Holy Scripture!"

Such then are the soldiers whom our leader St. Francis had —companions who could nourish with the marrow of the Holy Spirit and arm with heavenly weapons against the snares of the enemy not only the flock of Christ but also the Vicar of Christ with his venerable College of Cardinals.[2]

To the glory of Our Lord Jesus Christ, who is blessed forever and ever. Amen.

## 40     *How St. Anthony Converted the Heretics by Preaching to the Fishes*

Our Blessed Lord Jesus Christ, wishing to show how holy was His most faithful servant St. Anthony and how devoutly people should listen to his preaching and wholesome teaching, at one time among others rebuked the foolishness of the infidels and the ignorant and the heretics by means of irrational animals—fishes—just as in ancient times in the Old Testament He rebuked the ignorance of Balaam by the mouth of an ass.

For once when St. Anthony was in Rimini, where there was a great number of heretics, wishing to lead them back to the light of the true faith and onto the path of truth, he preached to them for many days and argued about the faith of Christ and about Holy Scripture. But they were stubborn and hardhearted, and not only did they not accept his holy teaching but, moreover, they refused to listen to him.

So one day, by an inspiration from God, St. Anthony went to the mouth of the river near the sea. And standing on the bank between the sea and the river, he began to call the fishes in God's name, as for a sermon, saying: "You fishes of the sea and river, listen to the word of God, since the faithless heretics refuse to hear it!"

And as soon as he said that, all of a sudden such a great

throng of large and small fishes gathered before him near the bank as had never been seen in that sea or river. And all of them held their heads a bit out of the water, gazing intently at St. Anthony's face. There you would have seen the big fishes staying close to the little ones, while the smaller ones peacefully swam or stayed under the fins of the larger fishes. You would also have seen the different types of fishes hasten to group themselves together and range themselves before the Saint's face like a field painted and adorned with a marvelous variety of colors. You would have seen schools of big fishes occupy the distant places in order to hear the sermon, like an army ranged for battle. You would have seen the middle-sized fishes take their positions in the center and stay in their places without any disturbance, as though they were instructed by God. And you would have seen a great and very dense crowd of small fishes come in a hurry, like pilgrims going to receive an indulgence, and approach closer to the holy Father as to their protector. And so first the smaller fishes near the bank, secondly the middle-sized, and thirdly the largest fishes, where the water was deeper, attended this divinely arranged sermon of St. Anthony—all in very great peace and meekness and order.

Then when all the fishes were in their places in perfect order, St. Anthony solemnly began to preach, saying: "My fish brothers, you should give as many thanks as you can to your Creator who has granted you such a noble element as your dwelling place, so that you have fresh and salt water, just as you please. Moreover He has given you many refuges to escape from storms. He has also given you a clear and transparent element and ways to travel and food to live on. Your kind Creator also prepares for you the food that you need even in the depths of the ocean. When He created you at the creation of the world, He gave you the command to increase and multiply, and He gave you His blessing. Later during the Flood, when all the other animals were perishing, God preserved you alone without loss. He has also given you fins so that with that additional power you can roam wherever you wish. It was granted to you, by order of God, to keep alive Jonas, the Prophet of the Lord, and to cast him onto dry land safe and sound on the third day. You offered the tribute money to Our Lord Jesus Christ, when as a poor man He had nothing to pay the tax. You were chosen as food for the Eternal King, Our Blessed Lord Jesus Christ, before His Resurrection and in a mysterious way afterwards. Because of all these things you should praise and bless the Lord, who has given you so many more blessings than to other creatures."

At these and similar words and preaching of St. Anthony, some of the fishes began to open their mouths, and all of them nodded their heads, and by these and other signs of reverence they praised God as much as they could.

Then St. Anthony, seeing how reverent the fishes were toward God the Creator, rejoiced in spirit and cried out in a loud voice: "Blessed be the Eternal God because the fishes of the waters give God more honor than heretical men, and animals lacking reason listen to His word better than faithless men!"

And the longer St. Anthony preached, the more the throng of fishes increased, and not one of them left the place which it had taken.

At this miracle the people of the city, including the abovementioned heretics, came running. And when they saw the marvelous and extraordinary miracle of the fishes listening to St. Anthony, all of them felt remorse in their hearts, and they sat down at his feet so that he should preach a sermon to them.

Then St. Anthony preached so wonderfully about the Catholic religion that he converted and brought back to the true faith of Christ all those heretics who were there, and the faithful he sent home with his blessing, strengthened in their faith and filled with joy.

St. Anthony also dismissed the fishes with God's blessing, and they all swam away to various parts of the sea, rejoicing and expressing their joy and applause in amazing games and gambols.

After this, St. Anthony stayed in Rimini for many days, preaching and reaping much spiritual fruit, both by converting heretics and by stimulating the piety of the clergy.[1]

To the glory of Our Lord Jesus Christ who is blessed forever and ever. Amen.

### 41     *About Brother Simon of Assisi and*
### *His Marvelous Life*

In the beginning of our Order, when St. Francis was still living, a certain young man of Assisi joined the Order and was called Brother Simon. The Almighty Lord God gave him such graces and consolations and raised him to such a degree of contemplation and elevation of mind that his whole life was a mirror of holiness, as I heard from those who were with him for a long time.

He was very rarely seen outside his cell. If he sometimes went among the friars, he was always eager to talk about God. He never had any schooling and he nearly always lived in the woods. And yet he spoke so profoundly and so loftily about God and the love of Christ that his words seemed supernatural.

Thus one evening when he went into the woods with Brother James of Massa to talk about God, they spoke so very sweetly and devoutly about Christ's love that they spent the whole night in that conversation. And in the morning it seemed to them that they had been there only a short while, as he who was with him told me.

This Brother Simon received such consolations from the Holy Spirit that when he felt a divine illumination and visitation of God's love coming over him, he used to lie down on his bed as if he wanted to sleep, because the sweet peace of the Holy Spirit required of him not only mental but also physical rest. And in such divine visitations he was often rapt in God and became completely insensible to material things.

For one time it happened that while he was thus rapt in God and seemed to be quite unconscious of the exterior world, though wholly burning within with divine love and graces, a friar who wished to prove by an experiment whether he really was insensible as he appeared, went and took a live coal from the fire and placed it on his bare foot. But Brother Simon did not feel the coal at all, and moreover he felt no pain and suffered no wound in his flesh, although that coal stayed on his foot until it had entirely burned itself out.

When this Brother Simon would sit down for meals with the friars, before he took any food for the body, he would take and give to his companions some food for the soul by speaking of God. Thus it happened one time that while he was speaking very fervently of God with the friars a certain young man of San Severino was converted to the Lord. In the world he had been noble and delicate in constitution and very sensual. But Brother Simon, when he received that young man into the Order and gave him the habit, kept in his charge the secular clothes he had taken off. And the young man stayed with Brother Simon in order to be instructed by him in the religious life.

But our enemy the devil, who strives to hinder every good, rushed upon that young man like a roaring lion, and by his evil breath, which sets coal on fire, enkindled within his flesh such burning torments that the boy lost hope of being able to resist so strong a temptation. Consequently he went to Brother Simon and said to him: "Give me back the clothes I wore in the world, because I can't stand the strain of this sensual temptation any longer!"

But Brother Simon felt great compassion for him and said to him: "Sit down here with me for a moment, my son." And while Brother Simon was pouring some beautiful words about God into the ears of that boy, he extinguished the flames of lust and took his temptation completely away.

Later the temptation returned several times, and the youth again asked for his clothes, but Brother Simon drove it away by talking to him about God.

Finally one night the temptation attacked him so much more violently than usual that he could not resist it for anything in the world, so he went to Brother Simon and said: "You must give me back my clothes now, because I simply cannot stay any longer!"

Then Brother Simon as a devout father had compassion on him and said, as he usually did: "Come, son, and sit beside me a while."

The distraught boy went to Brother Simon and sat down beside him. And while he was talking about God, the boy rested his head on Brother Simon's chest, because of his melancholy and depression. But Brother Simon, feeling very sorry for him, raised his eyes toward Heaven, and while he was praying to God with great devotion and compassion for the young man, he was rapt in an ecstasy, and finally his prayer was granted by God. And when Brother Simon came back to himself, the boy felt that he was completely freed from his temptation, as if he had never experienced it, so that the harmful ardor of the temptation was changed into the fervor of the Holy Spirit. And because he had been close to the live coal—Brother Simon —he became all afire with love for God and for his neighbor.

For one day when a certain criminal was captured and condemned to lose both his eyes, that young man courageously went, moved by compassion, to the governor while the council was in session. And with many tears and prayers he asked that he be given the grace that one of his eyes be extracted so that the criminal should not be deprived of both his eyes. But the governor and the council, seeing the youth's great fervor and burning charity, granted the criminal a complete pardon.

Moreover, one day when Brother Simon was praying in the woods and feeling a very great consolation from the Lord in his soul, a flock of birds, called rooks because of the great noise and clamor they make, began to disturb him with their cries, so he ordered them in the name of Jesus to go away and never to come back there again.[1] And it is wonderful to relate that, although that Place of Brunforte in the Custody of Fermo existed for over fifty years, those birds were never seen or heard again anywhere around the Place or district or entire region. And I, Brother Ugolino di Monte Santa Maria, stayed there for three years, and I observed that wonder in a sure way, and it was known among both the lay people and the friars of the whole Custody.[2]

To the glory of Christ. Amen.

## 42 About the Wonderful Miracles That God
### Performed through Some Holy Friars

In former times the Province of the Marches of Ancona was adorned and bright like the sky with brilliant stars that were the holy and exemplary Friars Minor who shone like stars above and below—before God and their neighbor—with radiant virtues, and who illumined the Order of St. Francis and the world by their example and teaching. Their memory is truly a blessing from God.

Among them some were like greater constellations that shone more brightly than others: for instance, first of all, Brother Lucido the Elder, who was indeed resplendent with sanctity and aflame with the love of God, and whose glorious preaching was inspired by the Holy Spirit and reaped marvelous fruit.[1]

Another was Brother Bentivoglia of San Severino, who was seen by Brother Masseo of San Severino raised up into the air at a great height while he was praying in the woods.

As a result of that miracle this Brother Masseo, who was then a pastor, left his pastorate and became a Friar Minor, and he lived such a saintly life that he performed many miracles before and after his death. His body rests in Murro.[2]

The above-mentioned Brother Bentivoglia, when he was once staying alone at Trave Bonanti nursing and taking care of a man suffering from leprosy, received an obedience from his superior to leave there and go to another Place which was fifteen miles away. Not wishing to abandon the sick man, with great fervor of charity he took him up and set him on his own shoulders. And burdened that way he carried him from early dawn until sunrise all that distance of fifteen miles, from the Place of Trave to the Place where he was sent, which was called Monte Sanvicino. If he had been an eagle, he could hardly have flown that distance in such a short time. Everyone in that region who heard about this divine miracle was filled with amazement and admiration.[3]

Another friar was Peter of Montecchio, a real saint, who was seen by Brother Servodeo of Urbino (at that time his guardian in the old Place of Ancona)[4] raised in the air about five or six cubits above the ground, that is, the pavement of the church, up to the feet of the Crucifix before which he was praying.

This Brother Peter, once while he was keeping the Lent of St. Michael with great devotion, on the last day of that Lent was praying in church, and he was heard talking with the most holy Archangel Michael and the Archangel talking with him, by a young friar who had carefully hidden under the high altar in order to observe him. And this is what they were saying.

The Archangel St. Michael said: "Brother Peter, you have labored faithfully for me, and you have afflicted your body in many ways. Now I have come to console you. So ask whatever grace you desire—and I will obtain it for you from the Lord."

Brother Peter answered: "Most holy prince of the heavenly army and most faithful defender of God's honor and most compassionate protector of souls, I ask you for this grace: that you obtain for me from God the forgiveness of all my sins."

The Archangel Michael replied: "Ask for another grace, because I will easily obtain that one for you."

But as Brother Peter did not ask for anything else, the Archangel concluded, saying: "Because of the faith and devotion which you have for me, I will obtain for you that grace which you request and many others."

When their conversation was over—and it lasted a great part of the night—the Archangel St. Michael went away and left Brother Peter intensely consoled.[5]

Brother Conrad of Offida was living in the days of that holy Brother Peter. When they were members of the community at the Place of Forano in the Custody of Ancona, one day Brother Conrad went into the woods to contemplate God, and Brother Peter secretly went after him in order to see what happened.

Now Brother Conrad began to pray very devoutly and with many tears to the Blessed Virgin Mary that she might obtain for him from her Son this grace: that he might be allowed to feel a little of that sweetness which St. Simeon felt on the day of her Purification when he held in his arms the Blessed Savior Jesus.

He earned the granting of his prayer by the most merciful Lady. For the glorious Queen of Heaven appeared with that Blessed little Son of hers in her arms in such dazzling splendor that it not only drove away the shadows but also outshone all lights. And approaching the holy Brother Conrad, she put in his arms that Blessed little Son who is more beautiful than the sons of men.

Brother Conrad took him with very great devotion and pressed his lips to His and clasped Him to his heart. And in these loving embraces and kisses he felt as though his soul were melting away with ineffable consolation.

Now Brother Peter was watching all this in the bright light, and he too felt a great sweetness in his soul. And he remained hidden in the woods. But when the Blessed Virgin Mary and her Son left Brother Conrad, Brother Peter hurried back to the Place, so as not to be seen by him.

Later when Brother Conrad returned, overflowing with joy and happiness, Brother Peter called him and said: "Oh, you heavenly man, you have had a great consolation today!"

Brother Conrad said: "What do you mean, Brother Peter? What do you know about what I have had?"

Brother Peter said: "I know very well—I know very well, you heavenly man, how the Blessed Virgin Mary visited you with her Blessed little Son."

When Brother Conrad heard that, he asked Brother Peter not to tell it to anyone, because as a truly humble man he wanted to keep secret the graces which God gave him. And after this the love between the two of them was so great that they seemed to have one heart and one soul in all things.[6]

Once in the Place of Sirolo this Brother Conrad by his

prayers freed a woman who was obsessed by the devil. And in the morning he immediately fled from that Place so that the mother of the liberated girl should not find him and he should not be acclaimed by a crowd of people. For Brother Conrad had prayed for her all that night, and he had appeared in a vision to her mother while he was liberating her.

To the praise and glory of Our Lord Jesus Christ. Amen.

### 43  *How Brother Conrad Converted a Young Friar*

The life of this Brother Conrad of Offida, a wonderful follower of Gospel poverty and the Rule of our Father St. Francis, was so saintly and full of merit before God that the Lord Jesus Christ repeatedly honored him with many miracles while he was alive as well as after his death.

Among others, once when he came on a visit to the Place of Offida, the friars asked him, for the love of God and of charity, to give a good talking to a certain young friar in that Place who was acting so childishly and foolishly that he was disturbing both the old and young members of the community very much, and he cared little or nothing for the divine office and the other regular practices of the religious life.

So Brother Conrad felt sorry for that young man and for the other friars whom he was disturbing. And yielding humbly to their request he called the boy aside. And in all charity he said such persuasive and inspired words of reproof to him that suddenly the hand of the Lord came over that youth, and by the power of divine grace he was changed into another man: from a child he became a mature man, so obedient, so thoughtful and kind, so devout, so peaceable and helpful and so eager to practice all virtues that, just as formerly the whole community had been disturbed by him, afterwards they all rejoiced because of his complete conversion to virtue. And they loved him very much, as though he were an angel.

As it pleased God, soon after his conversion that young man fell ill and died, and the friars grieved a great deal. And a few days after his death, while Brother Conrad, who had converted him, was praying devoutly one night before the altar of the friary, the soul of that friar came and greeted Brother Conrad affectionately, as a father. And Brother Conrad asked him: "Who are you?"

He replied: "I am the soul of that young friar who died recently."

And Brother Conrad said: "Oh, my dear son, how are you?"

He replied: "Beloved Father, by the grace of God and your teaching, I am well, because I am not damned. But on account of some of my sins which I did not fully expiate owing to lack of time, I am suffering very much in Purgatory. So I beg you, Father, as by your compassion you helped me when I was alive, to deign to help me now in my sufferings by saying some Our Fathers for me, because your prayers are very acceptable before God."

Brother Conrad willingly agreed and said one Our Father with the *Requiem aeternam*.

After he had said it, the soul said: "Oh, dear Father, what relief I feel now! I beg you to say it again."

And when he had prayed again, the soul said: "Holy Father, when you pray for me, I feel all refreshed, so I beg you not to stop praying for me!"

So Brother Conrad, realizing that the soul was thus helped by his prayers, said one hundred Our Fathers for him.

And when he had finished saying them, the friar said: "Dear Father, on behalf of Our Lord Jesus Christ I thank you for the charity you have shown me. May He give you an eternal reward for this kindness, because through your prayers I have been freed from all suffering! And now I am going to the glory of Paradise."

And after saying that, the soul went away.

Then Brother Conrad, in order to give joy and consolation to the friars, told them all that had happened during that night, and he and they were greatly consoled.

To the glory of Our Lord Jesus Christ. Amen.

### 44   How Brother Peter of Montecchio Was Shown Who Suffered Most from the Passion of Christ

At the time when the above-mentioned Brother Conrad and Brother Peter—two bright stars in the Province of the Marches and two heavenly men—were living together in the Custody of Ancona, at the Place of Forano (which they liked very much), there was so much love and charity between them that both seemed to have one heart and one soul, and they bound themselves together in this agreement: that in charity they must reveal to each other all the consolations which the mercy of God might grant to either one.

One day, after they had made that pact, it happened that Brother Peter was praying and meditating devoutly on the Passion of Christ. And His Most Blessed Mother and John the beloved Disciple were standing before Christ Crucified—and our blessed Father Francis was also there with his Stigmata. And there came to him the holy desire to know which of those three had suffered most from the Passion of Christ: the Mother who had given Him birth or the beloved Disciple who had rested on His breast or St. Francis who was crucified with Christ.

And while he was thinking these devout thoughts, weeping many tears, the Virgin Mary appeared to him with St. John the Evangelist and our blessed Father Francis, dressed in very noble raiment of heavenly glory; but St. Francis seemed to be dressed in a more beautiful garment than St. John.

And as Brother Peter was very frightened by this vision, St. John comforted him and said to him: "Do not be afraid, dear Brother, because we have come to console you and to clear up your doubt. Know therefore that the Mother of Christ and I grieved more than any other creature over the Passion of Christ, but after us St. Francis felt greater sorrow than any other. And that is why you see him in such glory."

And Brother Peter asked him: "Most holy apostle of Christ, why does the clothing of St. Francis seem more glorious than yours?"

St. John replied: "This is the reason: because when he was in the world, for the love of Christ he wore plainer clothes than I."

And having said these words, St. John gave Brother Peter a glorious garment which he was holding in his hand, and said to him: "Take this robe which I have brought to show you."

And when St. John wanted to clothe him in that robe, Brother Peter in amazement began to run and shout (for he was awake, not asleep, when he saw this): "Brother Conrad, dear Brother Conrad, come quick! Come and see something marvelous!" And at those words the holy vision vanished.

Then, when Brother Conrad came, he told him everything in detail. And they gave thanks to God. Amen.

### 45   About the Conversion, Life, Miracles, and Death of the Holy Brother John of Penna

When Brother John of Penna, one of the bright stars of the Province of the Marches, was still a young boy in the world, one night a very beautiful boy appeared to him and called him, saying: "John, go to Santo Stefano where one of My friars is due to preach. And believe his teaching and listen to his words, for I have sent him there. And after you have done that, you will have a long journey to make. And afterward you shall come to Me."

He immediately arose and felt a marvelous change in his soul. And going to Santo Stefano, he found there a great crowd of men and women who had come together from different villages in order to hear the word of God. And he who was to preach was a friar called Brother Philip, who was one of the first friars who came to the Marches of Ancona, when only a few Places had been founded in the Marches.

This Brother Philip rose up and preached with great devotion, not in the learned words of human wisdom, but announcing the Kingdom of God and eternal life by the power of the Spirit of Christ.

Now when the sermon was over, the above-mentioned boy, Brother John, went to Brother Philip and said to him: "Father, if you would receive me in the Order, I would be glad to do penance and to serve the Lord Jesus Christ."

The friar, being a holy and enlightened man, perceived the boy's marvelous innocence and ready will to serve God, and he said to him: "Come to see me in the city of Recanati on a certain day, and I will see that you are received." (For a Provincial Chapter was to be held in that Place then.)

In his innocence the boy reflected in his heart: "This will be the long journey that was revealed to me, which I am to make and then go to Heaven." He thought that would happen as soon as he was received in the Order. So he went and was received. But his expectation was not fulfilled then.

And during the Chapter the minister said: "Whoever wants to go to the Province of Provence by merit of holy obedience— I will send him there." Now when Brother John heard this, he felt a great desire to go there, thinking that perhaps that was the long journey he had to make before he went to Paradise. But he was too bashful to speak up. Finally he confided in Brother Philip, who had arranged for him to be received in the Order, and said to him: "Father, I ask you to obtain this grace for me: that I may be able to go and stay in Provence." For in those times the friars used to volunteer to go to foreign provinces so that they might be like pilgrims and strangers in this world and fellow citizens of the saints and servants of God in Heaven.

Brother Philip, seeing his simplicity and holy intention, obtained permission for him to go to that province. And Brother John set out with great joy, feeling sure that when he had finished that journey, he would go to Heaven.

But as it pleased God, he stayed in that province for twenty-five years, living a life of great and exemplary sanctity, but hoping every day that what had been promised to him would be fulfilled. And although he grew in virtue and holiness, and he was loved by both the friars and the lay people in all that province, he nevertheless could not see the least sign of his desire being granted.

One day while he was devoutly praying and weeping and lamenting to God that his exile and pilgrimage in this life were being prolonged too much, the Blessed Lord Jesus Christ appeared to him, at the sight of whom his soul melted with love.

And Christ said to him: "My son, Brother John, ask Me for whatever you want."

And he answered: "My Lord, I don't know what to say, because I want nothing but You. But I ask You only for this: that You forgive me all my sins, and give me the grace to see You again when I need You still more."

The Lord said to him: "Your prayer is granted." And after saying that, He vanished from his sight. And Brother John remained greatly consoled.

At last the friars of the Marches heard about his reputation for sanctity and arranged with the General that a written order be sent to him to return to the Marches. When he saw that order, he gladly set out, saying to himself: "This is the long journey after which I will go to God."

Now when he returned to his own province, he was not recognized by any of his relatives. But from one day to the next he waited and expected that God would have mercy on him and fulfill the promise that had been made to him.

But his life was still further prolonged, for he stayed on a good thirty years after his return to the Marches. And during that time he often served as guardian with great discretion. And the Lord performed many miracles through him.

Among a number of other gifts, he had the spirit of prophecy. For once when he was absent from his Place, one of his novices was attacked by the devil and so strongly tempted to leave the Order that he yielded and decided that he would leave as soon as Brother John came back to the Place.

But by the spirit of prophecy Brother John knew about that temptation and decision. And as soon as he came home, he called that novice and said to him: "Come, son—I want you to confess." And when he came, Brother John added: "First listen to me, son."

And then he told the novice all about his temptation, as God had revealed it to him. And he concluded: "My son, because you waited for me and did not want to leave without my blessing, God has given you this grace: that you will never leave this Order, but that you will die in this Order with the Lord's blessing."

And then that novice was strengthened in his good intention, and he stayed in the Order and became a holy friar.

And Brother John himself told me, Brother Ugolino, all these things.

Now Brother John was always a man with joy and peace of mind. He was silent and rarely spoke. And he was a man of great devotion and prayer, and especially after matins he did not go back to his cell, but stayed praying in church until dawn.

And one night after matins while he was praying fervently, an angel of the Lord appeared and said to him: "Brother John, your journey has come to the end which you have been awaiting so long. Therefore I announce to you on God's behalf that you may ask for whatever grace you desire—and also that you must choose either one entire day in Purgatory or seven days of suffering in this world."

And when Brother John had rather chosen seven days of suffering in this world, he suddenly fell ill with a number of different sicknesses in succession. For he was plagued with strong fevers and pains and gout in hands and feet and convulsions and intestinal troubles and many other sufferings. But what was worse than all the other afflictions was that a devil stood before him holding a large scroll on which were written all his sins and faults and failings of thought and deed, and the devil said to him: "Because of all these things which you thought and said and did, you are damned to the depths of hell!"

And the sick friar forgot all the good things that he had ever done, and that he was or ever had been in the Order. But he thought that he was utterly damned, as the devil was saying. So when he was asked by anyone how he felt, he would answer: "Bad—because I am damned!"

Seeing this, the friars of the Place sent for an old friar named Brother Matthew of Monte Rubbiano who was a very holy man and an intimate friend of Brother John.

Now Brother Matthew came to him on the seventh day of his tribulations and greeted him, saying: "How are you feeling, dear Brother?"

He replied: "Bad—because I am damned!"

Then Brother Matthew said: "How can you say that? Don't you remember that you often confessed to me, and I completely absolved you from all your sins? Don't you also remember that you have served God for many years in this holy Order? Besides, don't you remember that the mercy of God is greater than all the sins in the world, and that Christ Our Blessed Savior paid an infinite price to God our Father in order to redeem us? So you can be perfectly sure that you will be saved and not damned."

And then, when he had said that, as the seven-day period of Brother John's purgation was over, his temptation left him, and a feeling of consolation came over him. And with great joy he said to Brother Matthew: "Because you are tired and it is already time for bed, I want you to go and rest."

Now Brother Matthew did not want to leave him, but Brother John insisted so much that finally he left and went to get some rest.

And while Brother John remained alone with the friar who was taking care of him, Our Blessed Lord Jesus Christ appeared to him in a very bright light and sweet fragrance, just as He had promised to appear to him once more when he would need Him most. And He completely cured him of all his sicknesses.

Then Brother John joined his hands and gave thanks to God for having brought his long journey in this sad life to a happy end, and he was united for all eternity to his Lord Jesus Christ, like a chosen member to the head. And so with great joy and confidence and consolation he commended and gave up his soul to God and passed from this mortal life to eternal life with the Blessed Christ, whom he had desired and awaited for so long a time.

And this Brother John was buried in the Place of Penna San Giovanni.[1]

To the glory of Christ. Amen.

### 46   *How Brother Pacifico Saw the Soul of His Brother Going to Heaven*

In that Province of the Marches after the death of our Father St. Francis there were two brothers in the Order, Brother Humble and Brother Pacifico, both of whom were men of great sanctity and perfection.[1]

One of them, Brother Humble, lived in the Place of Soffiano and died there. But the other was a member of a community in a Place at some distance from him. And as it pleased God, when Brother Pacifico was staying in that distant Place, one day while he was praying in a solitary and lonely spot, the hand of the Lord came over him. And being rapt in ecstasy, he saw the soul of his brother, Brother Humble, ascend directly up to Heaven without any delay or hindrance.

Many years later it happened that the brother who lived on was made a member of the community at that Place of Soffiano where his brother had died and was buried. Now at that time, at the request of the Lords of Brunforte, the friars gave up the Place of Soffiano for another, so that they transferred the remains of the holy friars who had been buried there.[2] And when they came to the grave of Brother Humble among the others, his brother, Brother Pacifico, took up the bones very devoutly and washed them with excellent wine and then wrapped them in a white napkin, weeping over them and kissing them very reverently.

But the other friars who were present were surprised and shocked at this, because while he had a reputation for great holiness, it seemed to them that he was grieving for his brother out of a natural and worldly affection, and that he was showing greater devotion to those remains than to those of the other friars who had been no less saintly than Brother Humble and were worthy of the same honor as he.

Knowing that the friars were misjudging him, Brother Pacifico humbly explained to them: "My dear Brothers, do not be surprised because I have done something that I did not do to the others, for—blessed be God—it was not a natural affection that motivated me, as you thought. But I acted that way because, when my brother left this world and went to the Lord, I was praying in a solitary place far away from him and I saw his soul ascending straight up to Heaven. So I am certain that these bones of his are holy and are destined to rest some day in God's Paradise. That is why I am doing what you see. And if God had granted me such certainty regarding the other friars, I would have shown the same reverence for their bones."

Consequently, perceiving his good and holy motive, the

friars were greatly edified. And they praised God who performs such great wonders for His holy friars.

To the glory of Christ. Amen.

### 47   How the Blessed Virgin Appeared to a Holy Friar When He Was Ill

In the Marches of Ancona, in a certain solitary Place called Soffiano, there was in former times a certain Friar Minor (whose name I do not remember) of such great holiness and grace that he seemed to be godlike. And he was often rapt in the Lord.

Once when he was in a rapture and his mind was absorbed in God—for he had the grace of contemplation to a remarkable degree—various kinds of birds came to him and very tamely rested on his head and shoulders and arms and hands, and there they sang beautifully. When he came out of his contemplation, he was so overflowing with joy that he seemed rather like an angel, for then his face radiated in a marvelous way his communion with God, to such an extent that it aroused wonder and surprise in those who saw him.

He always remained alone and spoke very rarely, and he was in prayer or contemplation almost continually day and night. But when he was asked a question, he answered so pleasantly and wisely that he seemed more like an angel than a man. And the friars felt great reverence for him. He was pleasant to everyone and his conversation was always spiced with divine salt.

He persevered in this praiseworthy practice of the virtues until the end of his heavenly life. And by disposition of Divine Providence he became so mortally ill that he was unable to take any food. And he did not want to be given any medicine for his body. But he placed all his confidence in the heavenly doctor Jesus Christ and in His Blessed Mother. And he merited the grace of being visited and consoled in a wonderful way by the Blessed Virgin Mary, the Queen of Mercy.

For one day while he was lying alone and was preparing himself for death with all his strength, the Blessed and Glorious Mother of Christ herself appeared to him, accompanied by a throng of angels and holy virgins, amid a bright light, and she went close to the sick friar's cot. When he saw her, he was filled with inexpressible joy and consolation of both mind and body. And he began to beg her humbly to pray to her beloved Son that He might deign by His merits to lead him out of the dark prison of the flesh. And as with many tears he kept fervently begging her to do so, the Blessed Virgin Mary answered him, calling him by his name and saying: "Do not fear, my son, because your prayer is granted. For I have seen your tears. And I have come to give you a little consolation before you leave this life."

With the Blessed Mother of Christ there were three holy virgins, each of whom carried in her hands a box filled with an electuary that was so sweet in taste and fragrance that words cannot describe it. And as the Blessed Virgin Mary took one of those boxes and opened it, the whole house was filled with the perfume. And taking a spoon in her glorious hands, she gave a bit of the heavenly electuary to that sick friar. When he tasted it, he experienced such grace and sweetness that it seemed to him his soul would quickly leave his body. So he began to say to the glorious Virgin Mary: "No more, oh dear Mother of Jesus Christ and Blessed Lady—no more, oh blessed doctor, for I cannot bear such sweetness!"

But the merciful and kind Mother of God urged him on and consoled him by speaking a great deal to him about the Lord Jesus Christ, and she frequently made him take more of the electuary until that first box was empty.

Then as she took the second box and placed the spoon in it, the sick friar gently complained to her: "Oh Blessed Mother of God, if my soul has nearly melted from the perfume and sweetness of the first box, how can I bear the second? I beg you, oh Blessed above all the saints and holy angels, not to give me any more!"

Our Lady answered: "Son, you must take a little of this second box." And giving him a little of the second electuary, she said to him: "Now, my son, you have had enough. But rejoice, because I shall soon come back to you, and I shall lead you to the Kingdom of my Son which you have always longed for and desired."

And saying good-by to him, she vanished from his sight.

And he remained so comforted and consoled by the sweetness of that electuary, which had been brought from the apothecary of Paradise and administered to him by the hands of the Blessed Virgin Mary, that for several days he did not take any material food, but felt strong in body and mind, for it was not a medicine of this world but of Heaven. And he was given a profound spiritual insight, and his eyes were opened by such a radiant divine light that he clearly saw in the book of eternal life all who would be saved until Judgment Day.

And a few days later, on the last day of his life, while talking with the friars and rejoicing greatly in mind and body, he passed from this unhappy life to the Lord Jesus Christ.[1]

To the glory of Christ. Amen.

### 48   *How Brother James of Massa Saw in a Vision All the Friars Minor in the World*

Brother James of Massa—to whom God opened the door of His secrets and gave a perfect knowledge and understanding of Holy Scripture and of the future—was so saintly that Brother Giles of Assisi and Brother Mark of Montino used to say that they knew no one in the world who was greater in God's sight. Brother Juniper and Brother Lucido felt the same way. When Brother John, the companion of Brother Giles, was my spiritual director, I wanted very much to see him. For while I was asking Brother John about certain spiritual matters, he said to me: "If you want to be well instructed in the spiritual life, hasten to have some talks with Brother James of Massa, because Brother Giles wanted to be instructed by him. And nothing can be added to or taken away from his words, for his mind has penetrated into the secrets of Heaven, and his words are the words of the Holy Spirit. And there is no man on earth whom I have wanted so much to see."

This Brother James, about the beginning of the ministry of Brother John of Parma, was once rapt in an ecstasy while praying, and he remained unconscious for three days, so that the friars began to wonder whether he was dead. And in that rapture God revealed to him an understanding of Scripture and a knowledge of the future. And therefore, when I heard about it, my desire to see him and talk to him increased.

And when it pleased God that I have an opportunity to speak to him, I questioned him in this way: "If what I have heard about you is true, please do not hide it from me. For I heard that when you remained lying almost dead for three days, God showed you among other things what was going to happen in our Order. Brother Matthew, to whom you revealed it under obedience, said so."

For Brother Matthew, who was then Minister of the Province of the Marches, summoned him after that rapture and ordered him under obedience to tell him what he had seen.

Now Brother Matthew was a man of marvelous gentleness and holiness and simplicity. And he would often tell the friars in his talks to them: "I know a friar to whom God has shown all that will happen in our Order—and also some amazing secrets which, if they were uttered, would hardly be understood or even believed."[1]

Now Brother James revealed to me and told me, among other things, something very astounding, that is, that after many things which were shown to him concerning the condition of the Church Militant, he saw in a vision a certain very beautiful and high tree, and its roots were of gold, and its fruits were men, and all of them were Friars Minor. And the number of its principal branches corresponded to that of the provinces in the Order, and each branch had as many fruits as there were friars in that province. And then he knew the number of all the friars in the whole Order and in each province and also their name and face and age and condition and rank and position and their honors and graces and merits and faults.

And he saw Brother John of Parma standing on the highest part of the central branch of that tree, and on the tops of the branches which were around that central branch stood the ministers of all the provinces. And after this he saw Christ sitting on a very great white throne. And Christ called St. Francis and gave him a chalice full of the spirit of life, and sent him forth, saying to him: "Go and visit your friars. And let them drink from this chalice of the spirit of life, for the spirit of Satan will rise up and attack them, and many of them will fall and will not rise again." And Christ gave St. Francis two angels to go with him.

Then St. Francis came to offer the chalice of life to his friars as he had been ordered to do. And he began by offering it to Brother John, the Minister General, who accepted the chalice from St. Francis' hand and drank it all quickly and devoutly. And after he had drunk, he suddenly became all luminous and bright like the sun.

And after him St. Francis offered the chalice of the spirit of life to all the others, one after another, but very few of them accepted it with fitting reverence and devotion and drank all of it. Those few who did take it reverently and drank it all suddenly became as bright as the sun. But those who spilled it all or did not take it reverently became dark and black and deformed and horrible to see, like devils. And those who drank part but spilled part became more or less luminous or dark according to the degree of their drinking or spilling.

But shining more brightly than all the others on the tree was the above-mentioned Brother John who, having drunk more fully from the chalice of life, had a profound insight into the depths of God's true light, and in it he perceived that the whirlwind of a great storm was arising against that tree and would shake and tear its branches. Therefore he went down from the top of the branch where he had been standing, past all the branches, and hid himself in the solid part of the tree's trunk.

And while he gave himself to contemplation there, Brother Bonaventure, who had drunk part of the chalice and had spilled part, went up to the branch and place which Brother John had left. And when he was in that place, the nails of his fingers turned to iron and became as sharp and cutting as razors. And leaving his place, he wanted to attack Brother John with rage and fury, to hurt him. But seeing this, Brother John cried for help to Christ, who was sitting on the throne. And at his cry, Christ called St. Francis and gave him a very sharp flintstone and said to him: "Go and with this stone cut the nails of Brother Bonaventure with which he wants to tear Brother John, so that he cannot hurt him!"

Then St. Francis came and cut Brother Bonaventure's nails

as Christ had ordered him to do. And so Brother John stayed in his place, shining brightly.[2]

After this, a violent hurricane arose and struck the tree so strongly that the friars began to fall from it. And those who had completely spilled the chalice of the spirit of life fell first. And those who fell turned dark and were carried away by devils to realms of darkness and pain. But Brother John and those who had completely drunk the chalice were carried by angels to the realm of eternal life, light, and glory.

And he who saw the vision understood clearly and remembered every particular detail that he saw, such as the names and persons and places and ages and states of everyone whom he saw in the realms of light and darkness. And the hurricane and fierce storm lasted, with the permission of God's justice, until the tree was torn up by the roots and crashed to the ground and the wind blew it completely away.

Now as soon as that hurricane and storm stopped, from the root of the tree, which was of gold, came forth another tree that was all of gold and that produced golden fruits and flowers. Regarding that tree's growth, depth, fragrance, beauty, and virtue, it is better to be silent than to speak now.

But I do not want to omit one thing which he who saw this vision used to tell, for it sounded very noteworthy to me. For he said that the way in which the Order would be reformed would be very different from the way in which it was founded, because the working of the Holy Spirit, without there being a leader, will choose uneducated youths and simple, plain persons who are looked down upon. And without their having any example or teacher—even against the teaching and practice of the teachers—the Spirit of Christ will select them and fill them with holy fear and a very pure love of Christ. And when their number has increased in various places, then He will send them an utterly pure and saintly shepherd and leader, wholly conformed to Christ.

To the praise and glory of Christ. Amen.

### 49  *How Christ Appeared to Brother John of Alverna*

How glorious our blessed Father Francis is in the sight of God appears in the chosen sons whom the Holy Spirit added to his Order, for as Solomon says, the glory of the father is in his wise sons.

Among them shone in a very special way in our times the venerable and saintly Brother John of Fermo, who sparkled in the skies of the Order like a marvelous star owing to the radiance of his grace. (Because of the long time which he spent at the holy Place of Alverna and because he passed from this life there, he was also called Brother John of Alverna.)[1]

For when he was a boy in the world, he had the wise heart of an old man, and he longed with all his soul to take up the life of penance which keeps the mind and body pure. When he was still a little boy, he began to wear a breastplate of mail and an iron band on his flesh, and he used to carry the cross of abstinence every day. And especially while he was staying with the canons at St. Peter in Fermo, who lived in ease, before he received the habit of the holy Father, he used to avoid physical comfort and to practice self-control with amazing strictness, and he enjoyed inflicting the martyrdom of abstinence on his body.

But as his companions were so opposed to his angelic zeal that they took his breastplate away from him and interfered with his abstinence in various ways, inspired by God he thought of abandoning the world with its lovers and of offering up the flower of his angelic purity to the Crucified in the Order of St. Francis, in whom he had heard that the wounds of Christ's Crucifixion had been renewed.

Now after he had received the habit of the Friars Minor while still a boy and he had been committed to the care of a holy novicemaster for spiritual training,[2] he became so fervent and devout that when he heard that master speak of God, his heart would melt like wax near the fire, and interiorly he felt so inflamed with the sweet grace of God's love that he could not stay still exteriorly and endure such consolation, but in his spiritual intoxication he felt forced to get up and run or walk around the garden or the woods or the church, depending on how the interior fire and stimulus of the spirit impelled him.

Later, with the passing of time, God's grace made this angelic man grow continually in virtue and heavenly gifts and ecstasies and raptures, so that at times his mind was raised to the splendor of the cherubim, at times to the ardor of the seraphim, and at other times to the joys of the angels. And furthermore, sometimes it drew him on to the mystical kisses and intense embraces of Christ's love not only in interior spiritual graces but also in exterior signs, as with an intimate friend.

Thus it happened once that his heart became enkindled with the fire of God's love in an extraordinary way, and that flame lasted in him for three full years, during which he received marvelous consolations and divine visitations and was often rapt in God. In brief, during that time he seemed all on fire and aflame with the love of Christ. (And this was on the holy Mount Alverna.) [3]

But because God takes special care of His sons, giving them at different times either consolations or trials, either prosperity or adversity, depending on what He sees that they need to remain humble or to enkindle their longing for heavenly things still more—after the three years were over, while Brother John was staying in a certain Place—it pleased God in His goodness to withdraw that light and fire of divine love from him and to deprive him of all spiritual consolations, leaving him without love or light and utterly miserable and depressed and mournful. Consequently, when his soul did not feel the presence of his Beloved, in his anguish and torment he went through the woods, running here and there, anxiously seeking and calling aloud with tears and sighs for his dear Friend who had recently abandoned him and hidden, and without whose presence his soul could find no peace or rest. But nowhere and in no way could he find his Blessed Jesus Christ and enjoy as before the sweet spiritual consolations of His loving embraces.

And he endured that trial for many days, mourning and sighing and weeping and praying God in His mercy to give him back the beloved Spouse of his soul.

Finally, when it pleased God to have sufficiently tested his patience and inflamed his longing, one day while Brother

John was walking up and down in the woods where he had made himself a little path to walk on, being tired and unhappy and depressed he sat down there, leaning against a beech tree, and raised his tear-stricken face toward Heaven. And all of a sudden He who heals and lightens the weight of contrite hearts, Our Blessed Lord Jesus Christ, appeared on the path where Brother John had been walking, but He said nothing.

When Brother John saw Him and recognized Him, he immediately threw himself at His feet, and weeping uncontrollably he very humbly begged Him to help him, saying: "Help me, my Lord, because without You, my sweet Savior, I remain in darkness and grief. Without You, most gentle Lamb, I remain in worry and fear. Without You, Son of Almighty God, I remain in confusion and shame. For without You I am deprived of all that is good. Without You I am blind in the dark, because You are Jesus, the true Light of the World. Without You I am lost and damned, because You are the life of souls and the life of lives. Without You I am sterile and dry, because You are the God of Gods and the giver of graces. But in You I find all consolation because You are Jesus, our Redemption, love, and desire, our refreshing bread and wine who give joy to the choirs of angels and the hearts of all the saints. So enlighten me, most kind Master and compassionate Shepherd, because, though unworthy, I am Your little lamb."

But because the longing of holy men increases to greater love and merit when God delays in granting its fulfillment, the Blessed Christ went away from him along the path. Then Brother John, seeing that Christ was leaving without answering his prayer or saying anything to him, arose and ran after Him and again humbly threw himself at His feet, holding Him back with holy eagerness. And with fervent tears he implored Him, saying: "Oh, sweetest Jesus, have pity on me because I am suffering. Grant my prayer by the abundance of Your mercy and the truth of Your salvation. And give me back the joy of Your countenance and Your look, because the whole world is full of Your mercy. Lord, You know how intense my suffering is! I beg You to come quickly to the help of my darkened soul."

Again the Savior went away from him without saying anything to him or giving him any consolation. And it seemed as if He wished to leave as He went along the path. But He was acting like a mother with her baby when she withdraws her breast from him to make him drink the milk more eagerly, and he cries and seeks it, and after he has cried, she hugs and kisses him and lets him enjoy it all the more.

So Brother John followed Christ a third time with greater fervor and desire, weeping, like a baby following its mother or a boy his father or a humble pupil his kind teacher. And when he came up to Him, the Blessed Christ turned toward him and looked at him with a joyful and loving expression on His face, and He held out and opened His holy and merciful arms as the priest does when he turns to the people. And as He opened His arms, Brother John saw marvelous rays of light issuing from the holy breast of Christ that illuminated not only the whole forest but also his own soul and body with divine splendor.

Then the Holy Spirit suddenly revealed to Brother John the humble and reverent act which he should perform toward Christ. For he immediately threw himself down at Christ's feet, and the Savior showed him His blessed feet, over which Brother John wept so much that he seemed like another Magdalen. And he said devoutly: "I beg You, my Lord, not to consider my sins. But by Your most holy Passion and by the shedding of Your Precious Blood, deign to reawaken my soul to the grace of Your love, since it is Your commandment that we love You with all our heart and all our strength—and no one can fulfill that commandment without Your help. So help me, O most lovable Son of God, to love You with all my heart and all my strength!"

Now while Brother John was praying fervently lying at Christ's feet, he received so much grace that he felt completely renewed and pacified and consoled, like Magdalen. And then feeling again within himself the fire of divine love and knowing that the gift of divine love had returned to him, he began to give thanks to God and humbly to kiss the Savior's feet.

Then as he raised his head to look gratefully up at the Savior's face, Christ held out His most holy hands and opened them for him to kiss. And while He opened them, Brother John arose and kissed His hands.

And when he had kissed them, he came closer and leaned against the breast of Christ, and he embraced Jesus and kissed His holy bosom.[4] And Christ likewise embraced and kissed him.

And when Brother John kissed the holy breast of Christ, he perceived so heavenly a fragrance that if all the scents and perfumes in the world were fused together they would seem a putrid stench compared to that divine fragrance. Moreover the above-mentioned rays issued from the Savior's breast, throwing light into his mind interiorly and exteriorly and into everything around him. And in that embrace, fragrance, light, and holy breast of the Lord Jesus Christ, Brother John was rapt in ecstasy and utterly consoled and marvelously enlightened. For henceforth, because he had drunk from the fountain of the Lord's breast, he was filled with the gift of wisdom and the grace of God's word, and he often spoke marvelous supernatural words. And because from his belly flowed streams of living water which he had imbibed from the depths of the breast of Our Lord Jesus Christ, he therefore converted the minds of those who heard him and reaped wonderful spiritual fruit.

Furthermore, that fragrance and light which he had perceived endured within his soul for many months. And what is still more: on that path in the forest where the Savior's blessed feet had walked and at some distance roundabout he perceived that same light and fragrance for a long time, whenever he went there.[5]

When Brother John was coming back to himself after his rapture, the Blessed Christ disappeared. Yet afterward he always remained consoled and enlightened. For then he did not find the Humanity of Christ—as he who heard about it from Brother John told me—but he found his own soul buried in the depths of the Divinity. And this was proved by many clear manifestations.

For he used to utter such inspiring and profound and luminous words before the Roman Curia and before kings and barons and masters of theology and doctors of canon law that he moved all of them to wonder and surprise. Although Brother John was almost an uneducated man, he nevertheless solved and explained in an amazing way the most subtle and abstract problems concerning the Trinity and other deep mysteries of Holy Scripture.[6]

Now that Brother John was, as we have seen, raised up first to the feet of Christ with tears, then to the hands with graces, and third to the blessed breast with a rapture and rays of light—these are great mysteries which cannot be explained in brief words. But let him who wants to understand it read St. Bernard on the Canticle of Canticles, who there describes the successive groups: the beginners at the feet, those progressing at the hands, but the perfect at the kiss and embrace.

And that the Blessed Christ gave such grace to Brother John while saying nothing teaches us that, as the Good Shepherd, He strove more to feed the soul with divine grace than to make exterior sounds ring in the bodily ears, because the Kingdom of God is not in external things but in the innermost ones, as the psalmist says, "All His glory is within."

To the glory of Our Lord Jesus Christ. Amen.

### 50　*How Brother John of Alverna, While Saying Mass on All Souls' Day, Saw Many Souls Liberated from Purgatory*

Once when Brother John of Alverna was saying Mass on the day after All Saints' Day for all the souls of the dead, as the Church has ordained, he offered with such fervent charity and compassionate pity that most high Sacrament—which the souls of the dead desire more than all the other things we can do for them because of its efficacy—that he seemed to be consumed by the ardor of his devotion and his supernatural brotherly love.

When therefore during that Mass he reverently elevated the most holy Body of Christ and offered It to God the Father, praying to Him that for the love of His Blessed Son Jesus Christ, who had hung on the Cross to save souls, He might mercifully deign to free from the sufferings of Purgatory those souls whom He had created and redeemed, all of a sudden he saw an almost countless number of souls going out of Purgatory like innumerable sparks of fire issuing from a blazing furnace. And he saw them flying up to their heavenly home through the merits of Christ who hung on the Cross for humanity's salvation and who is offered up every day in that most holy Host for the living and the dead. For He is the Blessed God and Man, Light and Life, Redeemer and Judge and everlasting Savior. Amen.

### 51  *How Brother James of Falerone Appeared After He Died to Brother John of Alverna*

At the time when Brother James of Falerone, a man of great sanctity, was seriously ill in the Place of Mogliano in the Custody of Fermo, Brother John of Alverna, who was then staying in the Place of Massa, on hearing about his illness, began to pray fervently to God for him in mental prayer, with the heartfelt desire that Brother James might recover his health if it were good for his soul, because Brother John loved him as if he were his own father.

And while he was thus praying devoutly, he was rapt in an ecstasy and saw in the air a great throng of many angels and saints above his cell which was in the woods. And they shone with such brightness that they illuminated the whole countryside.

And among those angels he saw that sick Brother James for whom he was praying, standing there radiant with light and dressed in white clothes. He saw among them our blessed Father Francis adorned with the holy Stigmata of Christ and resplendent in great glory. He also saw and recognized the saintly Brother Lucido and Brother Matthew the Elder of Monte Rubbiano and many other friars whom he had never seen or known in this life, with many saints, and all of them were radiant with similar glory and brightness.

And while Brother John was gazing with great delight at that blessed throng of saints, it was revealed to him that the soul of the sick friar would certainly be saved and that he was destined to die from that illness, but that he would not go to Heaven immediately after dying because he had to be purified in Purgatory for a short while.

Now on seeing this, Brother John rejoiced so much over the salvation and glory of that friar that he did not grieve over the death of his body, but with great spiritual consolation he frequently called him, saying within himself: "Brother James, my dear Brother James, faithful servant of Christ and friend of God—Brother James, my beloved Father—Brother James, companion of the angels and of the saints!"

And so being sure of the death of Brother James and rejoicing over the salvation of his soul, he came back to himself and set out at once from the Place of Massa, where he had had this vision.

And he went to visit Brother James at Mogliano, where he found him so weak from his illness that he could hardly speak. And Brother John announced to him that he was going to die but that his soul would be saved and go in joy to the glory of eternal life, according to the certainty which he had been given by divine revelation.

Brother James, being assured of his salvation, was utterly filled with joy both in mind and countenance, and he made Brother John welcome with a beautiful smile and a happy expression on his features, thanking him for the joyful news he brought. And because Brother James loved him like a son, he commended himself fervently to Brother John, telling him that his soul was about to leave his body.

Then Brother John eagerly asked him to agree to come back to him after dying and tell him how he was—which Brother James promised to do if it pleased the Savior to allow him.

And after he had said that, as the moment of his death was approaching, Brother James began to recite with devotion these words of the psalm: "Oh, in peace—Oh, in Him— Oh, I will sleep— Oh, I will rest!" And after saying that verse, with a joyful and happy expression on his face, he left this life and went to the Lord Jesus Christ.

And after he had been buried, Brother John went back to the Place of Massa and waited for Brother James to carry out his promise to return to him on the day when he said he would. And while on that day he was waiting and praying, Christ appeared to him in a bright light with a great throng of angels and saints, but Brother James was not among them. So Brother John in great surprise fervently commended him to Christ.

Later, on the next day, while Brother John was praying in the forest of Massa, Brother James appeared to him, all in glory and joy, accompanied by angels.

And Brother John said to him: "Oh, holy Father, why did you not return and speak to me on the day you promised?"

Brother James answered: "Because I needed a little purifying. But at that same hour when Christ appeared to you, I appeared to the holy lay brother James of Massa while he was serving Mass—and he also saw the Host at the Elevation changed into an indescribably beautiful living Boy. And I spoke to that Brother and said: 'Today I am going to the Kingdom of God with that Boy, for no one can go there except through Him!' And at the same moment when you commended me to Christ, your prayer was heard and I was liberated."

And after saying that he went to the Lord. And Brother John was greatly consoled. Now Brother James of Falerone died on the Vigil of St. James the Apostle in July, and was buried in the Place of Mogliano, where he performs many miracles.[1]

To the glory of God. Amen.

### 52  *How Brother John Saw All Created Things in a Vision*

Because the above-mentioned Brother John of Alverna had completely renounced all the passing pleasures and consolations of this world and had placed all his affection and all his hope in God, the divine Goodness granted him new consolations and wonderful revelations, especially when the great Feast Days of Our Blessed Lord Jesus Christ came around.

So it happened once that when the Savior's Nativity was approaching, he was eagerly awaiting some consolation from God concerning the sweet Humanity of Christ. The Holy Spirit—who knows how to give Its gifts as It wishes, as to time and place, without regard to "him that wills, or him that runs, but to God who shows mercy"—granted to Brother John, not the consolation that he was awaiting regarding the Humanity of Christ, but such a great and intense and fervent love for the charity of Christ, by which He had humbled Himself to take on our humanity, that it seemed to him as though his soul was drawn out of his body and his soul and heart were burning a hundred times more than if he had been in a furnace. Being unable to endure that burning, he became frightened and panted and shouted out loud, because owing to the excessive intensity of his love he could not restrain himself from shouting.

Now at the hour when he felt that ardent love, so strong and sure a hope of his salvation came over him that if he had died then, he would not have believed at all that he had to pass through Purgatory. And that great love lasted, with interruptions, for half a year. But the fervor lasted more than a year, to such a degree that sometimes for an hour he seemed to be dying.

And after that time he received countless visitations and consolations from God, as I several times observed with my own eyes and as many others frequently observed. For because of his overflowing fervor and love he could not conceal the visitations, and many times I saw him rapt in ecstasy.

Among them, one night he was raised to such a marvelous light in God that he saw in the Creator all created things, both in Heaven and on earth, all disposed in their various realms, for instance how the choirs of blessed spirits are disposed under God—and also the earthly paradise and the Blessed Humanity of Christ. And he likewise perceived the lower realms. And he saw and felt how all created things are related to the Creator, and how God is above and within and without and around all created things.

Afterward God raised him above every creature so that his soul was absorbed and assumed into the abyss of the Divinity and Light, and it was buried in the ocean of God's Eternity and Infinity, to the point where he could not feel anything that was created or formed or finite or conceivable or visible which the human heart could conceive or the tongue could describe. And his soul was so absorbed in that abyss of Divinity and ocean or mass of light that it was like a drop of wine absorbed in a deep sea. And as that drop finds nothing in itself but the sea, so his soul saw nothing but God in all and above all, within all and without all things—yet three Persons in one God and one God in three Persons.

And he felt that eternal infinite love which led the Son of

God to incarnate out of obedience to His Father. And by meditating and pondering and weeping on that path of the Incarnation and Passion of the Son of God, he came to unutterable
insights. And he said that there is no other way by which the
soul can enter into God and have everlasting life except
through Christ, who is the Way, the Truth, and the Life.

In that same vision there was also shown to him everything
that was done by Christ from the fall of the first man until
the entrance into eternal life of Christ,[1] who is the head and
leader of all the elect who have existed since the beginning
of the world, who are, and who will be until the end, as has
been announced by the holy Prophets.

To the glory of Our Lord Jesus Christ. Amen.

### 53 *How While Saying Mass Brother John Fell Down As If He Were Dead*

Something wonderful and worthy of lasting fame happened
to that Brother John, as the friars who were present have
related.

Once when Brother John was staying in the Place of
Mogliano of the Custody of Fermo in the Province of the
Marches, during the first night after the Octave of St. Lawrence—within the Octave of the Assumption of the Blessed Virgin Mary—he arose before the time for matins. And while the
Lord filled his soul with grace, he recited matins with the friars.
But after saying matins, he went into the garden, because he
felt such sweet consolation from the great graces which he derived from those words of the Lord *Hoc est Corpus Meum*
(This is My Body) that he shouted out loud and repeated in
his heart *"Hoc est Corpus Meum."*

He was enlightened by the Holy Spirit regarding those
words, and the eyes of his soul being opened, he saw Jesus
Christ with the Blessed Virgin and a throng of angels and
saints. And he understood that saying of the Apostle that we
are all one body in Christ, and each of us is a member one of
another, and that with the saints we may grasp what is the
breadth, the length, the sublimity, and the depth, and know
the love of Christ that surpasses all knowledge, for it is wholly

in this Most Holy Sacrament which is brought into being when the words *Hoc est Corpus Meum* are said.

And when dawn came, stirred by divine grace, with those words on his lips, he went into the church in great fervor of spirit. And thinking no one saw or heard him—though a friar was praying in the choir and heard it—he was so troubled by the intensity of the grace that he could not prevent himself from shouting loudly three times.

And he remained in that condition until it was time for the Mass which he was to celebrate. So he went to vest. But when he reached the altar, the grace of fervent devotion increased within him, and the love of Christ also grew in him. And he was given a certain ineffable sense of God's presence which he could not express in words. He was afraid that this feeling and marvelous fervor might increase so much he would have to interrupt the Mass, so that he did not know what to do—whether to proceed or to wait.

However, as he had once had a similar experience, and the Lord had so tempered his emotion that he had not had to interrupt the Mass, he hoped that he might proceed this time. Nevertheless he feared what might happen, because such infusions of divine grace cannot be controlled by human beings.

When he had proceeded as far as the Preface of the Blessed Virgin, the supernatural illumination and sweet consolation of God's love increased so much within him that when he reached the *Qui pridie* he could hardly endure such overwhelming sweetness. Finally, when he came to the Consecration itself and began to pronounce the words of the Consecration over the Host, he kept repeating the first half of the formula—*Hoc est—Hoc est*—very often, and he was unable to go any further. And the reason why he could not go on was that he felt and saw the presence of Christ and of a throng of angels and saints, so that he almost fainted because of their grandeur which he felt in his soul.

Therefore the guardian of the Place anxiously came running to assist him and stood beside him, and a friar stood behind him with a lighted candle, while the other friars were watching in fear with many other men and women, including some of the most prominent persons in the province who were in the church to hear Mass, and all of them stood around the altar, waiting, and many were weeping, as women do.

But Brother John, almost beside himself with sweet bliss and joy, was standing there without finishing the Consecration because he saw that Christ did not enter into the Host or rather that the Host was not changed into the Body of Christ, until he added the other half of the formula, *Corpus Meum.*

Finally, after a long time, when it pleased God, Brother John, unable to bear the great majesty of Christ the Head, as the paradise of the Mystical Body was revealed to him, exclaimed aloud: *"Corpus Meum!"* The appearance of the bread immediately vanished, and in the host appeared the Lord Jesus Christ, the Blessed Son of God Incarnate and Glorified. And He showed him the humility and love which led Him to take flesh in the Virgin Mary and which makes Him come into the hands of the priest every day when he consecrates the host. And that humility held him in such sweet consolation and ineffable and unutterable wonder that he was not able to complete the remaining words of the Consecration. For as Brother John himself said, that humility and condescension of the Savior toward us is so marvelous that our body cannot endure it or words describe it. And as a result he could not proceed.

Therefore after saying *"Hoc est Corpus Meum,"* he was rapt in an ecstasy and fell backward, but was held up by the guardian who was standing beside him, for otherwise he would have fallen to the ground. And as the other friars and lay people who were in the church ran up, he was carried into the sacristy as if he were dead. For his body had turned cold like a corpse. And his fingers were so stiffly contracted that they could hardly be opened or moved. And he lay there unconscious from morning until terce. This happened during the summer.

Now as I was present and wished very much to know what God's mercy had done in him, almost as soon as he came back to himself I went to him and asked him for the love of God to consent to tell me all about it. And because he used to confide in me a great deal, by the grace of God he told me all about it.

And among other things he told me that before and while he was consecrating, his heart became liquefied like heated wax, and his body seemed to be without bones, so that he could not lift his arms or his hands to make the Sign of the Cross over the host. And he added that before he became a priest, it was revealed to him that he would faint that way during Mass. But as he had already said many Masses and that prophecy had not been fulfilled, he had thought that revelation had not come from God. Nevertheless about fifty days before the Assumption of the Blessed Virgin when this thing happened to him, it was revealed to him that it would happen to him around the Feast of the Assumption. But later he had forgotten that promise.[1]

To the praise and glory of Our Lord Jesus Christ. Amen.

Part Two

# THE CONSIDERATIONS ON
# THE HOLY STIGMATA

In this part we shall contemplate with devout consideration the glorious, sacred, and holy Stigmata of our blessed Father St. Francis which he received from Christ on the holy Mount Alverna. And because those Stigmata were five, like the five Wounds of Our Lord Jesus Christ, therefore this treatise shall have Five Considerations.

The First will be about the way St. Francis came to the holy Mount Alverna.

The Second will be about the life he lived and the conversation he had with his companions on that holy mountain.

The Third will be about the apparition of the Seraph and the imprinting of the most holy Stigmata.

The Fourth will be about St. Francis' going down from Mount Alverna after he had received the holy Stigmata and about his return to St. Mary of the Angels.

The Fifth will be about certain apparitions and revelations which were given after the death of St. Francis to some holy friars and to other pious persons concerning those glorious Stigmata.

### The First Consideration: How Count Orlando of Chiusi Gave Mount Alverna to St. Francis

Regarding the First Consideration, you should know that St. Francis, some time before he had the Stigmata of the Savior, moved by an inspiration from God, left the Valley of Spoleto to go to the Romagna with his companion Brother Leo.

And on their way they passed by the foot of the castle and walled village of Montefeltro, where at that time a great banquet and festival were being held to celebrate the knighting of one of the Counts of Montefeltro. When St. Francis heard from the villagers about the festivity that was taking place, and that many noblemen had gathered there from various districts, he said to Brother Leo: "Let's go up to that festival, for with God's help we will gather some good spiritual fruit."

Among the noblemen who had come to that meeting was a great and wealthy Count from Tuscany named Orlando of Chiusi in Casentino who, because of the marvelous things he had heard about the holiness and miracles of St. Francis, had a great devotion for him and wanted very much to see him and hear him preach.

St. Francis arrived at that village and entered and went to the square where all those noblemen were assembled. And in fervor of spirit he climbed onto a low wall and began to preach, taking as the theme of his sermon these words in Italian: "So great is the good which I expect that all pain is to me a delight." And under the dictation of the Holy Spirit he preached on this theme so devoutly and so profoundly—proving its truth by the various sufferings and martyrdoms of the holy Apostles and Martyrs, and by the severe penances of the holy Confessors, and by the many tribulations and temptations of the holy Virgins and of the other Saints—that everyone stood there gazing attentively at him, listening to him as though an angel of God were speaking. Among them, Count Orlando was touched to the heart by God through the marvelous preaching of St. Francis, and he decided to have a talk with him after the sermon about the state of his soul.

Therefore, when the sermon was over, he took St. Francis aside and said to him: "Father, I would like to speak to you about the salvation of my soul."

But St. Francis, who was very tactful, answered: "I am glad. But this morning go and honor your friends, since they invited you to the festival, and have dinner with them, and after dinner we will talk together as much as you wish."

Count Orlando therefore went to dine, and after dinner he returned to St. Francis and had a long talk with him about the state and salvation of his soul. And at the end Count Orlando said to St. Francis: "Brother Francis, I have a mountain in Tuscany which is very solitary and wild and perfectly suited for someone who wants to do penance in a place far from people or who wants to live a solitary life. It is called Mount Alverna. If that mountain should please you and your companions, I would gladly give it to you for the salvation of my soul."

Now St. Francis had a most intense desire to find some solitary place where he could conveniently devote himself to contemplation. So when he heard this offer, he first praised God who provides for His little sheep, and then he thanked Count Orlando, saying: "Sire, when you go home, I will send two of my companions to you, and you can show them that mountain. And if it seems suitable for prayer and penance, I very gladly accept your charitable offer."

And after he said that, St. Francis left. And when he had ended his journey, he returned to St. Mary of the Angels.

And likewise Count Orlando, after the knighting festival was over, returned to his castle named Chiusi, which is a mile away from Mount Alverna.[1]

After St. Francis had returned to St. Mary of the Angels, he sent two of his companions to Count Orlando. They searched for him, but because they did not know that part of the country they had great difficulty in finding his castle. When they arrived, he was very glad to see them, and he welcomed them with great joy and kindness, as though they were angels of God.

And wishing to show them Mount Alverna, he sent about fifty armed men with them, perhaps to protect them from wild animals. With this escort the friars climbed up Mount Alverna and explored it for a place where they might set up a house to live in. Finally they came to a part of the mountain where there was a small plateau that was very suitable for prayer and contemplation. And they decided in the name of the Lord to make their dwelling and that of St. Francis in that place.

With the help of the armed men who accompanied them, they cut down some branches with swords and built a little hut with the branches.

And having thus in the name of God accepted and taken possession of Mount Alverna and of the friars' Place on that mountain, with the count's permission, they left and went back to St. Francis.[2]

And when they came to him, they told him that the place was very solitary and suitable for contemplation. And they told him in detail how they had taken possession of it.

On hearing this news St. Francis was very happy. And praising and thanking God, he said to those friars with a joyful expression: "My sons, our Lent of St. Michael the Archangel is approaching. I firmly believe that it is the will of God that we spend that Lent up on Mount Alverna, which has been prepared for us by Divine Providence, so that for the honor and glory of God and the glorious Virgin Mary and the holy angels, we may merit from Christ to consecrate that blessed mountain with penance."

Then, having said that, St. Francis took with him Brother Masseo of Marignano of Assisi, who was a man of great wisdom and eloquence, and Brother Angelo Tancredi of Rieti, who was a man of very noble birth and had been a knight in the world, and Brother Leo, who was a man of the greatest simplicity and purity, because of which St. Francis loved him very much and used to reveal nearly all his secrets to him.

With those three friars St. Francis began to pray. And when their prayer was finished, he commended himself and the above-mentioned friars to the prayers of the friars who were staying behind. And with those three, in the name of Jesus Christ Crucified, he set out for Mount Alverna.

And as they were leaving, St. Francis called one of his three companions—Brother Masseo—and said to him: "Brother Masseo, you are to be our guardian and our superior on this journey. And while traveling and stopping together, we will follow our custom: either we will say the office or we will talk about God or we will keep silence. And we will not take any thought about eating or sleeping, but when the time for overnight rest comes we will beg for a little bread, and we will stop and rest in the place which God will prepare for us."

Then those three companions nodded. And making the Sign of the Cross, they set out.

And the first evening they came to a Place of the friars, and they stayed there overnight.[3]

The second evening, because of bad weather and because

they were tired and were unable to reach any Place of the friars or any village or house, when night came on with bad weather, they sought shelter in an abandoned and uninhabited church. And they lay down to rest there.

While his companions were sleeping, St. Francis began to pray. And he was persevering in prayer when, during the first watch of the night, a great number of the fiercest devils came with very great noise and tumult, and they began to attack and persecute him. One took hold of him here, another there. One pulled him down, another up. One threatened him with one thing, another scolded him for something else. And so they strove to disturb his praying in different ways.

But they were not able to do so because God was with him. And when St. Francis had endured those attacks of the devils for some time, he began to cry out in a loud voice: "You damned spirits, you can do only what the hand of God allows you. And therefore in the name of Almighty God I tell you to do to my body whatever God allows you. I will gladly endure it since I have no enemy worse than my body. And so if you take revenge on my enemy for me, you do me a very great favor."

Then the devils seized him with great violence and fury, and began to drag him around the church and to hurt him and persecute him much more than before.

And then St. Francis cried out and said: "My Lord Jesus Christ, I thank You for the great love and charity which You are showing me, because it is a sign of great love when the Lord punishes His servant well for all his faults in this world, so that he may not be punished for them in the next world. And I am prepared to endure with joy every pain and every adversity which You, my God, wish to send me for my sins."

Then the devils, having been humiliated and defeated by his endurance and patience, went away.

And in fervor of spirit St. Francis came out of the church and entered into a forest that was nearby. And there he gave himself to prayer. And praying and weeping and beating his breast, he sought Jesus Christ, the spouse and delight of his soul. And at last he found Him in the secret depths of his heart. And he spoke to Him reverently as to his Lord. Then he answered Him as his Judge. Next he entreated Him as a father. Then he talked with Him as with a friend.

During that night and in that forest, his companions, after they awoke, stood listening and wondering what he was doing. And they saw and heard him devoutly praying with tears and cries to God to have mercy on sinners. And they also saw and heard him weeping aloud over the Passion of Christ, as if he were seeing it with his own eyes.

That same night they saw him praying with his arms crossed on his chest, raised up above the ground and suspended in the air for a long time, surrounded by a bright cloud.

And so he spent that whole night in holy contemplation without sleeping.[4]

The next morning, as his companions knew that, owing to his exhaustion and lack of sleep during the night, St. Francis was too weak to be able to continue the journey on foot, they went to a poor local peasant and asked him, for the love of God, to lend his donkey for their Father, Brother Francis, who could not travel on foot. Hearing Brother Francis mentioned, the man asked them: "Are you friars of that Brother Francis of Assisi about whom people say so much good?"

The friars answered, "Yes," and that it was really for him that they were asking for the donkey.

Then with great devotion and care this good man saddled the donkey and led it to St. Francis, and with great reverence helped him get into the saddle.

Then they continued their journey, the peasant walking with them behind his donkey. And after they had gone a while, he said to St. Francis: "Tell me, are you Brother Francis of Assisi?"

St. Francis answered that he was.

"Well, then," said the peasant, "try to be as good as everyone thinks you are, because many people have great faith in you. So I urge you: never let there be anything in you different from what they expect of you."

When St. Francis heard these words, he did not mind being admonished by a peasant, and he did not say to himself, as many proud fellows who wear the cowl nowadays would say, "Who is this brute who admonishes me?" But he immediately got off the donkey and threw himself on his knees before the farmer and humbly kissed his feet, thanking him for having deigned to admonish him so charitably.

Then his companions and the peasant very devoutly helped him to his feet and set him on the donkey again. And they traveled on.[5]

When they had climbed about halfway up the mountain, because the summer heat was very great and the path was long and steep, the peasant began to suffer intensely from thirst, and he called ahead to St. Francis: "I am dying of thirst. If I don't have something to drink, I'll suffocate in a minute!"

So St. Francis immediately got off the donkey and began to pray. And he remained kneeling on the ground, raising his hands toward Heaven, until he knew by revelation that God had granted his prayer. Then he said to the peasant: "Run quickly to that rock, and there you will find running water which Christ in His mercy has just caused to flow from the rock."

The man ran to the place which St. Francis had shown him, and found a very fine spring that had been made to flow through the hard rock by the power of St. Francis' prayer. And he drank all he wanted, and felt better.

And it truly seems that that spring was produced by a divine miracle through the prayers of St. Francis, because neither before nor afterward was any spring ever seen there or anywhere nearby.

After he had done this, St. Francis, with his companions and the peasant, gave thanks to God for having shown them this miracle. And then they traveled on.[6]

And as they drew near to the peak that forms Mount Alverna itself, it pleased St. Francis to rest for a while under a certain oak tree standing by the path that is still there now.

While resting under the oak tree St. Francis began to study the location and the scenery. And when he was absorbed in this contemplation, a great number of all kinds of birds came flying down to him with joyful songs, and twittering and fluttering their wings. And they surrounded St. Francis in such a way that some of them settled on his head and others on his shoulders and others on his knees, and still others on his arms and lap and on his hands and around his feet. They all showed

great joy by their tuneful singing and happy movements, as
if they were rejoicing at his coming and inviting and persuading him to stay there.

Seeing this, his companions and the peasant were greatly
surprised. St. Francis rejoiced in spirit and said to them: "My
dear Brothers, I believe it is pleasing to Our Lord Jesus Christ
that we accept a Place and live a while on this solitary mountain, since our little brothers and sisters the birds show such
joy over our coming."

After saying these words, he arose and they journeyed on.
And at last they came to the spot which his companions had
first selected, where until then there was nothing but a very
poor little hut made of tree-branches.[7]

To the glory of God and of His Most Holy Name. Amen.

And this is the end of the First Consideration, namely, how
St. Francis came to the holy Mount Alverna.

### The Second Consideration: How St. Francis Spent His Time with His Companions on Mount Alverna

The Second Consideration deals with what St. Francis did with
his companions on that mountain.

In this connection you should know that when Count Orlando heard that St. Francis had come with three companions
to live on Mount Alverna, he was very happy. And the next
day he left his castle with many men and came to visit him,
bringing bread and other necessities for him and for his companions.

When he arrived up there, he found them praying. And going near, he greeted them.

Then St. Francis stood up and welcomed Count Orlando and
his men with great affection and joy. And afterward they began to talk together. And after they had talked and St. Francis
had thanked him for the holy mountain which he had given
them and for his coming, he asked Count Orlando to have a
poor little cell made for him at the foot of a very beautiful
beech tree that was about a stone's throw from the friars'
Place, because that spot seemed to him very suitable for de-

vout prayer. And Count Orlando had it made without delay.

Afterward, because evening was drawing near and it was time to leave, St. Francis preached a short sermon to them before they left.

Then, after he had preached and given them his blessing, since Count Orlando had to leave, he called St. Francis and his companions aside and said to them: "My dear friars, I do not want you to lack anything which you may need on this wild mountain, because of which you might have to give less attention to spiritual things. So I want you—and I say this once for all—just to send to my house for anything you need. And if you do not do so, I will really be offended."

After he had said this, he left with his men and returned to the castle.[1]

Then St. Francis had his companions sit down, and he gave them instructions regarding the way of life which they and whoever wished to live as religious in hermitages should lead. And among other things he especially stressed to them the observance of holy poverty, saying: "Don't pay so much attention to the charitable offer of Count Orlando that you should in any way offend our Lady Poverty. You can be sure that the more we despise poverty, the more will the world despise us and the greater need will we suffer. But if we embrace holy poverty very closely, the world will come to us and will feed us abundantly. God has called us to this holy Order for the salvation of the world. And He has made this contract between us and the world: that we give the world a good example and that the world provide us with what we need. So let us persevere in holy poverty, because it is the way of perfection and the pledge and guarantee of everlasting riches."

And after many beautiful and inspiring words and instructions on this subject, he concluded: "That is the way of life which I place upon myself and on you. And because I see that I am drawing near to death, I intend to stay alone and recollect myself with God and weep over my sins before Him. And let Brother Leo, whenever it seems right to him, bring me a little bread and a little water. And on no account let any lay persons come to me, but deal with them yourselves."

And after he had said those words, he gave them his blessing and went off to the cell by the beech tree. And his companions stayed in the Place with the firm intention of obeying the orders of St. Francis.[2]

A few days later St. Francis was standing beside that cell, gazing at the form of the mountain and marveling at the great chasms and openings in the massive rocks. And he began to pray, and then it was revealed to him by God that those striking chasms had been made in a miraculous way at the hour of Christ's Passion when, as the Gospel says, "the rocks split." And God wanted this to be manifested in a special way here on Mount Alverna in order to show that the Passion of Christ was to be renewed on that mountain in the soul of St. Francis by love and compassion and in his body by the imprinting of the Stigmata.

As soon as St. Francis had received this revelation, he shut himself up in his cell and recollected himself completely in his soul and prepared himself to meditate on the mystery of that revelation. And from that time, St. Francis, through constant prayer, began to experience more often the sweet consolations of divine contemplation, as a result of which he was many times so rapt in God that he was seen by his companions raised bodily above the ground and absorbed in God.[3]

In these contemplative raptures God revealed to him not only present and future things but also the secret thoughts and desires of the friars, as his companion Brother Leo experienced during those days.

For Brother Leo suffered a very great spiritual (not physical) temptation from the devil, so that there came to him an intense desire to have some inspiring words written by St. Francis' own hand. For he believed that if he had them, the temptation would leave him either entirely or partly. And although he had that desire, through shame or reverence he did not dare tell St. Francis about it. But the Holy Spirit revealed to the Saint what Brother Leo did not tell him. St. Francis therefore called him and had him bring an inkhorn and pen and paper. And with his own hand he wrote a Praise of Christ, just as Leo had wished. And at the end he made the sign of the Tau and gave it to him, saying: "Take this paper, dear Brother, and keep it carefully until you die. May God bless you and protect you from all temptation! Do not be troubled because you have temptations. For I consider you more of a servant and friend of God and I love you more, the more you are attacked by temptations. Truly I tell you that no one should consider himself a perfect friend of God until he has passed through many temptations and tribulations."

Brother Leo accepted that writing with fervent love and faith. And at once all temptation left him.

And going back to the Place, with great joy he told his companions what a grace God had given him in receiving those words written by St. Francis' own hand. He carefully put the paper away and kept it. And later the friars performed many miracles with it.[4]

From that hour Brother Leo, with great innocence and good intention, began carefully to observe and meditate on the life of St. Francis. He quietly tried as much as he could to see what the Saint was doing. And because of his purity he merited time and time again to see St. Francis rapt in God and raised above the ground. He found him outside the cell raised up into the air sometimes as high as three feet, sometimes four, at other times halfway up or at the top of the beech trees—and some of those trees were very high. At other times he found him raised so high in the air and surrounded by such radiance that he could hardly see him. Then Brother Leo would kneel down and prostrate himself completely on the ground on the spot from which the holy Father had been lifted into the air while praying.

When St. Francis was raised so little above the ground that he could reach him and touch his feet, what did that simple friar do? He would go to him quietly and embrace and kiss his feet and say with tears: "God, have mercy on this sinner. And through the merits of this very holy man, let me find Your grace and mercy."

And while Brother Leo was praying and recommending himself to God as before, through the merits of the holy Father, he experienced very great visitations of divine grace. And because of these things which Brother Leo frequently told about the Saint, he had such great devotion for him that very often he watched the hidden doings of St. Francis by night and day with holy ingenuity.

And one time among others, when he was standing there under St. Francis' feet and the latter were raised so high above the ground that Brother Leo could not touch him, he saw a scroll written in letters of gold come down from Heaven and rest on St. Francis' head. And on the scroll these words were written: HERE IS THE GRACE OF GOD. And after he had read it, he saw it return to Heaven.[5]

Through the gift of this grace of God that was in him, St. Francis was not only rapt in God in ecstatic contemplation, but he was also sometimes consoled by visitations of angels. One day while he was thinking about his death and the state of his Order when he was no longer alive, and he was saying, "Lord God, after my death what will happen to Your poor little family which in Your kindness You entrusted to this sinner? Who will console them? Who will correct them? Who will pray to You for them?" and similar words, an angel sent by God appeared to him and consoled him by saying: "I tell you on behalf of God that your Order will last until Judgment Day. And no one, no matter how great a sinner he is, will fail to obtain mercy from God if he has a heartfelt love for your Order. And no one who from malice persecutes your Order will be able to live long. Moreover, no one in your Order who is very evil and who does not amend his life will be able to persevere in the Order. Therefore do not grieve if you see some friars in your Order who are not good and who do not observe the Rule as they should. And do not think then that your Order is declining, because there will always be very many in it who will perfectly observe the Gospel life of Christ and the purity of the Rule. And immediately after their earthly life they will go to eternal life without passing through Purgatory at all. Some will live the life less perfectly, and they will be purified in Purgatory before they go to Paradise, but the period of their purgation will be entrusted to you by God. But do not worry about those who do not keep your Rule at all, says God, because He does not care about them."

And after the angel had said those words, he disappeared, leaving St. Francis greatly comforted and consoled.[6]

The Feast of the Assumption of Our Lady was then approaching, and St. Francis sought a convenient place that was more isolated and remote in which he might spend in greater solitude the Lent of St. Michael the Archangel, which began on the Feast of the Assumption.

Therefore he called Brother Leo and said to him: "Go and stand in the door of the oratory of the friars' Place, and when I call you, come to me."

Brother Leo went and stood in the doorway, and St. Francis walked some distance away and called loudly.

Hearing himself called, Brother Leo went to him. And St. Francis said to him: "Son, let's look for a more remote place, from which you cannot hear me when I call you."

And while they were seeking, they saw on the side of the mountain facing the south a spot that was isolated and perfectly suited to his purpose. But they could not reach it, because in front of it there was a very deep and fearful chasm in the rock. So with great effort they put a log across as a bridge and went over it.

Then St. Francis sent for the other friars and told them that he intended to spend the Lent of St. Michael in that solitary place, where he could pray alone, away from the others. And so he asked them to make a poor little hut for him there, where they could not hear him if he shouted.

And when the hut was made, St. Francis said to them: "Go back to your Place and leave me here alone, because with God's help I intend to spend this Lent here without distraction or disturbance of mind. And so none of you must come to me, and don't let any lay person come to me. But you, Brother Leo, come only once a day with a little bread and water, and once again at night at the hour for matins. And at that hour come silently, and when you reach the end of the bridge, just say: *'Domine, labia mea aperies.'* And if I answer inside, *'Et os meum annuntiabit laudem tuam,'* go across and come to the cell, and we will say matins together. But if I do not reply at once, then go right back."

And St. Francis said this because sometimes he was so rapt in God that he could not talk for a night and day, and he did not hear or feel anything with his bodily senses. Brother Leo very carefully observed this order.

And after he said this, St. Francis gave them his blessing, and they went back to the Place.[7]

Now the Feast of the Assumption came, and St. Francis began the holy fast with great abstinence and severity, mortifying his body and comforting his spirit by means of fervent prayers, watchings, and scourgings.

And while he was doing so he continually increased in virtue. And he prepared his soul to receive divine mysteries and illuminations, and his body to sustain the cruel attacks of the devils, with whom he often fought bodily.

Among other times, one day during this fast St. Francis came out of his cell in fervor of spirit and went to pray in a cavity nearby under a rock, below which there is a horrible and fearful precipice and a great drop to the ground. All of a sudden the devil appeared in a terrifying form, amid a great uproar, and began to beat him in order to throw him down.

Having nowhere to flee and being unable to endure the exceedingly cruel sight of the devil, St. Francis quickly turned around, with his hands and face and his whole body against the rock. And he commended himself to God, while groping with his hands for anything that he could grasp.

But as it pleased God, who never lets His servants be tried more than they can endure, suddenly by a miracle the rock to which he was clinging yielded to the form of his body and received him into itself. And as if he had put his hands and face into some liquid wax, the shape of his face and hands was imprinted on that rock. And thus with the help of God he escaped from the devil.[8]

But what the devil was not able to do to St. Francis at that time, namely, throw him down from there, he did later on, a good while after the death of St. Francis, to one of his dear and devout friars. One day while the friar was fitting in place some pieces of wood so that people could safely go there out of devotion to St. Francis and to the miracle which occurred there, the devil gave him a push while he was carrying a big log on his head that he wanted to place there, and made him fall with that log on his head. But God, who had saved and preserved St. Francis from falling, through his merits saved and preserved that devout friar of his from the danger of the fall. For as he fell, that friar with great fervor commended himself in a loud voice to St. Francis, who immediately appeared to him and set him down on the rocks below without any shock or injury. Now the other friars had heard his cry when he fell and they thought he was dead and dashed to pieces on the sharp rocks, since he had fallen from such a great height. So with great sorrow and weeping they took the stretcher and went down the other side of the mountain to fetch the pieces of his body and bury them. And when they had already come down the mountain, the friar who had fallen met them, carrying on his head the log with which he had fallen, and he was singing the *Te Deum laudamus* in a loud voice. As the friars were greatly amazed, he told them in detail how he had fallen and how St. Francis had saved him from all harm. Then all the friars came back to the Place with him, singing the *Te Deum* and praising and thanking God and St. Francis for the miracle he had performed for his friar.[9]

St. Francis, therefore, persevering in that fast, as we have said, although he endured many attacks from the devil, nevertheless received many consolations from God, not only through the visits of angels but likewise of wild birds. For during the whole of that forty days' fast a falcon that had its nest there near his cell would wake him up every night before matins by singing and beating its wings against the cell. And it would not leave until he arose to say matins. But at times when St. Francis was more tired or weak or ill, the falcon, like a tactful and compassionate human being, would sing somewhat later. And so St. Francis took a great liking for this holy "clock," because the falcon's thoughtfulness helped him to drive away all laziness and stimulated him to pray. Besides, it sometimes kept him company in a tame way during the daytime as well.[10]

Finally, pertaining to this Second Consideration, as St. Francis was greatly weakened in body, partly by his severe abstinence and partly by the attacks of the devils, and he wished to comfort his body with the spiritual food of the soul, he began to think of the limitless glory and joy of those who are blessed with eternal life. And then he began to pray that God might grant him the grace of tasting a little of that joy.

And while he was meditating on that thought, all of a sudden an angel appeared to him in a very bright light, holding a viol in his left hand and a bow in his right hand. And as St. Francis gazed in amazement at the angel, the latter drew the bow once upward across the viol. And immediately such a beautiful melody invaded St. Francis' soul and suspended all his bodily senses that, as he later told his companions, he wondered whether, if the angel had drawn the bow down again, his soul would not have left his body owing to the unbearable loveliness of the music.[11]

And that is all regarding the Second Consideration.

### The Third Consideration: About the Apparition of the Seraph and the Imprinting of the Holy Stigmata on St. Francis

Regarding the Third Consideration, that is, the apparition of the Seraph and the imprinting of the Stigmata, you should know that when the Feast of the Cross in September was approaching, Brother Leo went one night at the usual time to say matins with St. Francis.

And after he had called *"Domine, labia mea aperies"* from the end of the bridge, as he usually did and as he had been ordered to do by the Saint, St. Francis did not answer. Now Brother Leo did not go back, as St. Francis had instructed him, but with a good and holy intention he went across the bridge and quietly entered the Saint's cell. By the bright moonlight shining in through the door, he saw that he was not in the cell. Not finding him, he thought that he might be praying outside somewhere in the woods. So he came out and silently walked among the trees looking for him by the light of the moon.

And at last he heard St. Francis' voice speaking, and he went closer to hear what he was saying. In the moonlight he saw St. Francis on his knees, with his face lifted toward the sky and his hands held out to God, saying these words with fervor of spirit: "Who are You, my dearest God? And what am I, your vilest little worm and useless little servant?" And he repeated those words over and over, and he said nothing else.

Brother Leo marveled greatly at this, and he looked up and gazed at the sky. And while he was looking, he saw come down from the heights of Heaven a torch of flaming fire that was very beautiful and bright and pleasing to the eyes and that descended and rested on St. Francis' head. And he heard a voice come out of that flame and speak with St. Francis, and the Saint answered the speaker.

But seeing this and thinking himself unworthy to be so close to that holy spot where this marvelous apparition was taking place, and also fearing to offend St. Francis or to disturb him in his contemplation of such holy secrets, in case the Saint should hear him, he silently went back so that he could not hear what was said. And he stood at a distance, waiting to see the end.

And watching carefully, he saw St. Francis hold his hand out to the flame three times. And finally, after a long time, he saw the flame return to Heaven.

So Brother Leo went away, feeling reassured and joyful, and began to return quietly to his cell, so that the Saint should not hear him.

But as he was confidently leaving, St. Francis heard the sound of his feet on some twigs and leaves, and he said: "Whoever you are, I command you, in the name of Our Lord Jesus Christ, to stay where you are. Don't move from that spot!"

So Brother Leo obediently stood where he was and waited. And later he told his companions he was so terrified then that he would have preferred that the earth should swallow him up than to wait for St. Francis who, he thought, was angry with him. For Brother Leo took the greatest care not to offend his Father, so that through his fault St. Francis should not deprive him of his companionship. In fact, he felt such faith and love for the Saint that he did not care at all to live without him. And therefore whenever any friars were speaking about the Saints, Brother Leo used to say: "My dear friends, all the Saints are great, but St. Francis is also among the great ones because of the miracles which God performs through him." And he used to speak more willingly about him than about the others. So it is no wonder that he was terrified at his voice.

When St. Francis came up to him, he asked: "Who are you?"

Brother Leo replied, trembling: "I am Brother Leo, Father."

And recognizing him, St. Francis said to him: "Why did you come here, Little Brother Lamb? Did I not tell you many times not to go around watching me? Tell me under holy obedience whether you saw or heard anything?"

Brother Leo answered: "Father, I heard you talking and praying and saying often with great wonder, 'Who are You, my dearest God? And what am I, Your vilest little worm and useless little servant?' And then I saw a flame of fire come down from Heaven and speak with you, and you replied several times and held out your hand to it three times, but I don't know what you said."

Then Brother Leo knelt down before St. Francis and confessed the sin of disobedience which he had committed against his order, and with many tears he begged St. Francis to forgive him.

Then he asked very reverently: "Father, please explain to me the words I heard and also tell me those I did not hear."

Now St. Francis loved Brother Leo very much on account of his purity and meekness, and seeing that God had revealed to him or allowed the humble Brother to see some things, St. Francis consented to disclose and explain to him what he was asking.

And he said to him: "Little Brother Lamb of Jesus Christ, in those things which you saw and heard when I said those words, two lights were shown to my soul: one of the knowledge and understanding of the Creator, and the other of the knowledge of myself. When I said, 'Who are You, my dearest God?' then I was in a light of contemplation in which I saw the depths of the infinite goodness and wisdom and power of God. And when I said, 'What am I?' I was in a light of contemplation in which I saw the grievous depths of my vileness and misery, and therefore I said, 'Who are You, the Lord of infinite wisdom and good and mercy, that You deign to visit me, a most vile and abominable and contemptible worm?' And God was in that flame which you saw, and He spoke to me under the form of that flame, as He had formerly spoken to Moses.

"And among other things which He said to me then, He asked me to give Him three gifts. And I replied: 'My Lord, I am entirely Yours. You know that I have nothing but a habit and cord and breeches, and those three things are likewise Yours. So what can I offer or give to Your majesty? For Heaven and earth, fire and water, and everything in them are Yours, Lord. Who indeed has anything that is not Yours? Therefore when we offer You anything, we give You back what is Yours. So what can I offer to You, the Lord God, King of Heaven and earth and all creation? For what do I have that is not Yours?"

"Then God said to me: 'Put your hand in your bosom and offer me whatever you find there.' I searched and I found there a coin of gold that was so large and bright and beautiful that I had never seen one like it in this world, and then I offered it to God.

"God said to me again: 'Make Me another offering as before.'

"But I said to God: 'Lord, I do not have and do not love and do not want anything but You, and for love of You I have despised gold and all things. So if anything more is found in my breast, You put it there, and I give it back to You, the Ruler of all things.'

"And I did this three times. And after making the third offering, I knelt down and blessed and thanked God, who had given me something to offer. And I was immediately made to understand that those three offerings symbolized the holy golden obedience, the very great poverty, and the very radiant chastity which by His grace God has granted me to observe so perfectly that my conscience reproaches me nothing.

"And just as I put my hand in my bosom and offered and gave those three coins back to God who had placed them there Himself, so God infused into my soul the power always to praise and magnify Him with my voice and heart for all the good things and all the graces which He has granted to me through His very holy goodness.

"So those are the words which you heard when you saw me raise and hold out my hand three times. But be careful, Little Brother Lamb, not to go watching me any more. Now return to your cell with the blessing of God. And take good care of me. For in a few days God will do such astounding and wonderful things on this mountain that the whole world will marvel at them. For He will do something new which He has never done to any other creature in this world."[1]

And after saying those words, he had the Book of the Gospels brought to him, for God had placed in his mind the idea that what God wanted to do with him would be shown to him in opening the Book of the Gospels three times. So when the Book was brought, St. Francis gave himself to prayer. And when he had finished praying, he had Brother Leo open the Book of the Gospels three times in the name of the Holy Trinity. And it pleased Divine Providence that in those three openings the Passion of Christ always appeared before him. Thereby he was given to understand that as he had followed Christ in the acts of his life, so he had to follow Him and be conformed to Him in the afflictions and sufferings of the Passion before he left this world.[2]

And from that time St. Francis began to taste and feel more abundantly the sweetness of divine contemplation and divine visitations.

Among others he had one which immediately preceded and prepared him for the imprinting of the Stigmata, in this way. The day before the Feast of the Cross in September, while St. Francis was praying secretly in his cell, an angel appeared to him and said on God's behalf: "I encourage you and urge you to prepare and dispose yourself humbly to receive with all patience what God wills to do in you."

St. Francis answered: "I am prepared to endure patiently whatever my Lord wants to do to me."

And after he said this, the angel departed.

The next day came, that is, the Feast of the Cross. And St. Francis, sometime before dawn, began to pray outside the entrance of his cell, turning his face toward the east. And he prayed in this way: "My Lord Jesus Christ, I pray You to grant me two graces before I die: the first is that during my life I may feel in my soul and in my body, as much as possible, that pain which You, dear Jesus, sustained in the hour of Your most bitter Passion. The second is that I may feel in my heart, as much as possible, that excessive love with which You, O Son of God, were inflamed in willingly enduring such suffering for us sinners."

And remaining for a long time in that prayer, he understood that God would grant it to him, and that it would soon be conceded to him to feel those things as much as is possible for a mere creature.[3]

Having received this promise, St. Francis began to contemplate with intense devotion the Passion of Christ and His infinite charity. And the fervor of his devotion increased so much within him that he utterly transformed himself into Jesus through love and compassion. And while he was thus inflaming himself in this contemplation, on that same morning he saw coming down from Heaven a Seraph with six resplendent and flaming wings. As the Seraph, flying swiftly, came closer to St. Francis, so that he could perceive Him clearly, he noticed that He had the likeness of a Crucified Man, and His wings were so disposed that two wings extended above His head, two were spread out to fly, and the other two covered His entire body.

On seeing this, St. Francis was very much afraid, and at the same time he was filled with joy and grief and amazement. He felt intense joy from the friendly look of Christ, who appeared to him in a very familiar way and gazed at him very kindly. But on the other hand, seeing Him nailed to the Cross, he felt boundless grief and compassion. Next, he was greatly amazed at such an astounding and extraordinary vision, for he knew well that the affliction of suffering is not in accord with the immortality of the angelic Seraph. And while he was marveling thus, He who was appearing to him revealed to him that this vision was shown to him by Divine Providence in this particular form in order that he should understand that he was to be utterly transformed into the direct likeness of Christ Crucified, not by physical martyrdom, but by enkindling of the mind.[4]

During this marvelous apparition, all of Mount Alverna seemed to be on fire with very bright flames, which shone in the night and illumined the various surrounding mountains and valleys more clearly than if the sun were shining over the earth.

The shepherds who were guarding their flocks in that area witnessed this. And they were gripped by intense fear when they saw the mountain aflame and so much light around it, as they later told the friars, declaring that the fiery light remained above Mount Alverna for an hour or more.

Likewise, because of the brightness of that light, which shone through the windows of the inns in the district, some muleteers who were going to Romagna got up, thinking that the sun had risen, and they saddled and loaded their animals. And while they were on their way, they saw that light cease and the real sun rise.[5]

Now why those holy Stigmata were imprinted on St. Francis is not yet entirely clear. But as he himself told his companions, this great mystery is reserved for the future.

Brother Leo told this account to Brother James of Massa, and Brother James of Massa told it to Brother Ugolino di Monte Santa Maria, and Brother Ugolino, a good and trustworthy man, told it to me who am writing.[6]

During that seraphic apparition Christ, who appeared to St. Francis, spoke to him certain secret and profound things which the Saint was never willing to reveal to anyone while he was alive, but after his death he revealed them, as is recorded further on. And these were the words: "Do you know what I have done?" said Christ. "I have given you the Stigmata which are the emblems of My Passion, so that you may be My standard-bearer. And as I descended into Limbo on the day when I died and took from there by virtue of these Stigmata of Mine all the souls that I found there, so I grant to you that every year on the day of your death you may go to Purgatory and by virtue of your Stigmata you may take from there and lead to Paradise all the souls of your Three Orders, that is, the Friars Minor, the Sisters, and the Continent, and also others who have been very devoted to you, whom you may find there, so that you may be conformed to Me in death as you are in life."[7]

Now when, after a long time and a secret conversation, this wonderful vision disappeared, it left a most intense ardor and flame of divine love in the heart of St. Francis, and it left a marvelous image and imprint of the Passion of Christ in his flesh. For soon there began to appear in the hands and feet of St. Francis the marks of nails such as he had just seen in the body of Jesus Crucified, who had appeared to him in the form of a Seraph. For his hands and feet seemed to be pierced through the center with nails, the heads of which were in the palms of his hands and in the upper part of his feet outside the flesh, and their points extended through the back of the hands and the soles of the feet so far that they seemed to be bent and beaten back in such a way that underneath their bent and beaten-back point—all of which stood out from the flesh—it would have been easy to put the finger of one's hand as through a ring. And the heads of the nails were round and black. Likewise in his right side appeared the wound of a blow from a spear, which was open, red, and bloody, and from which blood often issued from the holy breast of St. Francis and stained his habit and breeches.[8]

Consequently his companions, before they knew it from him, nevertheless noticed that he did not uncover his hands or feet and that he could not put the soles of his feet on the ground. Later, finding that his habit and breeches were bloody when they washed them for him, they felt sure that he had the image and likeness of Christ Crucified clearly imprinted in his hands and in his feet and likewise in his side.

And although he tried hard to hide and conceal from them those glorious Stigmata, which had thus been clearly imprinted in his flesh, on the other hand he saw that he could scarcely hide them from his intimate companions. Nevertheless he feared to make public the secrets of God. So he was in an agony of doubt as to whether or not he should reveal the vision of the Seraph and the imprinting of the Stigmata.

Finally, urged on by his conscience, he called to himself some of his more intimate companions, and speaking in general terms, he explained his doubt to them without describing what had happened. And he asked for their advice.

Among those friars there was one called Illuminato who was very holy, and he was truly illumined by the grace of God. Realizing that St. Francis must have seen something marvelous, because he seemed almost stunned, he answered this way: "Brother Francis, you must know that God sometimes shows you His divine mysteries not only for yourself but also for the sake of others. So it would seem that you should rightly be afraid of being judged guilty of hiding your talent if you keep hidden something which God has shown you for the future good of many other persons."

Then St. Francis, being moved by these words—although at other times he used to say, "My secret to me"—with very great awe described the above-mentioned vision in detail, adding that Christ, who appeared to him, had said to him certain things which he would never tell anyone while he lived.[9]

Now although those very holy wounds, inasmuch as they were imprinted on him by Christ, gave him very great joy in his heart, nevertheless they gave unbearable pain to his flesh and physical senses.

Consequently, being forced by necessity, he chose Brother Leo, who was simpler and purer than the others. And he revealed everything to him, and he let him see and touch those holy wounds. And St. Francis entrusted his wounds only to him to be touched and rebound with new bandages between those marvelous nails and the remaining flesh, to relieve the pain and absorb the blood which issued and flowed from the wounds. When he was ill, he let the bandages be changed often, even every day in the week, except from Thursday evening all through Friday until Saturday morning, because he did not want the pain of the Passion of Christ which he bore in his body to be eased at all by any man-made remedy or medicine during the time when our Savior Jesus Christ had for us been arrested and crucified, had died and been buried. For the love for Christ, on that day of the Crucifixion he wished to hang, truly crucified with Christ in the sufferings of the Cross.

Sometimes it happened that when Brother Leo was changing the bandage of the wound in the side, St. Francis, because of the pain which he felt from the loosening of the bloody bandage, would put his hand on Brother Leo's chest over his heart. And from the contact of those holy hands on which were imprinted the venerable Stigmata, Brother Leo would feel such sweetness of devotion in his heart that he nearly fainted and fell to the ground. He would begin to sob and be rapt in a life-giving trance.

Lastly, regarding this Third Consideration, when St. Francis had finished the fast of St. Michael the Archangel, by divine revelation he made ready to return to St. Mary of the Angels. So he called Brother Masseo and Brother Angelo, and after many holy words and instructions, he commended to them as strongly as he could that holy mountain, saying that he had to go back to St. Mary of the Angels with Brother Leo. And after this, he said good-by to them and blessed them in the name of Jesus Crucified. And granting their request, he held out to them his very holy hands adorned with those glorious Stigmata, to see and touch and kiss. And leaving them thus consoled, he departed and went down the holy mountain.[10]

To the glory of Our Lord Jesus Christ. Amen.

*The Fourth Consideration: How, After the*
*Imprinting of the Holy Stigmata, St. Francis*
*Left Mount Alverna and Returned*
*to St. Mary of the Angels*

Regarding the Fourth Consideration, you should know that after the true love of Christ had perfectly transformed St. Francis into the true likeness of Christ Crucified, having finished the forty days' fast in honor of St. Michael the Archangel on the holy Mount Alverna, the angelic man Francis went down the mountain with Brother Leo and a devout peasant on whose donkey he rode, for owing to the nails in his feet he could not well go on foot.

When he came down from the mountain, the fame of his sanctity had already spread through the region, and the shepherds had reported how they had seen Mount Alverna all aflame and that this was a sign of some great miracle which God had done to St. Francis. So, when the people of the district heard that he was passing by, all of them—men and women, small and great—came out to see him and with devotion and desire tried to touch him and kiss his hands. As he was unable to deny them to the veneration of the people, although he had bandaged the palms, nevertheless to conceal the Stigmata still more, he bound them over again and covered them with his sleeves, and held out only his bare fingers for the people to kiss.

But even though he strove to hide and conceal the mystery of the glorious Stigmata in order to avoid all occasion of worldly glory, it pleased God, who had secretly imprinted those marks, openly to manifest many miracles for His glory by the virtue of those Stigmata, especially during this journey from Alverna to St. Mary of the Angels and later very many in various parts of the world, during the lifetime of St. Francis and after his glorious death, in order that the hidden and marvelous power of those Stigmata and the exceedingly great mercy and love of Christ for him to whom God had given them in a wonderful way might be manifested to the world by clear and evident miracles, some of which we shall record here.[1]

As St. Francis was drawing near a village on the border of the County of Arezzo, a woman came to him, weeping loudly and carrying in her arms her eight-year-old son. For four years he had had dropsy, and his stomach was so swollen that when he stood straight he could not see his legs or feet. The woman put her little boy down before St. Francis and begged him to pray to God for him. First, St. Francis began to pray. Then having prayed, he put his holy hands over the boy's stomach. At their contact all the swelling rapidly disappeared, and the boy was perfectly cured. Then St. Francis gave him back to his mother. She received him with intense joy, and took the child home, giving thanks to God and His Saint. And she gladly showed her cured son to everyone in the district who came to her house to see him.[2]

That same day St. Francis passed through Borgo San Sepolcro. And before he came near the town, crowds from the city and the farms ran to meet him. And many of them went before him with olive branches in their hands, crying out loudly: "Here comes the saint! Here comes the saint!"

And because of the devotion and desire that the people had to touch him, they pressed and thronged around him. But he went along with his mind raised and absorbed in contemplating God. Although he was touched or held or pulled, like someone who is unconscious he paid no attention at all to what was being done or said around him. And he did not even notice that he was traveling through that town or district.

Now when he had passed Borgo and the crowds had gone home and he reached a leprosarium a good mile beyond Borgo, he came back to himself like someone returning from the other world, and he asked his companions: "When will we be near Borgo?"

For his mind had been concentrating on and rapt in the splendors of Heaven and he had actually not perceived the changes of time and place or the people who met him. His companions learned by experience that this happened to him several other times.[3]

St. Francis arrived that evening at the friars' Place of Monte Casale, where there was a friar who was so cruelly sick and so horribly tortured by illness that it seemed more like a tribulation and torment of the devil than a natural sickness. For at times he would throw himself on the ground and roll around with a shocking expression, foaming at the mouth and shaking all over. At other times all his limbs were contracted or extended, or they would bend or twist or become stiff and hard. Sometimes when he was all rigid and tense, his heels would touch his head and he would jump up in the air and then suddenly fall flat on his back. When St. Francis, sitting at table, heard the friars tell about the serious and incurable sickness of this friar, he felt compassion for him. And he took a piece of bread which he was eating and made the Sign of the Cross over it with his holy stigmatized hands and sent it to the sick friar. As soon as the latter had eaten the bread, he was perfectly healed and never felt that illness again.[4]

When the next morning came, St. Francis sent two of the friars who were in that Place to stay at Alverna. And he sent back with them the peasant who had accompanied him behind the donkey that he had loaned him, as the Saint wanted him to return to his home with it.

While the friars were going with that peasant and entering the district of Arezzo, some men of that district saw them from a distance and rejoiced greatly, thinking that it was St. Francis, who had passed by there two days before. One of their women, who had been in labor for three days and could not be delivered, was dying, and they thought she would be safe and sound again if St. Francis laid his holy hands on her. But when the friars came near and the men realized that it was not St. Francis, they were very sorry. Yet though the Saint was not there in person, his power was not lacking, because their faith was not lacking. Then a wonderful thing happened! The woman was dying—she already showed the signs of death. But the men asked the friars whether they had anything which had been touched by the very holy hands of St. Francis. The friars reflected and searched carefully, and finally found nothing that St. Francis had touched with his hands except the halter of the donkey which he had ridden. With great reverence and devotion they took that halter and placed it on the body of the pregnant woman, devoutly calling on the name of St. Francis and faithfully commending her to him. And what more is there to say? The minute the woman had that halter on her body she felt freed from all danger, and she gave birth in joy and safety, without any difficulty.[5]

After St. Francis had been in that Place for some days, he left and went to Città di Castello. Then many of the citizens brought before him a woman who had been possessed by a devil for a long time, and they humbly asked him to free her because she was disturbing the whole neighborhood with mournful howling and piercing shrieks and barking like a dog. So St. Francis, having first prayed and made the Sign of the Cross over her, commanded the devil to leave her. And it immediately departed, leaving her sound in body and mind.[6]

And as the news of this miracle spread among the people, another woman with great faith brought to him a little boy of hers who was seriously ill with a cruel ulcer. And she reverently asked him to consent to make the Sign of the Cross over him with his own hands. Then St. Francis, granting her prayer, took the child and raised the bandage over the sore and blessed it, making the Sign of the Cross three times over the ulcer. Then he bound it up again with his own hands and gave him back to his mother. And because it was evening, she immediately put him to bed to sleep. The next morning when she went to take her little son from the bed, she found him unbandaged, and looking at him she saw he was perfectly healed, as if he had never had any illness, except that over the spot where the ulcer had been, the flesh had grown in the form of a red rose—rather as evidence of the miracle than as a token of the ulcer, because that rose remained there throughout his whole life and often inspired him with devotion to St. Francis, who had healed him.[7]

St. Francis then remained in that town for a month, at the eager prayers of the inhabitants. During that time he performed many other miracles. And then he left there to go to St. Mary of the Angels with Brother Leo and with a good man who loaned him his donkey, which St. Francis rode.

It also happened that, because of the great cold of the winter season and the roughness of the roads, after riding all day, they were not able to reach any place where they could stay overnight. So being forced by the snow and the darkness that was overtaking them, they took shelter under the brow of an overhanging rock to spend the night.

The good man to whom the donkey belonged, being uncomfortable and poorly protected and unable to sleep on account of the cold—for there was no way of making any fire—began quietly to complain to himself and to cry. And he blamed St. Francis for having brought him to such a place. Then St. Francis, hearing this, had compassion on him, and in fervor of spirit he stretched his hand out over him and touched him. It was a marvelous thing that as soon as that hand, which had been pierced and enkindled by the Seraph, touched the man, all sense of cold left him, and so much heat came over him, interiorly and exteriorly, that he felt as if he were near the mouth of a blazing furnace. Consequently, he was immediately comforted in mind and body, and he fell asleep. And as he himself later used to declare, he slept that night until morning among the rocks and the snow more sweetly than he had ever rested in his own bed.[8]

The next day they traveled on and reached St. Mary of the Angels. And when they were near it, Brother Leo looked up and gazed toward the Place of St. Mary. And as he looked, he saw a very beautiful cross, on which there was hanging the figure of Christ Crucified, going before the face of St. Francis, who was riding ahead of him. And he clearly saw that that wonderful cross went before the face of St. Francis in such a way that when he stopped, it stopped, and when he went on, it likewise went on, and wherever St. Francis went, it preceded him. And that cross was so bright that not only did it shine in St. Francis' face, but it also illuminated the air all around, and Brother Leo could see everything in a clear light. And it lasted until St. Francis entered the Place of St. Mary. This completely amazed Brother Leo and deeply touched him with compassion and inflamed him with interior devotion.[9]

When St. Francis arrived at the Place with Brother Leo, they were made welcome by the friars with the greatest joy and affection. And from that time until his death St. Francis stayed at that Place of St. Mary most of the time. And the fame of his sanctity and his miracles spread continually throughout the Order and throughout the world, although in his very deep humility he concealed, as much as he could, the gifts and graces of God and called himself a very great sinner.

At one time Brother Leo was wondering about this, and he foolishly said to himself: "Look—this man calls himself a very great sinner in public, and he came into the Order as an adult, and he is honored so much by God, and yet in secret he never confesses any carnal sin—can he be a virgin?" And he began to feel an intense desire to know the truth about this, but he did not dare ask St. Francis about it. So he turned to God and earnestly prayed that He would give him some assurance about what he wanted to know. He prayed a great deal and merited to be heard, and he received assurance through this vision that St. Francis was truly a virgin in body. For in a vision he saw St. Francis standing on a high and exalted place where no one could go or reach, and he was told in spirit that that very high and exalted place symbolized the perfection of virginal chastity in St. Francis, which was in reasonable accord with the flesh that was to be adorned by the holy Stigmata of Christ.[10]

Seeing that because of the Stigmata his physical strength was gradually diminishing and that he was no longer able to have charge of governing the Order, St. Francis set forward the date of the General Chapter. When all its members had assembled, he humbly made his excuses to the friars for the infirmity due to which he could no longer take care of the Order as far as discharging the duties of the Generalate was concerned, although he was not renouncing the position of General, since he could not do so, as he had been made General by the Pope, and so he could not give up the position or substitute a successor without the Pope's specific permission. But he appointed Brother Peter Catani as his Vicar, commending the Order to him and to the Provincial Ministers with all possible affection.

And having done this, St. Francis felt consoled in spirit, and raising his eyes and hands toward Heaven, he spoke thus: "To You, my Lord God, I commend Your family which You have committed to me until now—for now, owing to my infirmities which You know, my very dear Lord, I can no longer have charge of it. I also commend it to the Provincial Ministers—let them be held responsible to give an account to You on Judgment Day if any friar should perish through their negligence or their bad example or their overharsh correction."

And by those words, as it pleased God, all the friars at the Chapter understood that he was speaking of the Stigmata when he excused himself because of an infirmity. And as a result of their holy affection not one of them could hold back his tears.

And henceforth he left all the care and governing of the Order in the hands of his Vicar and of the Provincial Ministers. And he used to say: "From now on, since I have given up having charge of the Order because of my infirmities, I have no other duty but to pray to God for our Order and to give a good example to the friars. And I know for sure that if my infirmity should leave me, the greatest help I could give the Order would be to pray continuously to God for it, that He may govern, defend, and preserve it."[11]

Now, as was said above, St. Francis tried as much as he could to hide from everyone's eyes the very holy wounds which Christ the Son of God had miraculously imprinted on his hands and feet and side. And after he had received them he always traveled and lived with socks on his feet, and he concealed his hands with bandages so that nothing but the tips of his fingers were visible to his companions, recalling what the angel said to the holy Tobias: "It is good to hide the secret of the King." Nevertheless he could not prevent many friars from seeing and touching them in different ways, and particularly the wound in his side, which he tried to hide with special care.

Thus a friar who was serving him once persuaded him with devout cunning to take off his habit so as to shake the dust out of it. And when St. Francis removed it in his presence, that friar clearly saw the wound in the side, and by quickly placing his hand on his chest, he touched it with three fingers and measured how long and large it was. His Vicar also saw it in a similar way at that time. But Brother Rufino had an even clearer proof of it. He was a great contemplative. St. Francis sometimes used to say of him that no man in the world was holier than he, and because of his saintliness St. Francis loved him as a dear friend and used to give in to his wishes.

This Brother Rufino obtained proof about the Stigmata, and particularly the one in the side, for himself and for others, in three ways. The first was that, as he had to wash his breeches (which St. Francis wore so long that by pulling them up well he covered the wound in the right side with them), Brother Rufino carefully examined and inspected them, and each time he found that they were bloody on the right side. Consequently he realized for sure that it was blood that issued from that wound. But St. Francis scolded him when he realized that he was laying out his breeches in order to see that spot. The second way was once when Brother Rufino was scratching St. Francis' back, in order to make more certain about it, he deliberately passed his hand over it and put his large finger into the wound in the side, whereupon St. Francis shouted aloud in great pain: "God forgive you, Brother Rufino! Why did you do that?" The third way was when, wishing to see that venerable wound with his own eyes, that same friar once said to St. Francis with affectionate cunning: "Father, I beg you to grant me the very great consolation of giving me your habit and accepting mine, for the love of charity." Now Brother Rufino did this in order that, while St. Francis was taking off his habit, he might see with his own eyes the wound in the side which he had recently touched with his fingers. And so it happened. Yielding to Brother Rufino's affectionate request, although unwillingly, St. Francis took off his habit and gave it to him and accepted his. And then, because he had only that one, while he was taking it off, he was unable to cover himself in such a way as to prevent Brother Rufino from clearly seeing that wound.

Likewise Brother Leo and many other friars saw those Stigmata of St. Francis while he was living. Although because of their holiness those friars were reliable men whose mere word could be trusted, nevertheless, in order to remove any doubt from people's minds, they swore on the Holy Book that they had clearly seen them.

Several Cardinals who were intimate friends of St. Francis also saw them, and out of reverence for the Stigmata they composed and made beautiful and inspiring hymns and antiphons and texts in prose.

The Supreme Pontiff, Pope Alexander, while preaching to

the people before all the Cardinals (among whom was the saintly Brother Bonaventure, who was a Cardinal), said and confirmed that he saw with his own eyes the holy Stigmata of St. Francis when he was alive.[12]

The Lady Jacopa dei Settesoli of Rome, who was the most prominent lady in Rome in her time and was intensely devoted to St. Francis, saw and kissed them many times with the greatest reverence before St. Francis died and after he died, because she came from Rome to Assisi at the death of St. Francis as a result of a divine revelation. And it happened this way.

Some days before his death, St. Francis was lying sick in Assisi in the Bishop's Palace. And despite all the sickness, out of devotion he would often sing certain praises of Christ with some of his companions. And if he himself was unable to sing owing to his illness, he often made his companions sing. Now the men of Assisi, fearing that such a precious treasure should happen to be carried away from Assisi, had that Palace carefully guarded day and night by armed men. And while the Saint was lying there for many days, one of his companions said to him: "Father, you know that the people of this city have great faith in you and consider you a holy man, and so they may think that if you are as they believe, you should be thinking about death in this illness of yours, and that you should be weeping rather than singing, since you are so seriously ill. For you should know that your singing and ours, which you make us perform, is heard by many people in the palace and outside, because this palace is being guarded by many armed men on account of you, and they might be scandalized. So," said this friar, "I think that we would do well to leave here and all go back to St. Mary of the Angels, as this is not the right place for us among seculars."

St. Francis answered Brother Elias, who had said this: "Dearest Brother, you know that two years ago, when we were staying in Foligno, the Lord revealed to you the end of my life. Moreover, He has also revealed to me that that end will come in a few days, during this illness. And in this same revelation God has given me assurance of the remission of all my sins and of the happiness of Paradise. Until I had that revelation, I used to weep over death and over my sins. But after that revelation was given to me, I have been so filled with joy that I cannot weep any more, but I remain in bliss and joy all the time. And that is why I sing and shall sing to the Lord, who has given me the gift of His grace and an assurance of the bliss of glory in Paradise. But regarding our leaving here I willingly agree. However, you must prepare something to carry me, because owing to my sickness I am unable to walk."[13]

The friars therefore took him up in their arms and carried him on the way toward St. Mary of the Angels, accompanied by a crowd of people. When they reached a hospital that was on the way, St. Francis asked whether they had arrived that far, because as a result of his extreme penance and former weeping, his eyesight was impaired and he could not see well. So when he was told that they were at the hospital, he said to those who were carrying him: "Set me down on the ground and turn me toward Assisi."

And standing in the road, with his face turned toward the city, he blessed it with many blessings, saying: "May the Lord bless you, holy city, for through you many souls shall be saved, and in you many servants of God shall dwell, and from you many shall be chosen for the Kingdom of Eternal Life." And after he had said those words, he had himself carried farther on, to St. Mary of the Angels.[14]

And when they arrived at St. Mary, they carried him to the infirmary, and they laid him down there to rest. Then St. Francis called one of his companions and said to him: "Dearest Brother, God has revealed to me that I am going to live until a certain day and then die from this sickness, and you know that the Lady Jacopa dei Settesoli, who is very devoted to our Order, would be extremely sad if she knew about my death and was not present. So let us notify her that if she wants to see me alive, she should come here at once."

The friar answered: "You are right, Father; because of the great devotion she has for you, she would grieve intensely if she were not present at your death."

So St. Francis said: "Go and bring the inkhorn and pen and paper, and write as I tell you." And when the friar had brought them, St. Francis dictated the letter this way: "To the Lady Jacopa, servant of God, Brother Francis, the little poor man of Christ, sends his greetings in the Lord and fellowship in the

Holy Spirit of Our Lord Jesus Christ. You must know, my very dear friend, that the Blessed Christ by His grace has revealed to me that my life will come to its end soon. So if you want to find me alive after you have seen this letter, set out and hasten to St. Mary of the Angels. For if you do not come by a certain day, you will not be able to find me alive. And bring with you some haircloth in which to wrap my body and the wax needed for the funeral. I also ask you to bring me some of those things to eat which you used to give me when I was sick in Rome."

And while this letter was being written, it was revealed to St. Francis by God that the Lady Jacopa was coming to him and was near the Place and was bringing with her all those things which he was requesting in the letter. So after he had this revelation, St. Francis suddenly said to the friar who was writing the letter: "Don't write any more, because it is not necessary, but put the letter aside."

And all the friars were very much surprised that he did not allow the letter to be finished and did not want it to be sent. And then—a little while later—there was a strong knocking at the gate of the Place. And St. Francis sent the brother porter to open it. And when he opened the gate, there was the Lady Jacopa, the greatest noblewoman of Rome, with her two sons who were senators and with a throng of companions on horseback. She had come to St. Francis and had brought with her all the things which St. Francis had included in that letter.

On entering, the Lady Jacopa went right to the infirmary and came to St. Francis. Her arrival brought him great joy and consolation, and she also rejoiced on finding him alive and talking with him. And she had the cookies fetched which she had brought to St. Francis, and she gave him some to eat.

And after he had eaten some and was very comforted, the Lady Jacopa went to the feet of St. Francis and she knelt and took those very holy feet marked and adorned with the wounds of Christ, and she kissed and bathed them with her tears with such consolation and grace that she seemed to the friars who were standing around like another Mary Magdalen weeping and embracing and kissing the feet of another Christ. And the friars were unable to draw her away from the Saint's feet.

Finally, after a long time, they nevertheless raised her up and led her aside and asked her how she had come just at the right time and so well provided with everything that St. Francis needed while alive and when he would be buried. The Lady Jacopa answered that while she was praying one night in Rome, she heard a voice from Heaven saying to her: "If you want to find Brother Francis alive, go to Assisi at once, without delay. And take with you those things which you used to give him when he was sick in Rome, and take also those things which will be needed for his burial."

"And," she said, "I did so."

Moreover, she brought such a large supply of wax that it was sufficient not only for his funeral but also for all the Masses said over his body for many days.

The Lady Jacopa stayed until St. Francis died and was buried. And she with all her company gave very great honor to his remains at his funeral, and she paid for everything that was needed. Then she returned to Rome. But some time later, out of devotion to St. Francis she came again to Assisi. And there she ended her days in saintly penance and virtuous living and died a holy death. And it was her will that she be buried in the Church of St. Francis with great devotion. And so it was done.[15]

At the death of St. Francis, not only Lady Jacopa and her sons and her company saw and kissed his glorious Stigmata, but also many citizens of Assisi. Among them was a very well-known and prominent knight named Sir Jerome, who had great doubts and was skeptical about them, as St. Thomas the Apostle was about those of Christ. In order to make himself and others sure about them, he boldly moved the nails in the hands and feet and in an obvious way touched the wound in the side, in the presence of the friars and lay people. As a result, later he was a steadfast witness of that fact, swearing on the Book that it was so and that he had so seen and touched.[16]

St. Clare with her nuns also saw and kissed the glorious Stigmata of St. Francis. They were present at his funeral.

The glorious confessor of Christ St. Francis passed from this life on Saturday, the third of October, in the year of the Lord 1226, and he was buried on Sunday. That year was the twentieth of his conversion, when he began to do penance, and it was the second year after the imprinting of the Stigmata. And it was in the forty-fifth year from his birth.

Later, in the year 1228, St. Francis was canonized by Pope Gregory IX, who came in person to Assisi to canonize him.[17]

To the praise of Christ. Amen.

And this suffices for the Fourth Consideration.

### The Fifth Consideration: About Certain Apparitions to Saintly Persons Concerning the Holy Stigmata

The Fifth and last Consideration deals with certain apparitions and revelations and miracles which God performed after the death of St. Francis as a confirmation of his Stigmata and as a testimony of the day and hour when Christ gave them to him.

And in this connection it should be known that in the year of the Lord 1282, on the third day of October, Brother Philip, Minister of Tuscany, by order of Brother Bonagrazia the Minister General, commanded Brother Matthew of Castiglione Aventino, a man of great devotion and saintliness, to tell him under holy obedience what he knew about the day and hour when the sacred Stigmata were imprinted by Christ on the body of St. Francis, because he had heard that Brother Matthew had had a revelation about it. This Brother Matthew, under the obligation of holy obedience, answered him as follows:

"When I was a member of the community of Alverna during the month of May last year, one night I began to pray in the cell which has been built on the spot where it is believed that that holy apparition of the Seraph took place. And in my prayer I very fervently begged God to deign to reveal to someone the day and the hour when the sacred Stigmata were imprinted on the body of St. Francis. And as I was persevering in prayer and in this petition beyond the first watch, St. Francis appeared to me in a very bright light and said: 'Son, what are you asking God to reveal to you?' And I answered: 'Father, I am asking God to deign to reveal on what day and hour the Stigmata of the Lord's Passion were imprinted on you.'

"And he said to me: 'The Lord wishes you to know it, and

I will tell you. I am indeed your Father Francis—you know me well.' Then he showed me the Stigmata of his hands, feet, and side, and said: 'The time has come when God wishes to disclose for His glory what the friars have so far not sought to know. For He who appeared to me then was not an angel but was my Lord Jesus Christ in the form of a Seraph.[1] With His hands He imprinted in my body these five wounds as He had received those same holy wounds in His body on the Cross.'

"And describing the way in which the apparition occurred, St. Francis added: 'The day before the Exaltation of the Cross an angel came to me and told me on behalf of God that I should prepare myself to be patient and to receive what God might wish to do. And I answered that I was ready to suffer and to endure whatever God might deign to do. So the next morning, that is, the day of the Exaltation of the Holy Cross, which was a Friday in that year, I came out of my cell at the break of dawn in very great fervor of spirit, and I went to pray on this spot where you are now, a place where I often prayed. And while I was praying, there came down through the air from Heaven with great rapidity a crucified Young Man in the form of a Seraph, with six wings. At this marvelous sight I humbly knelt on this spot and began to contemplate devoutly the infinite love of Jesus Crucified and the infinite pain of His Passion. And the sight of Him aroused such compassion in me that I really seemed to feel that Passion in my body. And at His presence this whole mountain was shining with a golden light like a sun. And so, coming down that way, He came close to me and stood before me and said certain words to me which I have not yet revealed to anyone. But the time is drawing near when they shall be revealed, because the Order and the friars are in great need of them. Afterward Christ vanished from my sight and returned to Heaven. And I found myself marked like this with these wounds. Now go and confidently tell these things to your Minister, because this is the work of God and not of man.' And after saying those words, St. Francis blessed me, saying: 'My son, go in the name of the Lord!' And he went back to Heaven with a great throng of very radiant men."

The above-mentioned Brother Matthew declared that he had seen and heard all these things as they are truly written above, and that he had not been sleeping but was awake and conscious. And he took an oath to that effect, with his hand on the Bible, before the said Minister in his cell in Florence, when the latter questioned him about this under obedience.[2]

Another time a certain devout and holy friar, while reading the chapter on the Stigmata in the Legend of St. Francis, began to wonder with great anxiety of mind what must have been those very secret words that the Seraph said to him when he received the holy Stigmata and which St. Francis said he would not reveal to anyone while he was living in the body. And this friar said to himself: "St. Francis did not want to say those words while he was alive, but now, since he is no longer living in the body, maybe he would tell them if he was fervently prayed to do so." Believing therefore that they would do much good, the friar decided to pray that they be revealed. And henceforth he began devoutly to pray to God and to St. Francis that they might deign to disclose to him those secret words of the Seraph. And the friar persevered in that prayer every day for eight years, and in the eighth year he merited having his prayer granted in this way.

One day after eating he went with his brethren to the church to give thanks and praise to God. And after the office was over, he remained alone to pray in a certain part of the church. And while he was praying to God and St. Francis more fervently than usual, weeping many tears and burning with a more intense desire to know those words, a friar came in and called him, saying that the guardian had ordered him to accompany him to the village to get something which the Place needed. Therefore, without doubting that obedience is more meritorious than prayer, he immediately stopped praying as soon as he heard the superior's order, and humbly and obediently hastened out with that friar who had called him. And as it pleased God, in that act of prompt obedience he earned more merit than by his long praying.

Now when they went out of the gate of the Place, they met two foreign friars who seemed to have come from a distant country. One of them looked young, and the other old and thin. And because of the rainy winter weather they were muddy and wet. When that obedient friar saw them, he felt strong compassion and charity for them, and he said to his companion: "As our errand can wait a while, dear Brother, and these foreign friars are in real need of being charitably welcomed, please let me go first and wash this older one's feet, as he needs it most, and you can wash the younger one's. And then we can go on our errand."

So the other friar yielded to his companion's charity, and they went back to the Place and gave the foreign friars an affectionate welcome, taking them into the kitchen to get warm and dry. Eight other friars of the Place were also warming themselves at the fire. And after they had been near the fire for a while, they led the foreign friars aside to wash their feet, as they had agreed to do.

And while that devout and obedient friar was washing the feet of the older friar and removing the mud—because they were all covered with mud—he looked and saw that the feet were marked with the Stigmata! In amazement and joy he kissed and embraced the feet, crying aloud: "Oh, Brother, either you are Christ or you are St. Francis!"

On hearing his surprised outcry all the friars of that Place arose and gathered around to see the Stigmata. Then that elderly friar at their request allowed all of them to see and touch and kiss them with great awe and reverence. And as they were still more moved by amazement and joy, he said to them: "Do not doubt or fear, my dearest Brothers and sons. I am your Father, Brother Francis, who, by the will of God, founded three Orders. And I have been prayed to every day for eight years by this friar who is holding my feet—and today he especially prayed to me in the church after the praises which you recited there—that I should deign to reveal to him those secret words which the Seraph said to me when he gave me the Stigmata and which I never told anyone while I was alive. But today, because of his perseverance and his prompt obedience, for which he left the consolations of prayer, I have been sent to him by command of God in order to reveal to him in your presence what he wants."

Then St. Francis turned to that friar and said: "You must know, dearest Brother, that when I was on Mount Alverna, utterly absorbed in remembering the Passion of Christ, I received in my body His holy Wounds, and then Christ said to me: 'Do you know what I have done to you? I have given you the emblems of My Passion so that you may be My standard-bearer. And just as I went down into Limbo on the day of My death and, by the virtue and merits of those Wounds, drew out of there and led to Heaven all the souls that I found there, so I grant to you henceforth, in order that you be conformed to Me in death as you were in life, that every year on the day of your death you may go to Purgatory and, by the virtue and efficacy of your Stigmata, you may draw out of there all the souls of your three Orders—that is, the Minors, Sisters, and Continent—that you find there, and may lead them to the glory of Paradise.' Now I never told those words to anyone while I lived in the world, so that I should not be accused of boastful presumption and vainglory."

And after he had said these words, St. Francis and his companion suddenly disappeared. Later many friars heard this from those eight friars who were present during that vision and those words of St. Francis. (Brother Giacomo Raneto, a lector in Rome, said in a sermon that he had heard it from one of those eight friars.)[3]

St. Francis once appeared on Mount Alverna to Brother John of Alverna, a man of great holiness, while he was praying. And he stayed and spoke with him for a long time. And finally when he wanted to leave, he said to Brother John: "Ask me what you want."

Brother John said: "Father, I beg you to tell me something I have wanted to know for a long time, and that is what you were doing and where you were when the Seraph appeared to you."

St. Francis answered: "I was praying on that spot where the Chapel of Count Simon of Battifolle is now, and I was asking my Lord Jesus Christ for two graces. The first was that I should feel in my soul and in my body, as far as possible, all that pain which He had felt within Himself during His most holy Passion. The second grace I asked was that I should likewise feel in my heart that most intense love which He enkindled within Himself so as to endure such suffering for us sinners. And then God put it in my heart that He would let me feel both the one and the other, as much as possible for a mere creature. And that was fully accomplished in me during the imprinting of the Stigmata."

Then Brother John asked him whether those secret words which the Seraph had spoken to him were really as stated by the above-mentioned friar, who declared that he had heard St. Francis say them in the presence of eight friars. St. Francis replied that it was truly as that friar said.

Now Brother John also felt encouraged by the generosity of the giver to ask still more, and he said: "Oh, Father, I most earnestly beg you to let me see and kiss your glorious Stigmata, not because I have any doubts about them, but only for my consolation and devotion—for I have always longed to do so."

And St. Francis said to him: "Here, my son, are the Stigmata which you have desired to see." And he freely showed him his hands and feet and side, and offered them to him.

On seeing them, Brother John was overcome with amazement and fell down at his feet in fright. Then St. Francis raised him up, saying: "Arise and touch me." Consoled by the Lord, he gained confidence and began to touch those sacred Stigmata and kiss them and move the nails. And then, as he himself reported, he found out by experience that what Brother Bonaventure wrote in his Legend about those sacred Stigmata was true: that when they were pressed on one side, they extended still farther on the other side.

Finally he asked: "Father, what great consolation your soul must have had when you saw the Blessed Christ come to you and give you the marks of His holy Passion! If only God would let me feel a little of that sweetness now!"

Then St. Francis answered: "Do you see these nails?"

And Brother John said: "Yes."

"Touch once more this nail in my hand," said St. Francis.

Then with great reverence and fear Brother John touched that nail. And when he touched it, a scent suddenly came forth from it, spiraling up like smoke, as incense does. And entering through Brother John's nose, it filled his soul and body with such sweetness that he was immediately rapt by God in an ecstasy and became unconscious. And after the Blessed Father disappeared, he stayed in that rapture from that hour, which was tierce, until vespers. And for the next eight days he was unable to eat, and everything he saw seemed fetid to him.

Brother John never told anyone but his confessor about that

vision and intimate talk with St. Francis, until he was about
to die. But when he was near death, he revealed it to many
friars.[4]

A very devout and saintly friar of the Roman Province saw
this wonderful vision. He was united to another friar by a bond
of true affection and charity, and they loved each other after
death as they had while living. For when one of them died one
night and was buried the next morning in the first cloister before the entrance of the chapter room, that friar who survived,
at noon on the same day, while all the friars had gone to rest,
went to a corner of the chapter room in order to pray devoutly
to God and St. Francis for the soul of his beloved dead companion. And while he was persevering in prayer, with tears
and supplications, all of a sudden he heard the sound of many
persons going through the cloister. In great fear he quickly
looked at his companion's grave, and he saw St. Francis and
many of his friars standing around the grave at the entrance
of the chapter room. Looking beyond, he saw a great purga-
torial fire in the center of the cloister and the soul of his dead
companion burning in the middle of the fire. He looked around
the cloister, and he saw the Lord Jesus Christ walking in procession around the cloister with a great throng of angels and
saints.

And watching with intense amazement, he saw that when
Christ passed before the chapter room, St. Francis knelt down
with all those friars and said: "I beg You, my Most Holy Father and Lord, by that highest love and charity which You
showed to the human race in Your Incarnation, to have mercy
on the soul of this friar of mine that is burning in that purga-
torial fire there."

Christ did not answer or grant his prayer, but went on and
walked around the cloister with the throng of saints that followed Him. When He came back the second time before the
chapter room, St. Francis knelt down again with his friars as
before and prayed to Him thus for the soul of the dead friar:
"I beg You, Most Merciful Father and Lord, by the infinite
love and charity which You showed to the human race when
You died on the Cross for all men, to have mercy on the soul
of that friar of mine."

Again Christ passed on and did not answer. After going

around the cloister the third time, He came back by the dead friar's grave. Then St. Francis knelt down with the friars as before and prayed thus to Christ: "I beg You, Most Merciful Father and Lord, by that intense pain and consolation which I felt when You imprinted these Stigmata in my flesh, to have mercy on the soul of that friar of mine that is in the fire of Purgatory!" And he showed Christ the Stigmata in his hands, feet, and side.

On being prayed to by St. Francis this third time in the name of his Stigmata, Christ immediately stopped and looked at the Stigmata. And granting his prayer, He nodded and said: "I grant to you, Brother Francis, the soul of your friar."

And thereby He certainly wished both to honor and confirm the glorious Stigmata of St. Francis and openly to signify that the souls of his friars that go to Purgatory cannot be freed from suffering and led to the glory of Paradise in any way more easily than by virtue of his holy Stigmata, in accordance with the words which Christ said to St. Francis when He imprinted them on him. Now as soon as He had uttered these words, that fire in the cloister vanished and the dead friar appeared in glory with St. Francis, and ascended into Heaven with him and with Christ and all that blessed company of rejoicing angels and saints. Consequently, the friar who was his companion and who had prayed for him felt intense joy on seeing him freed from suffering and led to Paradise. And later he told the other friars all about the vision, and together with them he praised and thanked God. (I, Brother Francis Peri, heard of this miracle from Brother Luke of Pistoia when I was in Arezzo.)⁵ To the glory of Christ.

A noble baron named Landulf, of Massa di Santo Piero in the mountains near Gubbio, who was very devoted to St. Francis and finally received from his hands the habit of the Third Order, was given this assurance of St. Francis' death and his glorious Stigmata.

At the time when St. Francis' death was approaching, the devil entered into a woman of that village and cruelly tormented her. Moreover, he made her speak so intelligently in Latin that she defeated all the learned and educated men who came to debate with her. Now it happened that the devil went away from her and left her free for two days. And the third day he came back and afflicted her more cruelly than before. When the Baron Landulf heard about it, he went to this woman and asked the devil who was dwelling in her why he had left her for two days and on returning was tormenting her more severely than before.

The devil answered: "When I left her, it was because I met with all my companions who are in this region and we went in great strength to the death of that beggar Francis to dispute with him and take his soul. But as it was surrounded and defended by a throng of angels in greater numbers than we were, and it was carried to Heaven by them, we left, embarrassed by our defeat. So now I am giving back to this miserable woman what I neglected in those two days."

Then the Baron Landulf commanded him in God's name to tell the truth about the sanctity of St. Francis who, he said, was dead, and of St. Clare, who was alive. The devil replied: "I will tell you the truth about it, whether I want to or not. God the Father was so angry over the sins of the world that it seemed He would soon utter the final sentence against men and women to exterminate them from the world if they did not change for the better. But Christ, His Son, prayed for sinners and promised to renew His life and His Passion in one man—the poor little beggar Francis, through whose life and teaching He would lead many throughout the world to the path of truth and penance. And now, to show the world that He had done this in St. Francis, He wished that the Stigmata of His Passion, which He had imprinted on his body during his life, should at his death be seen and touched by many persons. Similarly, the Mother of Christ promised to renew her virginal purity and humility in a woman, Sister Clare, in such a way that through her example she would snatch many thousands of women from our hands. And so as a result of these promises God the Father was appeased and postponed His final sentence."

Then the Baron Landulf, wishing to know for sure whether the devil—who is the father of lies—was telling the truth in this matter, and especially regarding the death of St. Francis, sent one of his faithful squires to St. Mary of the Angels in Assisi to find out whether St. Francis was alive or dead. That squire on arriving there found out, and on returning reported to his master, that St. Francis had passed from this life precisely at the hour and on the day which the devil said.[6]

Omitting all the miracles of the Stigmata of St. Francis which may be read in his Legend, in concluding this Fifth Consideration it should be known that to Pope Gregory IX (as he later declared), when he was having some doubts about the wound in the side, St. Francis appeared one night, and raising his right arm a little, he uncovered the wound in his side. And he asked him for a vase, and he had one brought to him. And St. Francis had him place it under the wound in the side, and it seemed to the Pope that it really became filled to the brim with blood mixed with water which flowed from that wound. From that moment all doubt left him. And later, in agreement with all the Cardinals, he expressed his formal approval of the Stigmata of St. Francis, and gave the friars a special certificate with a hanging seal. And he did this at Viterbo in the eleventh year of his pontificate. And afterward in the twelfth year he gave another more comprehensive one.

Also Pope Nicholas III and Pope Alexander gave many privileges, whereby anyone who denied the Stigmata of St. Francis could be prosecuted as a heretic.[7]

And this suffices for the Fifth and last Consideration of the glorious Stigmata of our Father St. Francis. May God give us the grace to follow his life in this world in such a way that by virtue of his glorious Stigmata we may merit to be saved with him in Paradise!

To the glory of the Blessed Christ and His little poor Francis. Amen.

Part Three

# THE LIFE OF BROTHER JUNIPER

## 1 *How Brother Juniper Cut Off a Pig's Foot*
### *Just to Give It to a Sick Man*

One of the most elect first disciples and companions of St.
Francis was Brother Juniper, a man of such unshakable humility, patience, and self-contempt that the rushing waves of
temptation and tribulation could not move him. His patience
is said to have been so remarkable that no one ever saw him
disturbed, even when under great pressure. He reached such
a degree of self-contempt that he was considered stupid and
foolish by those who did not know how perfect he was. Therefore St. Francis, once when he was speaking about the outstanding virtues of his companions, said: "He would be a good
Friar Minor who had attained to Brother Juniper's contempt
of self and of the world."

Now one day Brother Juniper was visiting a certain sick friar
at St. Mary of the Portiuncula. And when he saw him suffering
very much from his illness, Brother Juniper's heart melted with
compassion and burned with fervent charity. So he asked the
friar: "Can I help you in any way? Do you want something
to eat?"

The sick friar answered: "I would love to eat a pig's foot
if I had one. . . ."

Brother Juniper quickly said: "Leave that to me—I'll soon
have one and prepare it the way you want!"

He went and took a knife from the kitchen and ran into the
fields, where he found a group of pigs feeding. He ran after
one of them, caught it, and cut off one of its feet with the

knife. Leaving the pig with its leg maimed, he came back and washed and dressed and cooked the pig's foot. And after he had prepared it well, he brought and served it with great kindness to the sick friar. The latter ate it very eagerly, to Brother Juniper's intense joy and consolation. And to entertain him, Juniper gleefully described how he had caught the pig.

Meanwhile, however, the man who was guarding the swine and who had seen him cut off the foot, told his master the whole story with great indignation. When the master heard about it, he went to the friars' Place and shouted at them, calling them hypocrites, thieves, forgers, bandits, and evil men for having with deliberate malice cut off one of his pig's feet. At all the noise he was making, St. Francis came out with the others and very humbly made excuses for his friars, saying that he had not known about what had happened. Yet to appease him, he promised that he would make good the damage. But the man would not calm down. Raging with anger, he uttered many curses and threats, repeating over and over that the pig's foot had been cut off with deliberate malice. He refused to accept any excuses or promises, and he left in unappeased anger and indignation, shouting curses and insults.

While the other friars stood around in amazement, St. Francis prudently thought the matter over and said to himself: "Could Brother Juniper have done this out of indiscreet zeal?" He immediately summoned Brother Juniper privately and asked him: "Did you cut off the foot of a pig in the fields?"

Then Brother Juniper, acting not like someone who has done something wrong but like one who believes he has performed a great act of charity, answered joyfully: "Dear Father, it is true I cut that pig's foot off. And now listen compassionately to the reason. I went to visit that sick friar . . ." And he told him the whole story.

On hearing it, St. Francis was very sad. And with zeal for justice, his face flushed, he said: "Oh, Brother Juniper, why did you bring this great disgrace on us? That man is quite right in being angry at us. And now maybe he is complaining about us and spoiling our reputation throughout the town—and he has good reason to do so! Therefore I now order you under holy obedience to run right after that man until you overtake him, and to throw yourself on the ground before him and ad-

mit your guilt to him. And promise to make good the damage
—and do it—in such a way that he will have no more reason
to complain against us. For this certainly has been a most serious wrong!"

Brother Juniper was very much surprised at these words, as
he marveled that anyone should be angry over such an act of
charity. For to him all these material things seemed like nothing, except if they were put to use in practicing charity. And
he replied: "Father, you can be sure I will quickly give him
full satisfaction. But why should he be so angry when something that belonged to God rather than to him was used to
perform such a real act of charity?"

Then he ran off and overtook the man, who was still so angry
that he had not an ounce of patience left. With intense joy
and fervor Brother Juniper told him all about the amputation
of the pig's foot, as though he had done him a great favor for
which he deserved a reward. The man's anger only increased,
and he became so enraged that he shouted insults at him, calling him a fool, a lunatic, and the worst kind of criminal—and
he almost struck him.

Brother Juniper was amazed at these ugly words, although
he rejoiced at receiving the insults. And because he thought
that the man had not understood what he had said (which
seemed to him a matter for joy rather than anger), he told
the same story over again. And he embraced the man, explain-
ing how it had been done only out of love, and urging the man
to congratulate him for doing such a good deed, and even inviting the man to give the rest of the pig for the same purpose.

Then that man was overcome by so much simplicity and
humility. And recovering his senses when he heard that the
cause of the deed had been an act of charity, he knelt down
and wept and admitted that he had been wrong in insulting
Brother Juniper and the other holy friars. And he acknowledged that perhaps he was greedy and ungrateful to God for
the good things which he possessed. So he went and caught
and killed the pig and had it cooked and well dressed. And
with great devotion and weeping he brought it to St. Mary
of the Angels and gave it to those holy friars to eat as compen-
sation for the wrong which he had done them.

Now St. Francis, considering the simplicity and self-con

tempt and patience under adversity of that holy Brother Juniper, said to his companions and the other friars who were standing around: "My Brothers, if only I had a great forest of such junipers!"

To the glory of Christ. Amen.

### 2    An Example of Brother Juniper's Great Power against the Devil

The proud devils could not endure Brother Juniper's presence because he was so humble and pure and innocent. For once a certain man who was possessed by a devil, acting in a strange and unusual way, left the road he was on and rapidly fled seven miles along side roads. When his relatives who were following him asked why he had so suddenly run away, he answered: "Because that stupid Brother Juniper was coming along that road—and I could not stand his presence!" They investigated and found that Brother Juniper had indeed come along at that time, as the devil said.

Therefore St. Francis used to say when possessed persons were brought to him to be healed, if the devil did not immediately leave them at his command: "If you do not go out of this person at once, I will have Brother Juniper come and deal with you!" Then the devil, fearing the presence of Brother Juniper and being unable to endure the virtue and humility of St. Francis, quickly went away.

To the glory of Christ. Amen.

### 3    How the Devil Plotted to Have Brother Juniper Condemned to Be Hanged

Therefore the devil, wishing to make Brother Juniper suffer by some worldly means, went to a very cruel tyrant named Nicholas, who was the lord of a castle and village and who was then at war with the city of Viterbo. And he said to him: "Sir, watch out for this castle of yours, because soon a great traitor will be sent here by the men of Viterbo to kill you and set fire to your castle. And I give you these clues that this is true: he goes around dressed like a poor man with tattered and patched clothes and a torn cowl hanging on his shoulders, and he is carrying an awl with which to kill you, and he has with him a flint and steel to set fire to this castle. And if you do not find this to be true, punish me any way you wish."

Nicholas the tyrant was very much surprised and frightened by these words, because the man who said them seemed to be trustworthy. So he immediately ordered that the gates should be carefully watched and that if a man with those signs should come, he should be brought before him at once.

Meanwhile Brother Juniper came to that village, and he was alone, for owing to his perfection he had been given permission by his minister to go about and stay without a companion as he pleased. And he met some rowdy boys who as a joke damaged and tore his cowl. He did not mind, but rather encouraged and helped them to make even more fun of him.

While the guards were watching at the gate, Brother Juniper came up with his habit mostly cut off—for he had given parts of it to some poor man on the way—and with his cowl torn, not looking at all like a Friar Minor. And as he clearly showed the signs that had been given them, they quickly rushed upon him, seized him, and led him before the tyrant. And when they carefully searched him for offensive weapons, they found in his sleeve an awl with which he used to mend his sandals, and also a flint which he carried to light a fire, because he used to have headaches and often lived in the woods and solitary places.

On seeing the signs in him which agreed with the devil's statement, Nicholas immediately ordered them to twist a cord around his head and tighten it with a bar. And they did so with such cruelty that the cord was almost buried in his flesh. Then they put him on the rack, and pulled and wrenched his arms and disjointed his whole body, without showing any mercy. And when in that condition he was questioned as to who he was, he answered: "I am a very great sinner." And when he was asked whether he wanted to betray the castle and give it over to the people of Viterbo, he replied: "I am a great traitor and do not deserve any good." And when asked whether he wanted to kill the tyrant Nicholas with that awl and to burn the castle, he answered: "I would do much greater and worse things if God allowed me to."

Then Nicholas, overcome by his fury, did not wish to continue the questioning, but without further delay angrily sentenced Brother Juniper as a traitor and murderer to be tied to a horse's tail and dragged through the village to the gallows and there to be hanged by the throat at once. Now at all this, Brother Juniper did not offer any excuses, and he showed no sorrow, but rather, like someone who rejoices in tribulations for the love of God, he looked very joyful and glad. And when the tyrant's order was being carried out, and Brother Juniper's feet were tied to the tail of a horse and he was dragged over the ground to be hanged, he did not complain or lament, but went along in all humility, like a gentle lamb being led to slaughter.

This sight and the sudden sentencing brought a great crowd of people on the run to see the prompt and cruel execution. And no one knew him. However, as God willed, a certain good man who had seen Brother Juniper being arrested and then sentenced, ran to the Place of the Friars Minor of that village and called the guardian, saying: "For God's sake, please come quickly, because a poor man has been arrested and immediately sentenced and is being led to execution! Come, so that he can at least commit his soul into your hands—because he seems like a good man to me and he has not had time for confession. And they are taking him to be hanged—but he does not seem to care about death or the salvation of his soul. Please come quickly!"

The guardian, who was a zealous and compassionate man, immediately hastened to him, to persuade him to confess and to try to save his soul. But when he arrived, the crowd that had gathered to see this execution had grown so large that he could not make his way through it. So he stood there and waited. And while he was waiting, he heard a voice in the crowd shouting: "Don't do that, you naughty fellows! That rope is hurting my leg!"

On hearing this, the guardian thought he recognized Brother Juniper's voice. He strenuously pushed his way through the crowd and succeeded in reaching him. And when he tore away the linen cloth which usually covered the face of the person to be executed, he realized at once that it was indeed Brother Juniper, and he was understandably amazed.

Then Brother Juniper, paying no attention to his sufferings and wounds, saw the guardian and said to him, half smiling: "Oh, guardian, how fat you are!"

Grieving and weeping, the compassionate guardian wanted to take off his own habit and give it to Brother Juniper, but the latter said with a smile and cheerful expression: "No, guardian, you are fat, and you would not look good without your habit. I don't want it."

Then the guardian tearfully asked the executioners and all the people standing around to wait a while for pity's sake, until he went to beg the tyrant Nicholas to have mercy on Brother Juniper. The executioners and the people sympathized with him, thinking that he was related to the prisoner, and they agreed to wait for the tyrant's answer.

Then the devout and compassionate guardian went to the tyrant Nicholas and said to him, weeping bitterly: "Sir, I can't tell you how amazed and how sad I am, because I believe that today in this place a greater sin and a greater wrong has been committed than was ever done in the days of our ancestors. But I believe that it was done through ignorance."

Nicholas listened patiently to the guardian and asked him: "What is the great crime and evil that has been committed in this place today?"

The guardian answered: "That one of the holiest friars in the whole world living today in the Order of St. Francis (for whom you have a special devotion) has been sentenced by you to a very cruel punishment—I fully believe without justification."

Nicholas said: "Now tell me, guardian, who he is. For perhaps without knowing it I have done a great wrong."

The guardian said: "He whom you condemned to death is Brother Juniper, the companion of St. Francis!"

Nicholas the tyrant was utterly astounded, because he had already heard about Brother Juniper's fame and his holy life. Overcome with horror, he trembled and turned pale. Then he ran quickly with the guardian to Brother Juniper and untied him from the horse's tail and set him free. And before all the people he threw himself on the ground in front of Brother Juniper, and weeping bitterly he humbly admitted his guilt for the harm and offense which he had caused to be done to this holy friar, and he begged to be forgiven: "I truly believe that the end of my evil deeds and my life is approaching. For since I have treated this holy man so cruelly without his being guilty —although I did not know it—God will not tolerate me any longer and I will soon die a violent death."

Brother Juniper generously forgave Nicholas the tyrant and went away, rejoicing in the Lord because he had conquered himself and had been willing to be despised for the love of Christ. And he left all the people very edified.[1]

To the glory of God. Amen.

### 4   *How Brother Juniper Used to Give Whatever He Could to the Poor, for the Love of God*

Brother Juniper had so much pity and compassion for the poor that when he saw anyone who was badly clothed or bare, he would immediately rip off his sleeve or cowl or some piece of his habit and give it to that poor man. And so the guardian ordered him under obedience not to give all or part of his habit to anyone.

A few days later it happened that he met a poor man who was almost naked and who begged Brother Juniper to give him something for the love of God. And Juniper said to him very compassionately: "My dear man, I have nothing to give you except my habit—and my superior has told me under obedience not to give it or part of it away to anyone. But if you pull it off my back, I certainly will not prevent you."

He was not speaking to a deaf man, for he immediately pulled the habit off, inside out, and went away with it, leaving Brother Juniper naked.

When he went back to the Place, the friars asked him where his habit was. And he answered: "Some good person pulled it off my back and went away with it."

And as the virtue of compassion grew in him, he was not satisfied with giving away only his habit, but to the poor he used to give books and ornaments for the altar and cloaks of the other friars and whatever he could lay his hands on. Consequently, when poor people came to Brother Juniper to beg, the friars used to take and hide the things they wanted to keep, so that Brother Juniper should not find them. For he used to give everything away, for the love of God and for His praise.

To the glory of Christ. Amen.

### 5 How Brother Juniper Cut Some Ringlets from the Altar and Gave Them Away

Once when Brother Juniper was at the friary in Assisi for the Feast of the Lord's Nativity, he was in the church near the main altar, which was very beautifully draped and decorated. At the request of the sacristan, he stayed to guard the altar while the sacristan went to get a bite to eat.

While he was devoutly meditating, a poor little woman begged him to give her something for the love of God. And he answered: "Wait a minute. I'll see if I can find anything to give you from this richly decorated altar."

Now there was on the altar a very costly frontal from which were hanging some silver ringlets.[2] And when Brother Juniper looked at the ornate altar, he saw the silver ringlets and said: "These ringlets are superfluous." And taking a knife, he cut all of them off the frontal and gave them to the poor little woman, out of compassion.

Meanwhile the sacristan, after eating three or four mouthfuls, began to remember the ways of Brother Juniper and to fear that in his zeal for charity he might do some damage to the richly decorated altar which he had left in his guard. So he quickly rose from the table and went to the church. And when, on looking over the ornaments of the altar, he saw that the ringlets had been cut away and stripped from the frontal, he became exceedingly angry and indignant.

Brother Juniper saw how excited he was and said: "Don't be upset about those ringlets, because I gave them to a poor little woman who was in great need. They were good for nothing here except to make a display of worldly vanity."

On hearing this, the sacristan became furious and immediately ran through the church and the whole city anxiously trying to find the woman. But not only did he not find her—he found no one who had seen her. So he returned to the friary and angrily took the frontal to the Minister General John Parenti,[3] who was then in Assisi, and said: "Father General, I demand justice from you against Brother Juniper, who has destroyed this frontal for me—and it was the finest one in the sacristy! Now look how he has ruined it and stripped away all the silver ringlets! And he says he has given them to a poor woman."

Brother John the General answered: "Brother Juniper did not do this—but your foolishness, because you assigned him to guard the altar! Don't you know his ways? I tell you I am surprised he did not give away the rest. However, I am going to correct him severely for this fault."

And after vespers were chanted, he summoned all the friars in chapter. And calling Brother Juniper before him, in the presence of the whole community he rebuked him very strongly about the ringlets. And as his anger increased, he raised his voice until he became rather hoarse.

Now Brother Juniper did not particularly mind those words, as he rejoiced in being blamed and humiliated, but he began to worry more about the General's hoarseness and to think of some remedy for it. So after receiving the scolding, he went into the city and had a bowl of porridge prepared with butter.

He returned late that night. And lighting a candle he took the bowl of porridge to the General's cell and knocked. On opening the door and seeing him holding the lighted candle and the dish, the General asked quietly: "What do you want at this hour? What is it?"

Brother Juniper answered: "Father, when you were scolding me in chapter for my faults, I noticed that your voice became hoarse from overstrain, I believe. So I thought of a remedy and had this porridge made for you with butter. Please eat it—I am sure it will relieve your throat and chest."

The General said: "What an hour for you to bother people!"

Brother Juniper replied: "Come—it was made for you. Please eat it. It will do you good."

But the General was angered by the lateness of the hour and his insisting, and said: "Go away, you brute! Do you think I am going to eat at this hour?"

As Brother Juniper realized that neither begging nor persuading would help, he said to him: "Father, since you do not want to eat—and this porridge was made for you—at least do this for me: hold the candle, and I will eat."

Then the General, who was a very pious and devout man, was won over by Brother Juniper's great compassion and simplicity and charity—for he had done it out of devotion—and he answered: "Well now, Brother, since you want to, let's both eat it together!"

And because of Brother Juniper's insistent charity, they both ate the bowl of porridge. And they were refreshed far more by their devotion than by the food.

To the glory of Christ. Amen.

### 6 How Brother Juniper Kept Silent for Six Months

By nature this servant of God had little patience when something insulting was done or said to him. But he made such strong efforts to control himself that with the grace of God he acquired that virtue in a short time.

Seeing therefore that he could not remain silent and refrain from answering when something unpleasant was said to him or when he was scolded, once, realizing that his tongue was doing him much harm, he decided to remain silent at all cost. And he arranged it this way in order to observe it better: on the first day he kept silent out of love for the Heavenly Father, the next day for love of Jesus Christ, the next for love of the Holy Spirit, the next for love of the Virgin Mary, the next for love of our Father St. Francis, and so on. Every day for love of some Saint, he remained silent and did not speak for six months. And although he suffered pain and anxiety within, nevertheless externally he forced himself not to reply, even though with great difficulty.

Now one time it happened that certain words were said that were extremely hard for him to bear, and he made such a violent physical effort and his suffering and violence were so great that blood gushed forth from his chest and he spat it out of his mouth.

On seeing it, Brother Juniper grieved intensely and went into the church before the crucifix, and there he devoutly complained and mourned over the great suffering and pain that he was enduring. And he said: "See, my Lord, what I am bearing for love of You!"

Then the Crucified Christ miraculously raised His right hand from the wood of the cross, where it was nailed, and laid it on the wound in His side and said: "And I—what am I bearing for you?"

And Brother Juniper was utterly amazed and frightened and shocked to the core of his being. And he felt such emotion in his soul and mind that from that moment he was changed into another man. For just as formerly he could not endure the least painful word without suffering, so henceforth, with the help of divine grace, he not only bore with joy the insults and offenses that were said or done to him, but he went out hunting for them as for precious stones for his soul.[4]

To the glory of Christ. Amen.

## 7　*How to Resist Temptations of the Flesh*

Now once when Brother Giles and Brother Simon of Assisi and Brother Rufino and Brother Juniper had come together to talk about God and the salvation of the soul, Brother Giles said to them: "What do you do about temptations of the flesh?"

Brother Simon answered: "I think of the vileness and foulness of such a sin, and that gives me a great horror of it, and that way I escape."

Then Brother Rufino said: "I throw myself on the ground and keep praying and begging for the mercy of God and the Blessed Mother until I feel myself completely freed from it."

Next Brother Juniper said: "When I hear the voice of such diabolical suggestions seeming to resound in the fortified town of my flesh, I immediately rush to shut the entrance of my heart, and as a secure guard of the fortress of my heart I concentrate on holy meditation and aspirations. So when those sensual suggestions come knocking at my door of my heart, I reply as from inside without opening the door: 'Go away! Go away, because the room is already taken, and so you cannot come in.' And that way I never let a sensual thought enter my heart. Consequently, seeing themselves defeated, they go away not only from me but from the whole neighborhood."

Then Brother Giles quickly said: "I agree with you, Brother Juniper, because a man can more safely and discreetly fight against that sin by running away. For within he has a traitor in his sensual desires, and outside the enemy's large and powerful army makes itself felt through the body's senses. But otherwise he has a mighty battle—and a rare victory. So flee from vice, and you will win."

To the glory of God. Amen.

## 8   *How Brother Juniper Humiliated Himself for the Glory of God*

Once Brother Juniper, wishing to humiliate himself thoroughly, stripped himself completely naked. He put his breeches on his head and tied his habit into a bundle with his cord and put it around his neck. And he went into Viterbo that way and went to the market place to be mocked. While he sat there naked, some children and boys understandably thought he was insane and mistreated him a great deal, mocking and insulting him, throwing mud and stones at him, and pushing him back and forth. After being derided and tormented by them for a long time, he went to the friary, still naked.

Now when the friars saw him, they were profoundly shocked and angry at him, especially because he had gone through the whole town like that, with his bundle on his head. They scolded him very severely and shouted serious threats at him. One of them said: "Let's put him in prison!" Another said: "He should be hanged!" And others: "He should be burned at the stake!" And others: "No penalty could be too great for the shocking example he has given today of himself and of the whole Order!"

And Brother Juniper listened cheerfully and answered humbly and with great joy: "You are right. I deserve all those punishments and still greater ones for giving such scandal."

To the glory of Christ. Amen.

### 9    *How Brother Juniper Played at Seesawing in Order to Humiliate Himself*

Once Brother Juniper came to stay in Rome, where his reputation for holiness had already spread. Therefore many Romans, out of devotion, went out to meet him. When that humble man saw them from a distance and realized why they were coming, he wondered how he could turn their devotion into scorn and mockery.

And so seeing two boys playing at seesawing on a plank set on a log, each sitting on the opposite end and going up and down, Brother Juniper quickly went over to them and removed one of them from his end of the plank and sat there himself and began to play at seesawing with the other boy.

Meanwhile the crowd of Roman people arrived. And when they saw him seesawing, they were astonished. However, they greeted him very reverently and waited for him to stop playing so that they might honor him by conducting him to the friary. But Brother Juniper paid little attention to their reverence and devout greeting or their waiting, for he seemed to be more interested in playing at seesawing. And after they had waited quite a while, some of them began to be bored and to say: "What a fool he is!" But some, knowing his ways, felt still greater devotion for him. Then, as he did not stop playing, all of them went away and left Brother Juniper seesawing.

And when they were all gone, Brother Juniper was very happy because he had seen some of them mocking him. So, rejoicing in their scorn, he went on his way and entered Rome in all meekness and humility, and came to the friary of the Friars Minor.

To the glory of Christ. Amen.

### 10    *How Brother Juniper Once Cooked for the Friars Enough Food for a Fortnight*

Once when Brother Juniper was in a certain small friary and all the other friars had to go out for some good reason, the guardian said to him: "Brother Juniper, we are all going out, so see to it that when we return you have a little food prepared to nourish the friars." Brother Juniper answered: "I'll be glad to do so. Leave it to me."

Now when all the friars had left, Brother Juniper began to think over this matter of cooking, and he said to himself: "What an unnecessary bother it is that every day some friar has to be lost in the kitchen, busy with this food and disturbed in trying to pray! Well, since I am left here to cook, this time I am going to cook so much that all the friars, and even more of them, will have enough to eat for a fortnight!"

And so he eagerly went to town and begged some cooking pots and collected some fresh and some salted meat and chickens and eggs and different kinds of vegetables. And he gathered and lit a lot of firewood. Then he filled all those pots with water and put them on the fire, and he put everything into the pots—chickens with feathers and eggs in shells and the vegetables, one thing after another—so that they should all cook together.

Meanwhile one of the friars who was a friend of Brother Juniper and used to approve of his simple ways, came back and was let in by the Brother. On entering the kitchen and seeing so many large pots boiling on the roaring fire, he was surprised and thought of Brother Juniper's simplicity. But he sat down by the fire and silently watched what he was doing. And he saw how he kept anxiously running from one pot to another, stirring their contents with a stick, and bringing more firewood and blowing on the fire and constantly keeping busy cooking, without a moment's rest. And because, owing to the intense heat, he could not get close to the pots to skim them, he took a board and tied it tightly to his body with a rope in order to protect himself from the heat. And then he jumped from one pot to another in a thoroughly entertaining way.

Meanwhile all the other friars returned. And after watching him with great amusement, that certain friar went out of the kitchen and said to them: "Brother Juniper certainly is preparing a wedding feast!" But they thought he was joking.

Then Brother Juniper took his pots off the fire and rang the bell for the meal. And when the friars had gone into the refectory, he came in with all that food he had cooked, all red-faced from his exertion and from the heat of the fire. And he said to them: "Have a good meal—and then let's go to pray, and no one need bother about cooking for the next fortnight because I have prepared enough today to last more than two weeks."

Then he set down on the table before the friars that hodge-podge of his which not a single hog in the city of Rome would have eaten, no matter how hungry it was. And he served them dishes of eggs in the shell and chickens partly covered with feathers. And the friars found on their plates the feathers which had fallen off when the chickens were boiled. Then, seeing that the other friars were not eating anything, Brother Juniper took a chicken with feathers and put it to his mouth, and without cutting it he tore it apart with his teeth. And he praised what he had cooked, like a salesman selling his wares, saying: "Such chickens are good for the brain—and this mixture will keep the body in good condition. Eat it—it will do you good!"

While the friars were struck with amazement and devotion by such simplicity and considered his self-control great wisdom, the guardian became very angry at his foolishness and wastefulness. And he scolded Brother Juniper very severely. Then the Brother immediately threw himself on his knees before the guardian and all the friars, and humbly admitted his fault, declaring that he was a very bad man. And he mentioned the sins which he had committed when he was in the world. And he said: "A certain man committed such and such a sin, and they tore out his eyes, but I should rather have my eyes torn out. Another man was hanged for his crimes—I should rather be hanged for my evil deeds, because I have wasted so many good things of God and of the Order!" And he went out, repenting bitterly, and would not let himself be seen by any of the friars all day long.

But the guardian said to the friars: "My dear Brothers, I wish Brother Juniper would waste as much every day—if only we had it—so that we might be edified like this. For it was his great simplicity and charity that made him do this."

To the glory of Christ. Amen.

## 11   *How Brother Juniper Once Went to Assisi for His Own Humiliation*

Once Brother Juniper was staying in the Valley of Spoleto, and he heard that there was a solemn celebration in Assisi. When he saw many devout pilgrims going there, he felt the desire to go to that festival. And the spirit of self-contempt came over him, and he stripped himself stark naked, without his breeches.⁵ And he went through Spello and two other villages that way, and passed through the center of Assisi and all the crowd and came to the friars' Place like that.

The friars were very much shocked and scandalized, and they rebuked him forcefully, calling him a lunatic and a fool and a disgrace to the Order of St. Francis, and declaring that he should be put in chains as a madman.

The General, who was staying in that Place then, summoned the friars and Brother Juniper and gave him a harsh and severe scolding in the presence of the whole community. And after many strong words of reproof he said to Brother Juniper: "Your fault is so great and serious that I don't know what penance I should give you."

Then Brother Juniper answered, like someone who takes pleasure in being humiliated: "I'll tell you, Father: that as I came here naked, so as penance I should go back naked along the same road to the place from which I came to this festival."

To the glory of Christ. Amen.

## 12   *How Brother Juniper Was Rapt in Ecstasy during Mass*

Once while Brother Juniper was hearing Mass very devoutly he was rapt in an ecstasy that lasted a long time, and so the other friars left him there alone. On coming back to himself, he went to them and said with great fervor: "Oh my Brothers, who in this life is so noble that he would not willingly carry a basket of manure from St. Mary's all through town, if he were given a house full of gold?" And he said: "Ah, why do we not want to endure a little shame in order to gain eternal life, which is better and more lasting than gold and a thousand worlds that soon vanish?"

### 13　*About the Grief That Brother Juniper Felt over the Death of His Companion, Brother Tendalbene*

Brother Juniper had as companion a friar whom he loved very much. His name was Tendalbene, and he had the virtues of obedience and patience in the highest degree. For if he were beaten all day long, he would never utter a single word of complaint or protest. And because his patience greatly edified others, he was sometimes sent to Places where the friars were hard to get along with and they persecuted him very much, but he endured it all very patiently, without complaining. When Brother Juniper told him to weep or to laugh, he would immediately do so.

Now, as it pleased God, this Brother Tendalbene died with a reputation for holiness.[6] And when Brother Juniper heard about his death, he felt more grief over it than he had felt from any earthly thing all his life. And expressing in words the intense sorrow which he felt within, he said: "I am miserable! Now I have nothing good left in this world." And he broke to pieces all the household utensils, saying that for him the whole world had been broken to pieces by the death of his dear and beloved Brother Tendalbene: "If it were not that I could not live in peace with the friars and they would not stand for it, I would go right to his grave and take his head, and from his skull I would make two bowls—from one of them I would always eat, out of devotion to his memory, and out of the other I would drink whenever I felt thirsty or wanted to drink."

To the glory of Christ. Amen.

14   *About the Hand That Brother Juniper Saw in the Air*

Once when Brother Juniper was praying—and perhaps he was thinking of doing something extraordinary—a hand appeared to him in the air, and he heard a voice saying to him: "Oh, Brother Juniper, without this hand you can do nothing."

He quickly arose and ran through the friary, gazing up at Heaven, dancing and shouting in a loud voice: "Indeed that is true, Lord! Indeed that is true!" And he kept on shouting that for a long time.

To the glory of Christ. Amen.

Part Four

# THE LIFE OF BROTHER GILES BY BROTHER LEO

## 1 *How Brother Giles Was Converted*

In order to arouse our devotion, so that we may labor more fervently in God's work, I have (although unworthy) sought to write down, for the glory of God and the edification of our souls, some words of the Lord and some of His great works which the Holy Spirit wrought in our most Blessed Father, Brother Giles, as I learned of them from his companions and as I very often heard them from our very holy Father himself. For he used to say: "The more we appreciate the good that the Lord performs in another, the more grace that good brings us, as long as we know how to cultivate and reap and preserve it, because the good is not of man but of God." He also used to say: "I am not good and spiritual as I ought to be, and I do not greatly appreciate and rejoice over another's good, and I do not grieve or feel compassion for the misfortune and tribulations of others, and so I am not profiting from the good and bad from which I should profit. So I sin against charity, my good diminishes, and I fall into sin."

In order that from the very beginning of his conversion the Lord might show us that He would build a great new edifice in His servant, He infused an extraordinary degree of grace into him even while he was still in secular clothes. For when, two years after the conversion of St. Francis, he heard from some of his relatives and from others how Brother Bernard of Quintavalle, following the Saint's example and counsel regarding the perfection of the holy Gospel, had sold all his possessions, and on the advice of St. Francis had distributed everything in his presence to many poor people gathered in the Square of St. George (where the Convent of St. Clare stands now), he immediately conceived the idea of speaking to St. Francis so that he might accept him and give him the habit, as St. Francis had done to Brother Bernard and to the holy Brother Peter, who were the first friars after St. Francis.

And because the word of God runs swiftly and blows where it pleases, he arose early the next morning and hastened to the Church of St. George, whose Feast was being celebrated that day. After praying fervently and attending Mass, he walked in the direction of the Church of St. Mary of the Portiuncula, where St. Francis was staying with those two brothers. Because Brother Giles did not know that Place, when he came to the crossroads near the leprosarium, he began to pray devoutly that the Lord would deign to direct him there without any trouble. The Lord had led him to the crossroads near the Place he was seeking. And while he was standing there, he began to think over this desire which he had just conceived.

And because the Lord is close to those who call upon Him in sincerity and He usually grants the prayers of His poor ones, just then St. Francis came from the nearby woods where he had been praying. Brother Giles was very glad to see him, and he prostrated himself on the ground at his feet.

St. Francis asked him what he wanted.

Kneeling humbly, he answered: "I want to be with you, for the love of God."

St. Francis said to him: "The Lord has given you a great gift. Suppose the Emperor came to Assisi and wished to select some citizen of the town to be his knight or chamberlain, there would be many who would strive for that honor. How much greater should you consider this gift that the Lord has chosen you from all of them and has called you to His court!"

Taking him by the hand and raising him to his feet, St. Francis led him to the above-mentioned church. And he called the holy Brother Bernard, saying: "The Lord has sent us a good brother." And they ate together, rejoicing in the Lord.[1]

## 2   How Brother Giles Was Given the Habit by
### St. Francis

Then St. Francis took Brother Giles with him and went to the town of Assisi to get a habit for him. And as they were walking along together, a poor woman humbly and reverently begged St. Francis to give her something "for the love of Christ"—and she repeated those words. But as he had nothing with which to help her, he did not reply, so she repeated the same words a third time.

On hearing this, Brother Giles, who was with the Saint, still in secular clothes, waited anxiously to be told to give her something, for his fear and awe of the Saint prevented him from venturing to answer.

Then the Saint turned to him with an angelic expression and said: "Let's give her your cloak—for the love of Our Lord Jesus Christ!"

Feeling intense joy over the order the Saint had given him, which he had been anxiously awaiting, he immediately took off his cloak and gladly handed it to the poor woman. And as he himself said, as soon as he had given away the cloak, he was filled with such consolation by the Holy Spirit as cannot be described in words.

And St. Francis gave him the habit that same day. Now after he received it, his joy at being covered with such poor clothing was so intense that neither heart nor tongue could express it.

## 3   About His Pilgrimage to St. James

In due time the number of friars in the Order increased to seven. Then St. Francis sent them out to different regions to urge the people to give praise to our Creator and Redeemer and Savior and to do wholesome penance. So Brother Giles went on a devout pilgrimage to St. James, and on that journey he suffered destitution, hunger, thirst, cold, and tribulation. But the Lord, who had begun to give him consolations from the beginning of his conversion, comforted him in all things at all times.

And he was satisfied with his one first habit. But during that journey he met a poor man, and being moved by charity, he took the cowl off his habit and gave it to him. And so he traveled on foot for twenty-one days without a cowl.

Then he returned to Assisi. And because he was a very devout and Catholic man, he went to St. Michael and to St. Nicholas at Bari. While traveling thus through the world, he would urge men and women to fear and love the Creator of Heaven and earth and to do penance for their sins.

Now one day when he was extremely tired from his journey and suffering from hunger, he took a rest and fell asleep by the wayside. When he awoke, he found by his head half a loaf of bread, as a favor from God who does not abandon those who place their hope in Him. And giving thanks to God, he ate it and felt strengthened.

### 4    *How He Went to Visit the Holy Sepulcher*

He also went beyond the sea and visited the Holy Land. And while he was staying at Acre, in order to earn his daily bread, he carried water from the fountain which was some distance away. Bearing a large jar on his shoulder, he went through the town telling men and women to take the water and to give him some bread for the love of God. For they had cisterns in the city, but the fountains were at a long distance outside.[2] This servant of Almighty God was not ashamed to humble himself and lower himself to any menial but honest work, so as to give a good example and to earn his bread by the labor of his own hands.

### 5    *How He Stayed with a Cardinal and Earned His Food*

Once when he visited the Lord Cardinal Nicholas, Bishop of Tuscoli,[3] he went out to help the men gathering olives and doing other menial jobs. He was given bread for his labor, and he brought it back to the Cardinal's house. And when the Lord Cardinal told him that as a poor man he should eat his bread, Brother Giles told him the saying of the Prophet: "Thou shalt eat of the labor of thy hands." For St. Francis taught that to the friars in the beginning and had it written in the Rule and confirmed it in his Testament when he was near death.

It would take a long time to tell all the labor, hunger, thirst, cold, want, and tribulations and humiliations that he endured, gratefully giving thanks to God for them, as he himself reported.

### 6   *About the Rapture*

Now when he returned from his pilgrimages, St. Francis, guided by the Holy Spirit, reflected that Giles was a man of God who always gave a good example, and he rejoiced fervently and told him to go wherever he wished. But Brother Giles answered that he did not want to go about and live in such liberty. Therefore in the seventh year after his conversion, St. Francis sent him to a hermitage called Favarone, in the plain of Perugia.[4]

And when God looked upon him and his many good works, the hand of the Lord came over him. And there—among other graces which God conferred on him—one night while he was praying, he was so filled with divine consolation that it seemed to him the Lord wished to draw his soul out of his body in order that he might clearly see some divine secrets and that he might be inspired to labor still more in the service of God.

He began to feel as if his body was dying, beginning with his feet, until his soul passed out of his body. And as it pleased our Creator who placed the soul in the body, while his soul was out of the body, it took great pleasure in gazing at itself, because of the remarkable beauty with which the Holy Spirit had adorned it. For it was exceedingly subtle and radiant, beyond all conception, as he himself declared when he was near death. Then that very holy soul was rapt in an ecstasy in which he contemplated some heavenly secrets which he revealed to no one. For he used to say: "Blessed is the man who knows how to keep and guard the secrets of God, as there is nothing hidden that may not be revealed when the Lord wishes and pleases. But I fear for myself, and so if things are to be revealed, I prefer that they be revealed by someone else than myself."

### 7   How the Devil Attacked Him

And because, with God's permission, the enemy of the human race always strives to trouble holy and perfect men, not long after that consolation it happened in the same hermitage that when he was entering his cell, having devoutly recited his prayers, he felt an angel of Satan behind him. Being unable to endure its terrifying presence, he gave himself to prayer and called on God in his heart, for he was unable to utter a word —and he was immediately liberated.

A few days later he asked St. Francis: "Father, is anything so terrifying that it cannot be endured as long as a man says one Our Father?"

St. Francis answered: "No one could endure seeing the devil as long as he said half an Our Father without dying immediately, unless he were helped by divine aid."

When he heard this, Brother Giles believed it was true, because of his experience.

Another time before this, when he was in Spoleto in a Church of St. Apollinaris (where the friars lodged in those days), he arose during the night and went into the church before the others. And while he was bowed in prayer there he felt the devil above him, crushing him and tormenting him. Although he prayed fervently, he could not get up, but he dragged himself as best he could to the holy-water font. And when he confidently sprinkled himself, he was immediately freed from the devil.

### 8   How He Saw the Lord Jesus Christ with His Own Eyes

In the eighteenth year of his conversion—the year when St. Francis passed from this world to Heaven—Brother Giles was

going with a companion to the hermitage of Cetona, and came
to the Place of the friars at Cibottola.⁵ While sleeping there
that night, he saw in a dream an emperor who treated him as
an intimate friend—which, as he himself said, was a presage
of the glorious grace and rapture which he was to have.

Then he and his companion arose and traveled to that
hermitage, where they spent the forty days' fast of St. Martin
in fervent devotion. And there Brother Giles saw St. Francis
in a dream and said to him: "I would like to have a talk alone
with you." St. Francis replied: "If you want to talk with me,
watch yourself."

When he had earnestly persevered there in prayer and devotion, one night three days before the Nativity of the Lord,
while he was praying fervently, the Lord Jesus Christ appeared
to him in such a way that he saw Him with his own eyes.
During this apparition Brother Giles uttered loud cries because
of the strong perfume, and it seemed to him that he was dying,
for he could not bear such bliss. His shouting greatly alarmed
the friars in the Place. He felt suddenly filled with an ineffable
perfume and an overwhelming spiritual sweetness. And so he
seemed to be in his last agony.

On hearing him, a certain friar was very much frightened,
and he went to Brother Giles' companion and said to him:
"Come to Brother Giles, because he is dying!" Arising at once,
he went to him and said: "What is the matter, Father?"

And Brother Giles answered: "Come, my son, because I
have been wanting to see you." For he loved his companion
very much and confided many things to him, because he had
trained him from his youth in a holy way of life. And Brother
Giles told him all that had happened to him. When the companion heard about it, he realized that the vision had been
given by God. And he went back to his cell.

The next day the companion returned to Brother Giles' cell.
And finding him weeping and lamenting, he urged him not
to grieve so much, as it might be fatal to his health.

He answered: "How can I not weep when I know myself to
be an enemy of God, and He has been so merciful to me and
has given me such a gift? So I am afraid of not doing His
Will." He said this because of the special grace which had
been given him by God. Feeling that he had been marvelously

changed and renewed by that grace, he said to his companion: "Until now I have gone where I wished and done what I wished, laboring with my hands. But now and henceforth I cannot do as I used to, but I must do as I feel guided within. Therefore I fear very much that others may ask me for what I cannot give them."

His companion said to him: "The Lord, who gives grace to His servant, also grants him custody of the grace. Nevertheless it is good for you to have the fear of God." And that answer pleased him.

He continued to enjoy that great and indescribable sweetness and blissful joy and divine odor from the third day before the Nativity of the Lord until Epiphany, though not continuously, but at intervals during the day and night. For his frail human nature could not long bear it when the dazzling brightness appeared. So he would pray fervently to the Lord not to place such a burden on him. And he would plead that he was not fit for it, as he was an uneducated and ignorant man and a simple peasant. But the more unworthy he considered himself, the more the Lord increased His grace in him. And he said in the end that God had breathed upon him as He had breathed upon the Apostles.

One night while Brother Giles was standing with his companion before his cell and they were speaking with loving devotion about the Lord's words, a bright light came and passed clearly between them. And when his companion asked him what it was, he answered: "Let it pass."

At that time there was a certain holy religious there to whom the Lord had revealed some of His secrets. And shortly before this happened to Brother Giles, he had seen in a dream the sun rising and setting where Brother Giles' cell was built. Later, on seeing Brother Giles so wonderfully changed by the hand of God and filled with a new spirit of grace, he said to him: "Carry tenderly the Virgin's Son."

## 9    *How after That Apparition He Was Easily Rapt in God*

After this, Brother Giles strove to preserve with the greatest care the grace which God had given him, for he used to say: "Above all graces and virtues, this is the highest virtue: to follow virtue and to preserve the grace that has been given to us." He also said: "The Apostles, after they received the gift of the Holy Spirit, had a hundred and a thousand times heavier burdens to bear in order to endure tribulations and preserve the grace that had been given to them."

From then on, he was always alone in his cell, watching, praying, fasting, and carefully keeping himself from every bad deed or word. And when anyone wished to tell him anything bad about another, he would say: "I do not want to know about another's sin." And he would say to the one who was telling it: "Be careful, Brother, not to see anything bad that does not concern you or do you any good."

The Lord therefore, finding him a good and faithful servant in little things, gave him greater gifts, of which he was worthy. And He increased so much the grace which He gave him that he could no longer hide it from men. For if anyone spoke to him about the glory of God and His sweetness or about Paradise, he would immediately fall into an ecstasy, and for a whole day and night he would stay motionless and not speak or move from the spot.

Consequently he withdrew not only from associating with lay people but also from his brethren and other religious. For he used to say: "It is safer for a man to save his soul with few than with many, that is, to be alone and be concerned with God and his soul. Because God alone, who created the soul, is the soul's friend—and not another." Thus he spoke from experience and said: "Oh, what a great and rare spiritual grace has he to whom it is granted to know his own soul! Only God knows it—and he to whom He wishes to reveal it."

Therefore he used to say about himself: "If St. Peter and St. Paul should come down from Heaven and tell me to satisfy the people who want to talk to me, I would not believe them."

And he used to say: "He who does good to his own soul also does good to the souls of his friends." And: "A man can lose many consolations and visitations of the Lord through his own fault which he may never recover again." And he mentioned as an example those who play dice: through one point of the dice, which is very small, a man may lose a great deal. So through a small sin, if a man does not know how to protect himself, he may lose a great advantage for his soul. St. Francis used to say the same thing. Therefore it is written: Beware lest you lose in laughter what you gained in grieving.

And so, because Brother Giles from the beginning of his conversion had not given his body any rest, but always devoted himself to God and the care of his soul, he found favor before the Lord and merited being honored by Him, as is evident in his heavenly revelations, which were such that we believe have been granted to few persons since the days of St. Francis.

### 10  *How He Used to Speak with Enthusiasm about That Vision*

Brother Giles used to praise the Place of Cetona, because of the mercy and extraordinary grace and privilege which the Lord showed him in that Place, above all other places on this side of the sea and beyond the sea, except for six places beyond the sea to which he used to compare it. And he used to say that people should go to that Place with greater reverence and devotion than to St. Michael or St. Peter or St. Nicholas or any place on this side of the sea, since the master is greater than the servant, and so Christ is greater than the other Saints. And he said that there could be a place similar to this, but not greater.

And when he said such things, his companion answered: "Father, it was a great thing that happened to St. Francis on Mt. Alverna in connection with the Seraph. And St. Christina and St. Catherine were noble virgins—and many other virgins and Saints that are honored in different countries."

To this Brother Giles replied: "My son, the creature is nothing compared to the Creator."

Another time when his companion Brother Gratian and Brother James and Brother Andrew of Burgundy were with Brother Giles, Brother Gratian said to Brother Andrew: "Is it found in Holy Scripture that Our Lord Jesus Christ would appear to anyone on this side of the sea after His Resurrection?" He said this in order to find out whether Brother Giles would answer.

Then Brother Giles suddenly replied very forcefully: "Did you ask: would the Lord appear on this side of the sea? He has indeed appeared less than twelve days' journey from this place!"

"Where was that, Father?" said Brother Andrew.

Brother Giles answered: "What you see, you see, and what you hear, you hear."

Then Brother Andrew said to him: "It is in fact written that the Lord appeared to St. Peter near Rome at a place that is called *Domine, quo vadis?*"

"I do not mean that place," replied Brother Giles, "because the one I mean was much greater than that. For I know a place where the Lord did something greater than He ever did to anyone on this side of the sea that I have heard of. The Lord may have done some things that I have not heard about, but of those that I have heard, this was greater than He has done to any man."

Brother Andrew said to him: "God did great things to St. Peter in Rome and to St. Francis in Assisi. These things you mention must be very great if they are greater than those."

"It is true that those were great," Brother Giles answered, "but the works of the Lord are one thing, and the Lord Himself is another." And he immediately added: "Your eyes, O Lord, are wonderful, and Your ears are ineffable—and Your other features are exceedingly marvelous!"

Brother Andrew said to him: "And where is that place?"

Brother Giles replied: "What you see, you see. And what you hear, you hear." Then he said: "Have you ever been to Chiusi?"

"No," said Brother Andrew, "but I have seen that country."

Brother Giles answered: "Good." And he added: "Do you know when those great things happened?"

Brother Andrew asked: "When?"

"In the year when St. Francis passed on," said Brother Giles. "And they lasted from the third day before the Lord's Nativity until the Vigil of Epiphany."

Brother Andrew said: "Did that event which you mention last all that time continuously or at intervals?"

"I don't say continuously," replied Brother Giles, "but at times both day and night." Afterward he said: "I have gone far in saying this."

Brother Andrew said to him: "I believe it is the Lord's will that His servants sometimes tell some secrets for the spiritual good of others."

"What happened then was not my fault," Brother Giles answered, "for I begged the Lord and told Him that such great things were not fit for me. But He is the Lord—and He does what He pleases."

### 11    *About the Vision Which He Had on Mount Pesulano*

Another time Brother Andrew said to Brother Giles: "The Lord did great things on Mount Alverna to St. Francis."

Brother Giles answered: "I know of no mountain on this side of the sea that is like Mount Pesulano."

Brother Andrew said: "Don't you think it is a very great thing if an angel appears to someone?"

"I am surprised at you, Brother Andrew," said Brother Giles. "Because if there were no Heaven or earth or angels or archangels or any creatures, the greatness of God would not be any less because of that. So it is a great thing when the Lord appears."[6]

Brother Andrew said to him: "I wish that a very beautiful church were built where the Lord did such great things."

"How right you are!" Brother Giles answered.

Brother Andrew said to him: "What name should be given to that church?"

"The name of the Feast of Pentecost!" replied Brother Giles.

"Do you think," said Brother Andrew, "that the Holy Spirit has ever since come upon anyone as He came upon the Apostles at Pentecost, that is, in the form of fire?"

Brother Giles answered: "If I glorify myself, my glory is nothing." And he added: "Let's not talk about this any more."

O holy and indeed most holy Giles, to whom the Lord deigned to give such glory! For he would say about himself, as though speaking of someone else: "St. Paul says that he was rapt twice, whether in the body or out of the body, adding 'I don't know—God knows.' But what if God should give someone perfect certainty about it?"

## 12   *How He Was Rapt in Ecstasy While Speaking of God*

Once when Brother Giles was staying at the friars' Place at Agello in the County of Perugia, he came back to the friars to eat at the usual time of vespers. And after supper he began to speak to the friars who were there some divinely inspired words filled with consolation and ardent devotion. And while he was thus aflame with saintly fervor he made their hearts burn within them.

And then in a holy silence he fell into a rapture before them and remained enraptured almost until the cocks crowed for the first time. And the moonlight was very bright. When he left the friars and was walking toward his cell, all of a sudden such a dazzling light appeared that it completely absorbed the moonlight. When the friars saw it, they were astonished. But Brother Giles came back, as he had not gone far, and said to them: "What would you have done if you had seen greater things?" And he added: "He who does not see great things believes that small things are great." And after saying that, he went and shut himself up in his cell.

## 13   *How the Devils Tempted Him with Pride*

And because the devils cannot harm and trouble holy and perfect men by terror, they turn to another method and temptation: pride and vanity. One night when he was praying in his cell in a Place near Perugia, he heard the devils standing near him and saying: "Why is this man striving so hard? He is already a saint. He is already anointed. He is already an ecstatic." Later he asked a certain companion, in whom he confided a great deal, what this meant, especially the word "ecstatic," which he did not understand. And he answered: "Don't pay any attention to it, Brother, because it was a temptation of the devil."

Another time in the same Place, when he was under an olive tree, a friar said to him: "Father, what do the learned men say about this contemplation?" And because he did not want him to fall into an ecstasy as he usually did when he heard such things, that friar added, as if dismissing the subject: "The learned men say many things."

But Brother Giles suddenly exclaimed: "Do you want me to tell you what I think? Contemplation is fire—unction—ecstasy —savor—rest—glory!"

And that friar was quite amazed at those profound words which he uttered with such fervor.[7]


### 14   How Helpful His Correction Was

Once when Brother Giles humbly and charitably corrected a certain friar who deserved correction, the friar was angry. But that night someone appeared to him in a vision and said: "Brother, do not be angry at Brother Giles' correction, because he who believes him will be blessed." The next morning that friar went to Brother Giles and asked him to correct him severely.


### 15   About an Attack by the Devil at Cetona before His Death

When Brother Giles was drawing close to the day of his death, in order that the Lord might give him a crown and rest after his great labors and struggle and victory, he began to endure more attacks than usual, so that he might be tested in all things. And one night when he wanted to give his body some rest after he had prayed for a long time, the devil seized him and forced him into such a narrow place that he could not move at all. While he was anxiously trying to arise, Brother Gratian, who was taking care of him, began to hear him a little. And when he came closer to the cell, he clearly heard him breathing hard, and he thought and said to himself: "If you go near and he is praying, let him pray on, but if it is something else, you will see what it is."

And so he went to the door of the cell and began to listen. And when he heard him struggling, he called to him, saying: "What is the matter, Father?"

And he said: "Come in, son. Come in!"

He tried to open the door, but as he could not, he said: "Why can't I open the door?"

"Push!" Brother Giles said. "Push strongly, son, and you will quickly open the door! Because I am pressed against the door by enemies and I can't get up."

The friar pushed against the door with all his strength and forced it open. On entering the cell where Brother Giles was lying, he tried with all his might to lift him up, but could not.

Brother Giles said: "Let us leave ourselves in the hands of the Lord."

The friar agreed, although unwillingly. But after he had let him stay a while, he grasped him firmly and dragged him out of that narrow place.

And after Brother Giles had rested a little, he said to his companion: "Why does the devil try so hard to interfere with God's graces?" And he also said to his companion: "You did a good deed, son, in coming to me. May God reward you for it!"

And his companion said to him: "Why did you do this, Father? Why didn't you call me? How guilty we would have felt if you had died—for you and we would be greatly blamed!"

Brother Giles answered: "What is it to you if my enemies take their revenge on me?" And again he said: "Why does the devil try so hard to interfere with God's graces? For if this happened once, it would be bearable—or twice or three or four times. But he tries all the time. Yet you should know this for sure: the more he tries to interfere, the lower he descends, because he is opposing God. For my serving God was not my doing in the beginning but God's. And the end will likewise be His, because of His mercy. It is not surprising that the devil persecutes a sinner so much, since he knows that he is conceived and born in sin, for he sees him ascending to that place from which he himself fell. So he has often tormented and does torment me, and does not give me any rest."

### 16　*About Another Attack by the Devil at Cetona*

Again one night near the Feast of St. Benedict while Brother Giles was praying to the Lord, the devil wanted to interfere with the grace that God was giving him, and he terrified Brother Giles to such a degree that he began to shout in a frightening way: "Help, Brother, help!"

On hearing him, Brother Gratian, who was in a cell near him, awoke and quickly arose and went to him, calling aloud: "Don't be afraid, Father! Don't be afraid! I'll help you!" And going into his cell, he said: "What was the matter, Father?"

Brother Giles said to him: "Don't worry, son. Don't pay any attention to it."

And Brother Gratian answered: "Let me stay here with you, since the enemy is tormenting you so much."

"God reward you, son," the Father said to him. "It was good of you to come to me. Now go back to your cell."

Indeed in the evening after supper when Brother Giles returned to his cell, he would say: "I expect to be martyred tonight."

Again once when he was talking with a companion, he said: "From the beginning of the world until now, no Order has existed that is better or more effective for serving God than the Friars Minor."

### 17　*About a Divine Consolation Which He Had in the Same Place*

Once when Brother Giles was very close to his last days of life, while he was walking away from his cell he said to one of his companions with unutterable joy: "What do you think of this, my son? I have found a great treasure so bright and radiant that no human tongue can describe it. I am plundering joy! What would you say, son, if you were showered with blessings by God?"

And he often repeated this. For when he said it, he was so overflowing with joy and fervor that he seemed to be intoxicated with the Holy Spirit.

When a certain friar told him to come and eat, he answered: "I have the best food of all, son."

And the friar replied, as though tempting him: "Don't bother about such things, Father. Come and eat."

But the saint did not take his answer as a joke, and said: "Brother, you did not speak well. I would rather have you give me a slap strong enough to draw blood."

No doubt his most holy soul had already realized that his Beloved, as He had told him, wished to draw it from its tabernacle to enjoy in Heaven that most glorious treasure which he merited to find at the beginning of his conversion and to preserve. For the Lord fulfilled his longing by granting him that death which he had foretold and so long desired.

Once when a friar told him that St. Francis had said that a servant of God should always want to die and die as a martyr, Brother Giles answered: "I want to die no better death than that of contemplation."

As a matter of fact at a certain time he had gone to the Saracens out of a desire to die as a martyr for the love of Christ, and after he returned and had been found worthy of climbing to the heights of contemplation, he said: "I am glad I did not die then as a martyr."


## 18  *About His Happy Death*

As his death drew near, he began to have a high fever. And because he suffered from a cough and pains in the head and chest, he could not eat or sleep or rest. Day and night therefore the friars carried him about on his bed so that he might find rest.

Now on the vigil of St. George the Martyr, that night at the time for matins, they had carried him thus on his bed and had let him lay his head down on the bed, and he seemed to be resting that way. And with his eyes and mouth closed, without further delay, his very holy soul was caught up in a rapture to its home in Paradise above.

O holy—most holy—Giles, on that same day when the Lord inspired and led you to St. Francis to follow him and when he clothed you in the religious habit—fifty-two years later on that same day the Lord led you into the fellowship of the citizens of Heaven!

A certain holy person at that time saw in a vision that the Lord went to meet him with a host of angels and blessed souls and received him in the air before he ascended into Heaven and conducted him up in honor, amid the singing of the angels.

Blessed Brother Giles possessed seven very praiseworthy and wholesome and perfect qualities. From the beginning of his conversion and every day until the day he died, he became more and more perfect. Accordingly it is believed that the Lord generously multiplied His grace in him and filled him with still more powerful gifts. The first is that he was an intensely faithful and loyal Catholic. The second, that he was reverent. The third, devout. The fourth, patient and compassionate. The fifth, considerate. The sixth, obedient. The seventh, that he was beloved by God and men because of the graces which were showered on him.

He shone in many miracles during his life and after his death. He who wrote this experienced it himself. Amen.

Here ends the life of Blessed Giles which was compiled and written by Brother Leo with his own hand. God be praised forever![8]

# Part Five

# THE SAYINGS OF BROTHER GILES

## Prologue

Because "the word of God is living and efficacious and more piercing than any two-edged sword"—*living* by giving life to the dead, *efficacious* by giving medicine to the sick, and *more piercing than any two-edged sword* by penetrating the hard-of-heart—"and reaching unto the division of soul and spirit" by separating vices from virtues, it seems fitting and wholesome that the sayings of the servants of God which are drawn with inexpressible joy of heart not from human wisdom but from the wellsprings of the Savior Jesus Christ, should be recorded for the edification of later generations.

And so to the glory and honor of Almighty God and the edification of our fellow men who may read or hear them, we have made a written record that is most helpful for the soul of the honey-sweet sayings of Brother Giles which he spoke from the fullness of his heart in spiritual conversations.

### 1 On Virtues and Graces and Their Effects, and Conversely on Vices

The graces of God and the virtues are a ladder and road to climb to Heaven, but vices and sins are the road and ladder to go down to hell.

Vices and sins are poison. Virtues and good deeds are an antidote.

Grace attracts grace. And one vice leads to another vice.

Grace does not wish to be praised. And vice does not wish to be despised—that is, a man who has grace does not want to be praised and does not seek praise. And the man who has vices does not want to be despised or blamed—which comes from pride.

The mind finds peace in humility. Patience is its daughter. Purity of heart sees God. Devotion assimilates Him.

If you love, you will be loved. If you fear, you will be feared. If you serve, you will be served. If you treat others well, others will treat you well.

Blessed is he who loves and does not therefore desire to be loved. Blessed is he who fears and does not therefore desire to be feared. Blessed is he who serves and does not therefore desire to be served. Blessed is he who treats others well and does not desire that others treat him well. And because these are great things, the foolish do not attain them.

There are three very great and useful things—whoever has them cannot fall into evil. The first is: if you bear in peace, for God's sake, all the tribulations that may happen to you. The second is: if you humble yourself more in everything you do and receive. The third is: if you love faithfully those good things that cannot be seen with your eyes.

Those things that are more scorned and shunned by worldly men are honored and valued by God and His saints. And those that are more loved and embraced and honored by worldly men are more hated and shunned and scorned by God and His saints. Men hate everything that should be loved and love what should be hated.

Once Brother Giles asked a certain friar: "Have you a good soul?"

He answered: "I don't know, Brother."

Brother Giles said: "Holy contrition—holy humility—holy charity—holy devotion—and holy joy make the soul holy and good."


## 2  *On Faith and the Incomprehensibility of God*

All that we can think, see, tell, and touch is nothing compared to what we cannot think, tell, see, or touch.

All the wise and holy men who have been, are, and will be, who have spoken or will speak of God, have not said or ever will say anything about God compared to what He is, except as the prick of a needle is compared to Heaven and earth and all creatures that are in them—and more than a thousand times less. For all Holy Scripture speaks to us as a mother uses baby talk with her little son, because otherwise he could not understand her words.

Brother Giles once said to a certain secular judge: "Do you believe that the gifts of God are great?"

The judge answered: "I do."

Brother Giles said to him: "I will show you that you do not believe it." And he added: "How much is all your property worth?"

"It is worth perhaps a thousand pounds," replied the judge.

Brother Giles said to him: "Would you give it for ten thousand pounds?"

"Yes, very willingly," he answered.

Brother Giles said to him: "It is certain that all earthly things are nothing compared to heavenly things. So why do you not give up the former for the latter?"

The judge replied: "Do you believe that any man practices all that he believes?"

Brother Giles answered: "Holy men and women have tried to practice the good things which they believed and were able to do. And they have fulfilled by holy desire what they could not achieve in practice. Their holy desire made up for what was lacking in their practice. If anyone had perfect faith, he would reach a point where he would be given complete certainty. So if your faith is good, your deeds will be good."

What harm can any evil do to a man who looks forward with perfect faith to a great and everlasting good? And what good can any good do to a man who expects a great and everlasting evil? What good can the angels and all the saints in Heaven restore to a man who has lost the best of all good things? How can he be consoled and who could console him? No one except a visitation from God.

Yet no sinner should ever despair of God's mercy as long as he lives. For there is hardly a tree so thorny and knotted that men cannot make it smooth and beautiful. So likewise there is no sinner in this world so bad that God cannot adorn him in many ways with grace and virtues.

### 3    *On Love*

Love is greater than all the other virtues.

Blessed is he who is not satiated with those things that he should always desire.

Brother Giles said to a certain friar who was his spiritual friend: "Do you think I love you?" That friar answered: "I do." Brother Giles said to him: "Don't believe that I love you, because the Creator is the only one who truly loves a creature, and the love of the creature is nothing compared to the love of the Creator."

And another friar said: "Brother Giles, what is it that the Prophet says: 'Every friend will walk deceitfully?'" Brother Giles answered: "Therefore I am deceitful to you because I do not make your good mine. For the more I made your good mine, the less deceitful would I be to you. And the more someone rejoices over his neighbor's good, the more he shares in it. So if you want to have a share in the good of all, rejoice in the good of all. Make the good of others your own if it pleases you, and make the evil of others your care if it displeases you. That is the way of salvation: that you rejoice over your neighbor's good and grieve over his evil, and think good of others and evil of yourself, and honor others and despise yourself."

He who does not want to honor others shall not be honored. And he who does not wish to know shall not be known. And he who does not wish to endure fatigue shall not rest.

To develop piety and kindness is a work that is more fruitful than any other work.

Whatever is without love and charity is not pleasing to God and His saints.

A man becomes poor through his own works and rich through divine works. So a man must love the works of God and despise his own.

What is greater than to know how to praise the gifts of God and to reprove oneself for one's bad actions? I wish I had studied in that school from the beginning of the world, if only I had lived, and I wish I could study in it until the end of the world, if only I were to live—considering and praising the gifts of God and considering and reproving myself for my wrongdoings. And if I were imperfect in reproving myself for my wrongdoings, I would not want to be imperfect in meditating on the gifts of God.

You see how actors and minstrels praise highly those who give them a little piece of clothing—what then should we do for the Lord our God?

You ought to be very faithful in the love of Him who wishes to free you from all that is evil and who wants to give you all that is good.

### 4 On Holy Humility

No one can come to the knowledge of God except through humility. The way to go up is to go down.

All the dangers and great falls that have happened in the world would never have happened except for holding the head high, as can be seen in him who was created in Heaven and in Adam and the Pharisee in the Gospel and many others. And all the great good that has happened has been done by bowing the head, as can be seen in the Blessed Virgin, the publican, the good thief, and many others.

Brother Giles also said: "If only we could have a heavy weight that would always make us bow our head!"

A friar said to him: "How can we avoid this pride?"

"Lift your hands," he said, "and put your mouth where your feet are. If you think over the gifts of God, you must bow your head. And if you think over your sins, you must likewise bow your head. Woe to him who wants to be honored for his wickedness!"

A great degree of humility in man is to know that he is always opposed to his own good. I also think that the fruit of humility is to give back what does not belong to us and not to appropriate it for oneself—that is, to attribute all good things to God, to whom they belong, and all bad things to oneself.

Blessed is he who considers himself as vile in the eyes of men as he finds himself vile in the sight of God.

Blessed is he who judges himself now, because he will not come to another judgment.

Blessed is he who walks with faith under the judgment and obedience of another. For the Apostles also did that after they were filled with the Holy Spirit.

Let him who wants to have peace and quiet look upon every man as his superior.

Blessed is he who does not wish to make an appearance in his words and habits that is different from the one which God's grace has made for him.

If someone were to be the holiest man in the world and to consider himself the vilest—that would be humility.

Humility is not good at speaking, and patience does not venture to speak.

Humility seems to me to be like lightning. For as lightning strikes terrible blows and afterwards none of it can be found, so humility dissolves all evil and is the enemy of all sin and makes a man look upon himself as nothing.

Through humility man finds peace with men before God. For if a great king wished to send his daughter to some place, he would not put her on an untamed, proud, and stubborn horse, but on a gentle horse that was easy to ride—so the Lord does not bestow His grace on the proud but on the humble.

### 5   On the Holy Fear of the Lord

The holy fear of the Lord expels all evil fear and protects those good things which cannot be expressed in words or even thought of. It is not given to all to have this fear, for it is a very great gift.

The fear of God rules and governs a man and makes him come into the grace of the Lord. If a man has that grace, the fear of the Lord preserves it, and if he does not have it, it leads him to it. All rational creatures that have fallen would never have fallen if they had had this gift. This holy gift is given only to saintly men and women. The more grace a man has, the more humble and godfearing he is. And this virtue, which is less practiced by men, is not smaller than the others.

With what security can a man who has offended his God

so much that he deserves death go into the presence of God? Blessed is the man who knows for sure that he is in a prison in this world and that he has always offended his God.

A man ought to fear very much that his pride may cause his fall.

Always fear and beware of yourself—and of anyone like yourself.

There is no perfect security for a man while he is among his enemies. Our enemy is our flesh. It is always an enemy fighting our soul along with the devils. So a man should have a greater fear of himself than of anything else in the world, so that his own malice should not overcome him. For it is impossible for someone to ascend to the grace of God or to persevere in it without a holy fear and a holy dread. He who does not have it has a sign that he will perish.

This fear makes us obey humbly and bow our head down to the ground under the yoke of holy obedience.

Again, the more fear we have, the more we pray. And it is no small thing to be given the grace of holy prayer.

No matter how great they seem, the works of men are not to be judged according to the opinion of men but according to the judgment and pleasure of God. And so it is good for us to have holy fear at all times.

### 6   On Patience

He who would bear tribulations patiently for God's sake would quickly attain to great grace and would overcome this world and already have one foot in the other world.

Whatever a man does, whether good or evil, he does it to himself. So you should not be angry if anyone offends you, but you ought to have compassion for his sin.

Bear with patience the offenses which your neighbor commits against you—for God's sake, for your neighbor's sake, and for your own sake.

The readier someone is to bear tribulations and offenses for God's sake, the greater he is before God and no more. And the weaker he is in enduring tribulations and sufferings for

God, the less he is before God, and he does not know what God is.

If anyone says something bad to you, help him. And if someone says something good to you, offer it to God. But if he says something bad to you, you ought to help him by saying something worse about yourself.

If you want to do your part well, do it badly and the other's part well—that is, praise his deeds and words and criticize your own. And if you want to do your part badly, do the contrary. So when someone competes with you, lose if you want to win. For in the end when you think you have won, you will find that you have lost. Therefore the way of salvation is the way of losing.

We are not good bearers of tribulation because we are not good seekers of spiritual consolation. For he who would faithfully work in himself and on himself and for himself would easily bear all things.

Don't offend anyone. And if someone commits an offense against you, bear it patiently for the love of God and for the remission of your sins. For it is much better to endure one serious offense without complaining than to feed a hundred poor people for many days and to fast every day for many days until the stars come out at night. What good is it for a man to despise himself and mortify his body with fasts and prayers and watchings and disciplines and not be able to endure a single offense from his neighbor, for which he would receive a greater reward than for those things which he bears by his own choice? And this is a warning sign, because his hidden pride is put to the test by the insult which he receives.

Men expiate their sins more by bearing tribulations without complaining than by weeping.

Blessed is he who always has his sin and the goodness of God before his eyes and who patiently bears all tribulations and trouble, for he can look forward to a great consolation.

Blessed is he who does not seek or desire any consolation from any creature under Heaven.

A man should not expect God to reward him if he is humble and calm only when he is satisfied with everything.

He who always keeps his sins before his eyes will not weaken in any tribulation.

You should receive every good thing you have as from God and all bad things as from your sins. For if one man were to do all the good that all the men in the world have done, are doing, and will do, nevertheless if he really looked within himself, he would find himself always opposed to his own good.

A certain friar said to him: "What shall we do if great tribulations come in our time?"

Brother Giles answered: "If the Lord should make stones and rocks rain from Heaven, they would not hurt us if we were what we should be. If a man were what he should be, evil would be changed into good for him. For just as good itself is twisted into evil for a man of ill will, so evil is changed into good for a man of good will. For all great good things and great bad things are within man, where they cannot be seen."

The worst devils come running to us when we endure great infirmity and great labor and great hunger and great insults.

If you wish to be saved, do not ask that anyone should do justice to you.

Holy men do good and suffer evil.

If you know that you have offended the Lord your God, the Creator and Lord of all creatures, you should know that it is right that all should persecute you and avenge the offense that you have committed against your Lord.

You ought to bear patiently the offenses and wrongs that are done to you, because you have no right to justice against anyone, since you deserve to be punished by all.

It is a great virtue for a man to overcome himself. If you overcome yourself, you overcome all your enemies and you attain all that is good.

It would be great virtue if anyone let himself be overcome by men, because such a man would be the master of this world.

If you wish to be saved, try not to hope for any consolation that any mortal creature can give you. Because falls due to such consolations are greater and more frequent than those due to tribulations.

It is a noble quality in a horse that, although it is running very fast, yet it can be turned by its rider from one road and directed into another. Thus a man inflamed with anger ought to let himself be ruled by someone who corrects him.

The mere remembrance of God ought to induce a man—as far as he is concerned—to pay others to give him slaps and blows and drag him around by the hair.

Once a certain friar was grumbling in his presence about some difficult order that had been given him. And the holy Brother Giles said to him: "My friend, the more you grumble, the more you burden yourself. And the more devoutly and humbly you bow your head under the yoke of holy obedience, the lighter and sweeter it will be for you. You do not want to be blamed in this world—yet you want to be honored in the other? You do not want to be cursed—yet you want to be blessed? You do not want to labor—yet you want to rest? You are deceived, because through blame we come to honor, through being cursed we obtain blessings, and through labor, rest. The proverb is true: he who does not give what he is sorry to lose cannot have what he desires. Don't be surprised if your neighbor offends you sometimes, because even Martha, who was holy, wished to stir up the Lord against her own sister. But Martha complained unjustly against Mary, because the more Mary lost the use of her body, the more she worked than Martha, for she had lost speech, sight, hearing, taste, and movement. Try to be kind and good, and fight against vices, and bear tribulations and humiliations with patience. For there is nothing else to do but to overcome yourself, because it is a small thing for a man to draw souls to God unless he overcomes himself."

## 7   On Holy Solitude and Watchfulness of Heart

The lazy man loses this world and the other, without doing any good to himself or others. It is impossible to acquire virtues without trouble and effort.

If you can be safe, don't put yourself in danger. He who works for God and for the everlasting Kingdom is safe.

A young man who rejects work rejects the Kingdom of Heaven.

If something is not worth while, then neglecting it does not matter or hurt, because if no good comes from it, the evil does no harm.

Just as an evil idleness is a way to go to hell, so a holy idleness and quiet are a way to go to Heaven.

A man should be very careful to preserve the grace that God has given him and to work faithfully with it, for men often lose the fruit for leaves and the grain for straws. God gives the fruit to some and allows them to do without the leaves, but to some He gives both, and some lack both.

I think it is greater to preserve the good things that God gives than to acquire them. He who knows how to acquire them but does not know how to store them up will never grow rich. Yet to know how to store them up and not to know how to acquire them is not a great thing.

Many acquire much but do not grow rich because they do not guard what they have gained. And some gain bit by bit and grow rich because they guard well what they have.

What a flood of water the Tiber River would collect if it did not keep flowing!

Men ask God for a gift that has no measure and no limit, yet they want to serve Him within a measure and limit. So he who wants to be loved and rewarded without limit should serve and love without measure and limit.

Men fail to attain perfection because of their own negligence.

Once the holy Brother Giles said to someone who wished to go to Rome: "When you are on the way, don't draw to yourself what you see, so that it does not hinder you. And learn how to prefer good money to false. For the enemy is very clever, and he has many hidden traps."[1]

Blessed is he who makes good use of his body for the love of Almighty God and who does not seek any reward short of Heaven.

If a man was extremely poor and someone said to him: "Brother, you can have this thing of mine to put to good use for three days, and for this you will receive an unlimited treasure," would not that poor man, if he was sure this was true, eagerly strive to put that thing to good use? The thing which is loaned to us by God is our flesh, and the whole time of our life is like three days. So if you want to enjoy happiness, work at earning it, for if you don't work, how should you rest?

If all the fields and vineyards in the world belonged to one man and he did not cultivate them or have them cultivated, what produce would he get from them? But another man who had a small number of fields and vineyards and cultivated them well would get produce from them for himself and for many others.

If someone wants to do wrong, he hardly asks for any advice. But when he wants to do something good, he tries to get advice from many.

A common proverb says: "Don't put the pot on the fire near your neighbor's hedge."

A man is not blessed if he has a will to do good, unless he tries to carry it out by doing good deeds, because that is why God gives men His grace—to put it into practice.

Once a man who, it seems, was a tramp said to the holy Brother Giles: "Brother Giles, give me the consolation of an alms." Brother Giles replied: "Try to live right—and you will have consolation."

Unless a man prepares a place for God within himself, he will never find a place among the creatures of God.

Who would not be willing to do what is better in this world not only for his soul but also for his body? Yet we are unwilling to do what is good for the soul or the body.

I could swear to this truth: that he who makes the Lord's yoke lighter for himself makes it heavier, and he who makes it heavier makes it lighter.

If only men would do what is best even for their body in this world! He who made the other world made this one, and He can give in this world the good things which He gives in the other. For the body feels the graces of the soul, because the good and evil of the soul have an effect on the body.

Then a friar said to him: "Perhaps we will die before we know our own good and experience any good." Brother Giles answered: "Tanners know about skins, shoemakers about shoes, smiths about iron, and so on in other crafts. But how can a man know a craft he has never practiced? Do you think that great lords give great gifts to stupid and insane men? They do not."

Just as good deeds are the way to all good, so evil deeds are the way to all evil.

Blessed is he whom nothing under heaven shall disedify and

whom everything he shall see and hear or know shall edify, and who shall try to make good use of all things.

## 8   *On Contempt of the World*

Woe to the man who gives his heart and desire and energy to the things of this world and on their account gives up and loses the things that are of Heaven and last forever!

The high-flying eagle would not fly so high if it had one of the beams of St. Peter's Church tied to each wing.

I find many people who work for their body and few who work for their soul. For many work for the body—breaking rocks, tunneling into mountains, and working in many other occupations that are hard on the body. But who labors so energetically and eagerly for his soul?

A greedy man is like a mole that does not believe there is any treasure or any other good but to burrow into the ground and live in it. Yet there are other treasures that it does not know about.

The birds of the air and the beasts of the earth and the fishes of the sea are satisfied when they have enough food for themselves. But since man is not satisfied with the things of this world and always longs for others, it is clear that he was not made primarily for those but for others. For the body was made for the sake of the soul, and this world for the sake of the other world.

This world is this kind of field: he who has a larger part of it has the worst part.

He also used to say that St. Francis did not like the ants very much because they were too anxious about collecting their food, but he liked the birds more because they "do not gather into barns."

## 9   *On Holy Chastity*

Our flesh is like a hog that runs eagerly into the mud and enjoys being in the mud.

The flesh is like the insect that always likes to wallow in the dung of horses.

Our flesh is the devil's boxer. Our flesh is the devil's forest.

The devil does not give up hope to get a man as long as he sees that he has flesh.

A man who has a borrowed animal makes as much use of it as he can—that is what we ought to do with the body.

It is impossible for a man to attain to grace unless he gives up sensuality.

Although a man who has an animal makes it work hard carrying heavy burdens, and although he feeds it well, still it will not go along the road right without being guided by a rod. That is the way it is with the body of a man who does penance.

A friar said: "How can we protect ourselves from the vices of the flesh?" The holy Brother Giles answered him: "He who wants to move big rocks and large beams tries to move them more by skill than by strength. And we must proceed in the same way in this case."

Every vice wounds chastity. For chastity is like a clear mirror that can be obscured just by breathing on it.

It is impossible for a man to come to the grace of God while he takes pleasure in sensual things. So you can turn this way and that, up and down, to one side and the other, but there is nothing else to do than to fight against the flesh that wishes to betray you day and night. He who overcomes it overcomes all his enemies and attains all that is good.

He also used to say: "Among all the other virtues I would give first place to holy chastity."

A friar said to him: "Isn't charity a greater virtue than chastity?" The holy Brother Giles answered him: "And what is more chaste than charity?" And he often used to say, singing: "O holy chastity, what are you? What are you? You are such and so great that foolish people do not know what you are and how great you are!"

A friar said to him: "What do you mean by chastity?" Brother Giles replied: "By chastity I mean to keep guard over all the senses with the grace of God."

Once when Brother Giles was praising chastity very much, a married man came up and said to him: "I keep away from all women except my wife—is that enough for me to do?" He answered: "Don't you think a man can get drunk on the wine in his own glass?" He said: "Yes, he can." And the holy Brother Giles said: "That is the way it is in this case."

Someone else said to him: "Brother Giles, the Apostle seems to mean only a widow when he says, 'She who gives herself up to pleasure is dead while she is still alive.'" Brother Giles answered him: "Although that saying may refer to widows, still that saying applies wherever it applies."

And the holy Brother Giles said to those who were standing around: "Some land that has not been farmed for a long time, where many thorns and such things have grown, and now it is almost like a forest—it is a very hard job to dig there. So it is with an unhappy sinner who has spent a long time in sin and is full of vices. A great deal of work in preaching and discussing has to be spent on him before you can lead him to the road to salvation and good works."

After that he said: "Just look, O man, at what you love and why you love it: Heaven or earth—the Creator or the creature—light or darkness—the flesh or the spirit—good or evil—and then you will be better able to separate the good from the bad and see what you ought to love and what you ought to hate."

## 10 On Resisting Temptations

Great grace cannot be possessed in peace, because many conflicts always arise against it. The more grace a man has, the more the devil attacks him. But a man should not on that account stop being guided by his grace, because the harder the battle, the greater will his crown be, if he wins.

But we do not have many hindrances because we are not what we should be. Yet if someone walked well in the way of the Lord, he would not feel tired or bored, but in the way of the world he feels tired and bored to death.

A friar answered: "You seem to be saying two things that contradict each other." The holy Brother Giles replied: "Don't the devils run after a man of good will more than after the others? That is a hindrance! And if a man sold his cheap merchandise for a thousand times more than it was worth, would he feel tired? Now the contradiction is solved! So I say that the more virtue a man has, the more he is pursued by vices, and he must hate them all the more. You gain virtue from every vice that you conquer. And you will receive a greater reward from the vice that troubles you most—if you conquer it."

Whatever may be the reason for which a man fails to walk in the Lord's way—that is the cause of his losing his reward.

Someone said to him: "I am often tempted by the worst kind of temptation, and I have often asked the Lord to take it away from me—and He does not take it away." The holy Brother Giles answered him: "The better the armor with which a king arms his soldiers, the more bravely he wants them to fight."

Then a friar asked him: "What can I do to go willingly to prayer when I feel dry and lacking in devotion?" He replied: "Suppose a king has two servants, one of whom is armed, but the other is unarmed, and they have to go to war. The one who is armed goes bravely to war, but the other who is unarmed says this to his lord: 'My lord, as you see, I have no weapons. But because I love you I will go into battle even without weapons.' Now the king on seeing the faithfulness of that servant says to his attendants: 'Go and prepare armor to adorn this faithful servant of mine, and place on him the emblem of my own armor.' So too if someone goes into the battle of prayer as if without arms, because he feels dry and lacking devotion, God sees his faithfulness and places the emblem of His armor on him.

"With temptations it is as sometimes happens to a farmer who sees a forest of trees and briars on a section of his land which he wants to cultivate and sow with grain, but he is exhausted with much labor and sweating and trouble before he can gather any grain there, and at times he is almost sorry he undertook that job on account of the work and worry it brings him. For, first, he sees the forest that has to be cleared of shrubs—but he sees no grain. Second, he works hard and cuts down the trees and extracts the roots of the trees—but he does not see the grain. Third, he breaks up the soil and prepares it—but he does not see the wheat for which he is working so much. Fourth, he plows the soil again. Fifth, he sows it. Sixth, he weeds it. Seventh, he reaps it. Eighth, he threshes it. And he works very hard at all those things. Ninth, he stores it away with great joy, almost forgetting all the labor because of the rich harvest that he finally obtains from it. And he endures many other labors besides these, and he blesses them all on account of the joy that the sight of the good harvest gives him."

Again someone said to him: "What can I do? For if I do any good, I become vain about it, and if I do bad, I am depressed and almost fall into despair." The holy Brother Giles answered: "You do right in grieving for your sin. However, I advise you to grieve moderately. For you must always believe that God's power to forgive is greater than your power to sin. If God has mercy on some great sinner, do you think He abandons a smaller sinner? But don't stop doing good because of the temptation to vanity. For if a farmer wishing to throw seed on the ground says to himself: 'I don't want to sow this year because, if I sow, birds may come and eat that seed,' and if therefore he does not sow, he would not have any produce from his land to eat. But if he sows, although some of the seed perishes, still he will have most of it. That is the way it is with the man who is tempted to vanity and fights against it."

A friar said to Brother Giles: "It is written of St. Bernard that he once said the seven penitential psalms and did not think of anything but what he was saying." The holy Brother Giles answered: "I think it is a greater thing if an armed camp is strongly attacked, and the sentinel of the camp defends himself manfully and bravely."

## 11 On Penance

Once a secular judge said: "Brother Giles, how can we lay people ascend to the life of grace and virtue?" Brother Giles replied: "First, a man must be sorry for his sins, then make a good confession, then humbly do the penance given him, and afterwards keep himself from all sin and from all occasion of sin. Finally he should do some good deeds."

Blessed is that evil that is turned into good for man, and cursed is that good that is turned into evil for man.

A man ought to bear bad things willingly in this world, because Our Lord Jesus Christ gave us an example of this Himself.

Blessed is he who shall grieve for his sins and weep day and night and shall not be consoled in this world until he arrives in that place where all the desires of his heart shall be fulfilled.

## 12 *On Prayer and Its Effects*

Prayer is the beginning and fulfillment of all good. Prayer illumines the soul, and by it all good and evil is known.

Every sinner should pray this prayer to the Lord—that He may give him to know his own misery and his sins and God's gifts.

He who does not know how to pray does not know God.

All who would be saved must of necessity, if they have the use of reason, turn to prayer in the end.

Suppose a very shy and simple woman had an only son whom she loved dearly and he was arrested by the king for some crime and was led away to be hanged—would not that woman, although shy and simple, scream, with disheveled hair and bared breast, and run to ask the king to free her son? Who —I ask you—taught that simple woman to make a petition for her son? Did not necessity and her love for her son make that shy woman (who previously hardly went beyond the threshold of her house) almost daring, running and screaming through the streets among men? And did it not make a simple person wise? Just so he who truly knew his own evils, dangers, and losses would be able to pray well—and would want to do so.

A friar said to him: "A man should feel very sorry when he cannot find in prayer the grace of devotion." Brother Giles answered: "I advise you to go slowly. For if you had some good wine in a glass and some sediment was under the wine, would you shake the glass and mix the wine with the sediment? That is not the thing to do. And if the grindstone of a mill sometimes does not make good flour, the miller does not immediately smash it with a hammer, but he repairs that grindstone slowly and gradually, and afterwards it makes good flour. Do likewise yourself, and reflect that you are not at all worthy to receive any consolation from God in prayer. For if someone had lived from the beginning of the world until now and were to live on until the end of the world, and every day while he prayed his eyes shed a dishful of tears, he would not be worthy then at the end of the world that God should give him even one single consolation."

A friar once asked him: "Why does a man suffer more temptations when he is praying to God than at other times?" The holy Brother Giles answered him: "When someone has a lawsuit against some opponent in the court of a prince, if that man goes to the prince to suggest that something be done against his opponent, the latter on hearing about it objects with all his power so that the decision should not be given in favor of the former. That is the way the devil acts against us. For if you spend time in conversation with others, you will often see that you do not feel many attacks of temptation. But if you go to pray to refresh your soul, then you will feel the burning arrows of the enemy against you. However, you should not give up prayer on that account, but you should stand firm. Because that is the way to our home above, and he who gives up prayer because of it is like a man who runs away from battle."

Someone said to him: "I see many who seem to have the grace of devotion and tears as soon as they go to pray. But I can hardly feel anything while praying." Brother Giles replied: "Labor faithfully and devoutly, because the grace that God does not give you at one time He may give you at another time. And what he does not give you one day or one week or month or year, He could give you another day or another week or month or year. Place your labor humbly in God, and God will place His grace in you as it may please Him. A metalworker making a knife strikes many blows on the iron out of which he is making the knife before the knife is finished. But finally the knife is finished with one blow."

A man ought to be very anxious about his salvation. For if the whole world were full of men right up to the clouds, if that were possible, and only a single one of those men were to be saved, nevertheless each one should correspond to his graces in order that he might be that one. For to lose Heaven is not to lose a shoestring. But unfortunately for us, there is One who gives, but there is none who receives!

Another time a friar asked Brother Giles: "What are you doing, Brother Giles?" He answered: "I am doing wrong." But the other said again to Brother Giles: "What wrong are you doing—you a Friar Minor?" And Brother Giles said to another friar who was standing there: "Brother, who is more ready— God to give His grace or we to receive it?" He replied: "God is more ready to give it to us than we are to receive it." The holy Brother Giles said to him: "And do we do good?" That friar answered: "No indeed—we do wrong." Then Brother Giles turned to the one who had asked him what he was doing, and said: "There you are—it is clear that I told you the truth when I answered that I was doing wrong."

He also said: "Many good deeds are commended in Holy Scripture, such as to clothe the naked, feed the hungry, and many others. However speaking of prayers the Lord says: 'For the Father seeks such to adore Him.' Good deeds adorn the soul, but prayer is something very great."

Holy religious are like wolves who hardly go out except for some great necessity, and then they stay out only a short while.

A certain friar who was a close friend said to Brother Giles: "Why don't you sometimes go out to see laymen who want to have a talk with you?" Brother Giles answered: "I want to satisfy my neighbor with profit to my own soul. Don't you believe that sometimes I would rather give a thousand pounds—if I had them—than to give myself to my neighbor?" The friar replied: "I believe it." "And do you believe," said Brother Giles, "that sometimes I would rather give four thousand pounds than to give myself to my neighbor?" "I believe it," he answered. Brother Giles said to him: "The Lord says in the Gospel: 'Whoever has left father and mother and brothers and sisters, etc., for My Name's sake, shall receive a hundredfold in this world.' Now there was a certain man from Rome who joined the Order of Friars Minor whose property was said to be worth sixty thousand pounds. So it is something great which the Lord God gives in this world that is worth a hundred times sixty thousand pounds! But we are blind and see as through a veil. If we see a man who has much grace and virtue, we cannot bear his perfection. If someone were truly spiritual, he would hardly want to see or hear or spend time with anyone except for a very important reason, but he would always want to be alone."

He also said about himself: "I would rather be blind than

to be the handsomest or the richest or wisest or noblest man in the world." Someone said to him: "Why would you rather be blind than to have those things?" "Because," he replied, "I am afraid they might hinder me on my way."

Blessed is he who neither thinks nor says nor does anything that is blameworthy.

### 13 On Contemplation

Brother Giles once asked a certain friar: "What do those wise men say that contemplation is?" But he said: "I don't know." Said he: "Do you want me to tell you what I think it is?" And he said: "I do." And the holy Brother Giles said: "There are seven degrees in contemplation: fire—unction—ecstasy—contemplation—taste—rest—glory.

"I say *fire,* that is, a certain light that comes first to enlighten the soul. Then the *unction* of ointments from which a certain marvelous odor arises that follows that light, as mentioned in the Canticle: 'in the odor of thy ointments,' and so forth. Then *ecstasy:* for once the odor is felt, the soul is rapt and is withdrawn from the physical senses. So there follows *contemplation:* for after it is thus withdrawn from the physical senses, it contemplates God in a wonderful way. Afterward follows *taste:* for in that contemplation it feels a marvelous sweetness which is mentioned in the Psalm: 'Taste and see,' and so forth. Then *rest:* because once the spiritual palate has tasted the sweetness, the soul rests in that sweetness. Lastly follows *glory:* because the soul glories in such rest and is refreshed with intense joy, so the Psalm says: 'I shall be satisfied when Thy glory shall appear.' "[2]

He also said: "No one can ascend to the contemplation of the Divine Majesty except through fervor of spirit and frequent prayer. Man is enkindled by fervor of spirit and ascends to contemplation when his heart, along with the rest of his being, is fully disposed to it so that it desires or can think of nothing else except what it has and feels."

The contemplative life is to give up all earthly things for the love of God, to seek only heavenly things, to pray constantly, to read spiritual books often, and to praise God continually by hymns and canticles.

To contemplate is to be separated from all and to be united to God alone.

He also said: "He is a good contemplator who, if he were to have his hands and feet cut off and his eyes taken out and his nose, ears, and tongue cut off, would care for or desire to have no other members or anything else that can be thought of in the whole world besides what he has and feels, because of the greatness of the most sweet, ineffable, and unutterable odor, joy, and consolation that he experiences—just as 'Mary sitting at the Lord's feet' received so much of the sweetness of the word of God that no part of her being could or wished to do anything but what it was doing. And that is why she did not reply by word or deed to her sister who was complaining that she was not helping her, and Christ took her part, answering for Mary who was unable to reply."

## 14    On the Active Life

As there is no one who merits to attain to the contemplative life unless he has first been faithfully and conscientiously trained in the active life, it is necessary that the active life be lived with earnest effort and all care.

He would live the active life well who—if it were possible— would provide food for all the poor people in the world, would clothe them all, give them an abundance of all the things they needed, and build all the churches and hospitals and bridges this world needs—and if afterward everyone in the world considered him a bad man, and he knew this well and wanted to be considered nothing but bad, and if he did not on that account give up any of his good works but gave himself still more fervently to every sort of good work, like a man who does not want or desire or expect any merit from it in this world, considering how Martha, when she was busy with much serving asked her sister to help and was reproved by the Lord, yet she did not stop doing her good work. So too someone who is living the active life well should not stop doing his good works because of any criticism or scorn, since he does not expect any earthly but an everlasting reward.

He also said: "If you find grace in prayer, pray—and if you don't find grace in prayer, pray, because the Lord has accepted even goat's hair as an offering."

Sometimes a king is more pleased by the foot of someone doing a small job for him than by the whole body of another man doing a much larger job for him, because the Lord sees the heart.

When the Lord confided the ministry of preaching to St. Peter, he said that He had retained the greater part for Himself, saying to him: "And you, once you are converted, confirm your brethren."

### 15 On the Continuous Practice of Spiritual Caution

If you want to see well, pluck out your eyes and be blind. If you want to hear well, be deaf. If you want to walk well, cut off your feet. If you want to work well, cut off your hands. If you want to love well, hate yourself. If you want to live well, die to yourself. If you want to make a good profit, know how to lose. If you want to be rich, be poor. If you want to enjoy pleasure, afflict yourself. If you want to be secure, always be afraid. If you want to be exalted, humiliate yourself. If you want to be honored, despise yourself and honor those who despise you. If you want to have good things, endure evil things. If you want to rest, work. If you want to be blessed, desire to be cursed. Oh, what great wisdom it is to know how to do this! But because these are great things, they are not given to all.

If a man were to live a thousand years and not have anything to do outside himself, he would have enough to do within, in his own heart, nor would he be able to bring the work to perfect completion—he would have so much to do only within, in his own heart!

He who does not make of himself two persons—a judge and a master—cannot be saved.

No one should wish to see or hear or speak anything unless

it is for his own spiritual good, or to proceed further in any way.

He who does not want to know shall not be known. But unfortunately for us those who have the gifts of God do not realize it, and those who do not have them do not seek them.

Man conceives God as he wishes. But God is always just as He is.

### 16  *On Useful and Useless Knowledge and on Preachers of the Word of God*

He who wants to know enough should bow his head enough and do enough and drag his belly on the ground, and the Lord will teach him enough.

The highest wisdom is to do good deeds, to guard oneself well, and to think of God's judgments.

Once he said to a man who wanted to go to the university in order to learn: "Why do you want to go to the university? The height of all knowledge is to fear and love God—those two things are enough for you. A man has as much knowledge as he does good and no more. So don't rely on your own wisdom, but strive to work with all care, and put all your reliance on those deeds of yours. Therefore the Apostle says: 'Let us not love in word or tongue, but in deed and in truth.' Don't concentrate too much on being useful to others, but concentrate more on being useful to yourself."

Sometimes we want to know much for others and little for ourselves.

The word of God does not belong to him who bears or speaks it but to him who puts it into practice.

Many men who did not know how to swim have gone into the water to help those who were drowning, and they have drowned with those who were drowning. First, there was one misfortune, and then there were two.

If you work well for the salvation of your own soul, you will be working well for the salvation of all your friends. If you do right by yourself, you will do right by all your well-wishers.

A preacher of the word of God is put there by God to be a light, a mirror, and a standardbearer for the people of God.

Blessed is he who so directs others on the right way that he himself stays on it, and so urges others to run that he does not stop running, and so helps others that they become rich and he himself does not thereby become poor.

I believe that a good preacher speaks more to himself than to others.

I believe that he who wishes to draw the souls of sinners should fear greatly that he may himself be drawn to evil. "How so?" a friar asked him. And he said: "Turn your eyes away that they should not behold vanity. Those who speak do not comprehend, and those who listen do not understand."

Someone said to him: "What is better: to preach well or to act well?" He answered: "Who earns more merit: the man who goes to the Church of St. James or the man who shows others the road to take to St. James?"

I see many things that are not mine. I hear many things that I do not understand. And I say many things that I do not do. So it seems to me that a man is not saved by seeing, hearing, and speaking.

## 17   On Good Words and Bad Words

He who speaks good words is "like the mouth of God," and he who speaks bad words is like the mouth of the devil.

When God's servants come together anywhere for conversation, they should discuss the beauty of the virtues so that the virtues should be pleasing to them. For if they are pleasing to them, they will practice them, and if they practice the virtues, they will always love the virtues still more.

The more vices a man has, the more necessary it is for him to talk about the virtues. For just as someone very easily falls into vices by frequent evil conversation about vices, so by frequent holy conversation about the virtues he is drawn and disposed towards the virtues.

But what shall we say? For we cannot speak good about good, nor can we speak evil about evil. So what shall we say? For regarding good we cannot say how good it is, or regarding the evil of guilt and punishment how bad it is, as both are incomprehensible to us.

I think it is no less a virtue to know how to remain silent well than to know how to speak well. And it seems to me that men should have a neck like a crane's, so that their words would go through many joints before they came out of the mouth.

## 18 *On Persevering in Good*

What good does it do a man to fast, pray, give alms, mortify himself, and receive great graces from Heaven—and not reach the haven of salvation?

Sometimes a ship appears on the sea that is beautiful, large, new, and full of rich treasure. But some disaster happens to it and it does not reach port safely but sinks miserably—what good did all its excellence and beauty do it? Again sometimes there is a ship on the sea that is small, ugly, old, contemptible, and not full of treasure. And with great difficulty it escapes the dangers of the sea and safely reaches port. That alone is worthy of praise. This happens also with men in this world. So it is right that we should all fear.

Although a tree has grown, yet it is not large all at once. And if large, it is not in bloom. And if in bloom, nevertheless it does not immediately bear fruit. And if it bears fruits, they are not large at first. And if they are large, yet they are not ripe. And if ripe, nevertheless all of them do not reach the mouths of those who eat them, but many fall down and rot away or are eaten by pigs or other animals.

Someone said to him: "May the Lord make you end well!" Brother Giles answered: "What good would it do me if I went begging for the Kingdom of Heaven for a hundred years, if I did not end well? I think the two great good things for men are to love God and always to keep oneself from sin. He who had those two good things would have all that is good."

## 19 *On the Religious Life and Its Security*

Brother Giles used to say about himself: "I would rather have a little of God's grace in the religious life than a great deal in the world, because there are more dangers and fewer aids in the world than in a religious order. But a sinful man has more fear of what is good for him than of what is bad for him, because he is more afraid of doing penance and joining a religious order than he is of staying in sin or remaining in the world."

A layman asked Brother Giles' advice as to whether or not he should become a religious. The holy Brother Giles answered: "If a very poor man knew that a valuable treasure was hidden in some public field, would he ask anyone's advice whether he should go after the treasure in a hurry? How much more should men hurry to dig up the heavenly treasure!" When he heard this, that man joined a religious order, after selling all his property.

Brother Giles also used to say: "Many enter the religious life and do not practice those things that are a basic part of the religious life. And they are like a farmer who would put on the armor of Roland but not be capable of using it in battle. For not all men are able to ride the horse Bayard, or if they rode it, could keep from falling off. I don't think it is much to enter the court of a king, nor do I think it much to receive gifts from a king. But I do think it is a great thing to know how to remain in a royal court by doing the right thing. The court of the Great King is the religious life—to enter it and to receive some gifts from God in it is not much. But to be able to live in it by doing the right thing and to persevere devoutly and conscientiously in it to the end is a great thing. For I would rather live as a layman and yearn devoutly and anxiously for the religious life than to be a religious and be tired of it."

The glorious Virgin Mary, Mother of God, came from ancestors who were sinners, and she was never in any religious order—yet she is what she is.

A religious should believe that he neither can nor knows how to live except as a religious.

Once he also said to his companion: "From the beginning of the world until now there has never appeared a religious order that is better or more advantageous than the Order of Friars Minor."

He also said: "It seems to me that the Order of Friars Minor was truly sent into this world for the great benefit of men. But woe to us unless we are such men as we should be! The Order of Friars Minor seems to me to be the poorest and the richest in the world. But this seems to me to be our greatest vice: that we wish to walk too high. He is rich who imitates the rich man. He is wise who imitates the wise man. He is good who imitates the good man. He is handsome who imitates the handsome man. And he is noble who imitates the noble man— that is, Our Lord Jesus Christ."

## 20   *On Obedience and Its Usefulness*

The more a religious is restricted under the yoke of obedience for the love of God, the more fruitful will he be. And the more a religious is obedient and subject to his superior for the honor of God, the poorer and purer from sin will he be before the other men of this world.

A truly obedient religious is like a well-armed knight riding on a good horse who passes safely among enemies and no one can harm him. But a religious who grumbles at obeying is like an unarmed knight riding on a bad horse who, when passing among the enemy, falls and is immediately captured, chained, wounded, imprisoned, and sometimes put to death.

A religious who wants to live according to his own will wants to go into the fire of hell.

As long as the ox holds its head under the yoke, it fills the barns with grain. But the ox that does not hold its head under the yoke and wanders around may think it is a great lord— but the barns are not filled with grain.

The great and the wise humbly put their heads under the yoke of obedience. But the foolish withdraw their heads from under the yoke and do not want to obey.

Sometimes a mother nourishes and takes good care of her son, and after he has grown up, he does not obey his mother because of his pride, but makes fun of her and looks down on her. The mother is the religious order, and the son is the religious who, after it has nourished and taken good care of him, later looks down on it and makes fun of it and does not want to be obedient.

I think it is greater to obey a superior for the love of God than to obey the Creator Himself giving some command in person.

Now it seems to me that if someone had so much grace that he spoke with angels, if he were called by someone whom he had promised to obey, he should interrupt his talk with the angels and obey the human being. Because while he is under someone's orders in this world, he is bound to obey the man who is his superior, for the sake of the Creator. And this is the proof: because the Lord, as we read in the first book of Kings, did not disclose His will to Samuel before he had Heli's permission.

He who has put his head under the yoke of obedience, and later, to follow the way of perfection, withdraws his head from under the yoke of obedience—that is a sign of great hidden pride.

A good habit is the way to all good, and a bad habit is the way to all evil.

### 21   On Remembering Death

If someone had lived from the beginning of the world until now and had always suffered from evil as long as he lived, and were soon to go to all good, what harm would all the evil that he suffered do him? And if someone always had all good things from the beginning of the world until now and he were now to go to all evil, what good would all the good that he had do him?

A layman said to him: "I would like to live a long life in this world and have everything in abundance." He answered him: "If you were to live a thousand years and be the lord of the whole world, when you died what reward would you get from the flesh that you served? But a man who does right and takes good care of his soul for a short while will receive an indescribable reward in the future."

Part Six

# ADDITIONAL CHAPTERS

## 1 How St. Francis Abhorred the Name "Master"

Francis, the humble imitator of Christ, knowing that the name "Master" was only appropriate for Christ by whom all things were made, used to say that he would gladly wish to do all things, but he did not want to be a master or be known by the name "Master" lest by such a name he should seem to be acting against the saying of Christ in the Gospel that forbids anyone to be called "Master," because it was better for him to be humble with his poor little knowledge than—if it were possible—to perform great deeds and presume to go against the humble words of so glorious a Master. For the name "Master" is appropriate only for the Blessed Christ, all of whose acts are perfect. And so he commanded that no one on earth should presume to be called "Master," because in Heaven there is only one true Master without any defect: the Blessed Christ who is God and man, light and life, the maker of the world, who is glorious and to be praised forever. Amen.[1]

## 2 Concerning the Marvelous Statue That Spoke to St. Francis

One night when St. Francis was devoutly praying to Almighty God in the Place of St. Mary of the Angels, a very wonderful vision appeared before his bodily eyes: a great statue similar to the one which King Nabuchodonosor saw in a dream. For

it had a head of gold and a very beautiful face, and its chest
and arms were of silver, its abdomen and thighs of bronze,
its legs of iron, and its feet partly of iron and partly of clay,
and it was dressed in sackcloth, which seemed to make it blush
for shame.

Now St. Francis, gazing at the statue, was greatly amazed
at its indescribable beauty and its wonderful size and also at
the shame that it seemed to feel about the sackcloth in which
it was dressed.

And while he was gazing with wonder at its extremely beautiful head and face, the statue itself spoke to him, saying:
"Why are you so amazed? God has sent you this example so
that you may learn from me what is to happen to your Order
in the future.

"My golden head and very beautiful face that you see is
the beginning of your Order, based on the perfection of the
Gospel life. And just as the substance of gold is more valuable
than all other metals, and as the position of the head and face
is superior to that of the other members, so the beginning of
your Order will be of such great value because of the golden
fraternal charity, and of such great beauty because of the angelic purity, and of such great loftiness because of its evangeli-
cal poverty that the entire world will be astounded. And Queen
Saba—that is, Holy Mother Church—will marvel and rejoice in
heart when it sees in the first chosen friars of your Order such
Christlike beauty and splendor of spiritual wisdom shining as
in angelic mirrors. And blessed will be those who conform
themselves utterly to Christ and strive to imitate the virtues
and customs of that first precious metal, the golden head, by
adhering more to its heavenly beauty than to the deceptive
flowers of the world.

"Now the chest and arms of silver will be the second state
of your Order, which will be as inferior to the first as silver
is to gold. And just as silver has great value and brightness
and sonorousness, so in that second state there will be many
friars who will be so brilliant in Holy Scripture and the light
of holiness and the sublimity of the word of God that some of
them will be made popes and cardinals and many will be bishops. And because a man's strength is shown in his chest and
arms, so in that time the Lord will raise up in your Order men

who will be outstandingly brilliant in both knowledge and virtue and who will defend this Order and also the entire Church by knowledge and virtue from the many attacks of the devils and various attacks of faithless men. But although that future generation will be admirable, nevertheless it will not attain the very perfect state of the first friars, but compared to them it will be like silver compared to gold.

"After it there will be a third state in your Order that will be like the bronze abdomen and thigh. Because as bronze is considered of less value than silver, so those of the third state will be inferior to the first and second. And although they will spread in numbers and distance over a great part of the world, like bronze, nevertheless there will be among them some 'whose God is their belly' and for whom 'the glory' of the Order 'is in their shame,' and 'who mind' only 'earthly things.' And although, because of their knowledge, they will have an amazing eloquence 'like sounding brass,' yet alas, because they will be lovers of their belly and their body, they will be in the eyes of God (as the Apostle says) like sounding brass or a tinkling cymbal, because while uttering heavenly words and begetting spiritual offspring by showing to others the fountain of life, they themselves will be fatally arid and will adhere without interior grace to the earth. May the mercy of God succor them! Amen.

"After them will come a fourth terrible and frightening state which is now shown to you in the iron legs. For just as iron overcomes and dissolves bronze, silver, and gold, so that state will be of such ironlike hardness and depravity that the coldness and horrible blight and metallic morality of that dangerous time will sweep into oblivion whatever good the golden charity of the first friars and the silver truth of the second and the bronze, though resounding, eloquence of the third have erected in the Church of Christ. However, as the legs support the body, so those friars will support the body of the Order by some hypocritical rusty strength. And therefore both the iron belly and legs will be hidden by clothing, because those friars will have the habit of the Order and piety, but 'within they will be ravenous wolves.' But those rusty and ironlike friars serving only their belly—although they may hide it from the world, yet it will be evident to the Lord, because by the hammer of their perverse life they will reduce to nothing their most precious gifts. Therefore, like the hardest iron, they will be afflicted with the fire of tribulations and the hammer of terrible trials, so that they will be melted down not only by the fires and burning coals of the devils but also of secular authorities, in order that such powerful persons may suffer torments from powerful men. And because they sinned by irreverence and hardness, they will be cruelly tortured by irreverent men. As a result of those trials they will be stirred to such impatience that, just as iron resists all metals, they will set themselves in opposition to everyone, and thus they will stubbornly oppose not only secular authorities but also their spiritual superiors, thinking that they can resist everything, like iron. And thereby they will greatly displease God.

"Now the fifth state will be partly of iron, referring to the above-mentioned hypocrites, and partly of earth, referring to those who give themselves completely to worldly business. And as you see burnt clay and iron appearing together in the feet, although they can in no way unite, so will it be in the last state of this Order: for a great abomination and division shall arise among the earthly ambitious hypocrites who are hardened by the mire of temporal things and the desires of the flesh, for like clay and iron they cannot come together because of their great discord. And they will despise not only the Gospel and the Rule, but also with their clay and iron feet—that is, with their perverse and impure cravings—they will tread upon all the discipline of this holy Order. And just as clay and iron are separate entities, so many of them will be divided among themselves both interiorly by living in a state of contentiousness and exteriorly by adhering in a partisan way to secular despots. As a result they will arouse the hostility of everyone to such a point that they will hardly be able to enter or reside in towns or openly wear the habit. And many of them will be punished and liquidated by frightful tortures at the hands of seculars, who despise such abominable feet. All this will happen to them because they have wholly turned away from the golden head. But in those perilous days those who turn back to the warnings of that precious head shall be blessed, for the Lord will try them like gold in a furnace and will crown them and welcome them into eternity like a victim of a holocaust.

"Now this habit that I seem to be ashamed of is holy poverty. Although it is the jewel and splendor of the whole Order and the unique custodian and crown and basis of all holiness, nevertheless those degenerate sons, lacking all virtuous efforts, will, as we said, be ashamed of that most holy poverty, and putting aside their coarse habits, they will select and obtain, even by simony, expensive and ostentatious robes. But blessed and happy will be those who persevere to the end in what they have promised to the Lord!"

And after saying this, that statue vanished.

St. Francis was greatly amazed at all this, and like the good shepherd, weeping tears, he commended his present and future sheep to Almighty God.

May Our Lord Jesus Christ be praised and glorified forever! Amen.[2]

### 3 *How Brother Rufino Liberated a Possessed Man*

Now Brother Rufino, because of his intense concentration of mind on God and his angelic peace of soul, whenever someone called him, would answer in such a serious and gentle and strange tone that he seemed to be coming back from another world. Once when his companions called to him to go for some bread, he answered like a diviner in a trance.

And while he was begging for bread in Assisi, a tightly bound, possessed man was being led by a large group of men to St. Francis in order that he might free him from the devil. When the man saw Brother Rufino from a distance, he immediately began to shout and thrash around with such fury that he broke his bonds and leaped away from the men. They were amazed at such an extraordinary seizure and urged him to tell them why he was being tormented more than usual.

He answered: "Because that poor little friar—that obedient, meek, holy Brother Rufino going about with his sack—burns me up and crucifies me by his saintly virtues and humble prayers. And so I cannot remain in this man any longer!"

And after saying that, the devil left him at once.

When Brother Rufino heard this—as those men and the cured sick man were acting very reverently toward him—he gave praise and honor to Our Lord Jesus Christ. And he urged them in all things to glorify God and the Savior, Our Lord Jesus Christ, from whom this and all good things come and who is blessed forever. Amen.[3]

## 4  *How St. Francis Foretold a Terrible Famine*

St. Francis not only gave Brother Leo marvelous consolations during his lifetime, but he also appeared to him frequently after he died.

Once while Brother Leo was praying devoutly, St. Francis appeared to him and said: "Oh, Brother Leo, do you remember when I was in the world I predicted that a great famine would come over the whole world, and I said I knew of a certain poor little man for the love of whom God would spare the world and not send the scourge of famine as long as he was alive?"

Brother Leo answered: "I remember very well, dear Father."

And St. Francis said: "I was that creature and that poor little man for love of whom God did not send the famine among men, but out of humility I did not want to reveal it. But now you should know for sure, Brother Leo, that after I have left the world a terrible and universal famine will come over the world, so that many men will die of hunger."

And so it happened that about six or nine months after he had said those words, such a great famine spread everywhere that people ate not only the roots of plants but also the bark of trees, and a great number of them died from hunger.

The innocence of Brother Leo and the divine friendship and sublime gift of prophecy of St. Francis are evident from this.[4]

To the glory of Our Lord Jesus Christ. Amen.

### 5 *How Blood Came Out of a Picture of the Stigmata of St. Francis*

How worthy of admiration were those wonderful Stigmata of the holy Father was demonstrated in a notable miracle which occurred in a certain friary of the Friars Preachers. For there was in that community a certain Friar Preacher who had such a heartfelt hatred for St. Francis that he could not see him in a picture or hear a word about him or really believe that he had been marked with the holy Stigmata. So when this friar was a member of the community of that convent beyond the mountains, in the refectory of which was a painting of St. Francis with the holy Stigmata, he, moved by faithlessness and hatred, secretly went and cut the sacred Stigmata out of the holy Father's picture with a knife so that not a single trace of them was to be seen.

But the next day, when the friar sat down at mealtime and glanced at the picture of St. Francis, he saw the Stigmata there in the places where he had cut them out, but looking more recent than before. He angrily thought that he had not completely cut them out the first time. And watching for a moment when no one was in the room—for he who does evil hates the light—he went and cut out the Saint's Stigmata a second time, in such a way however that he did not destroy the stone on which the picture was painted.

Now on the third day when the friar sat down at the table, he looked at the picture of St. Francis—and he saw those sacred Stigmata seeming more beautiful and new than they had ever appeared before. Then the friar, being darkened by evil and aroused by wickedness, added a third sin to his second. And he said to himself: "By God, I am going to erase those Stigmata so that they will never appear again!"

And as before he waited for a time when he would not be seen by men, forgetting that all things are bare and open to the eyes of God. Then with intense fury he took a knife and dug the marks of the Stigmata out of the picture, cutting out the color and the stone.

But just as he finished digging, blood began to flow from

the openings, and it gushed out violently and stained the friar's face and hands and habit. He was terrified and fell to the ground as if he were dead. Meanwhile the blood was flowing in streams from the openings in the wall which the unhappy man had made where the Stigmata had been.

Then the friars of the house came and found him lying there like a corpse. And they were very sorry when they realized what an evil deed he had committed. Moreover, seeing that the blood continued to flow, they tried to stop up the openings with pieces of cotton, but they could not restrain the streams of blood. So fearing that lay people would perceive it and as a result they would suffer scandal and scorn, they thought of pleading devoutly to St. Francis to help them. So the prior and all the friars in the community bared their backs before the picture of St. Francis and gave themselves the discipline and prayed, weeping tears and begging St. Francis mercifully to forgive the offense of that friar and to deign to stop the flow of blood.

And because of their humility, their prayers were immediately granted. The blood ceased flowing, and the holy Stigmata remained to be venerated in their beauty by all.

From that time the friar was exceedingly devoted to St. Francis. And as the friars of the Place of Alverna have testified, that friar went up to Mount Alverna out of devotion, and he brought some of the bloodstained cotton with him and gave it to those friars.

Moreover out of devotion he came to St. Mary of the Angels, and he very devoutly visited all the Places of St. Francis with great reverence and weeping. For wherever he could find events or relics connected with St. Francis, he would burst into tears in such a devout way that he would make others weep too. He also described all the above-mentioned miracles before many Friars Minor in Alverna and Assisi (when his companions were absent so that they should not consider these matters to reflect on their Order). By the merits of St. Francis that friar became so devoted to the Franciscans that sometimes when he could not see them, he nevertheless remained united with them by the bond of brotherly charity in God.[5]

To the glory of Our Lord Jesus Christ. Amen.

## 6 *How the Lady Jacopa Visited Brother Giles*

When Brother Giles was staying in Perugia, the Lady Jacopa dei Settesoli, a noble Roman lady who was very devoted to the Friars Minor, came to see him. Later a Brother Gerardino of the Order of Minors, a very spiritual man, also arrived to hear his edifying conversation.

And while several other friars were standing there, Brother Giles said these words in Italian: "Because of what a man can do, he comes to what he does not want."

Now Brother Gerardino in order to provoke Brother Giles to speak, said: "I am amazed, Brother Giles, that a man, because of what he can do, comes to what he does not want, since a man can of himself do nothing. And I can prove that in a number of ways. First, to be capable of doing something presupposes being, and a thing's functioning depends on its being, as fire warms because it is hot. But of himself a man is nothing. Therefore the Apostle said: 'If any man thinks himself to be something, whereas he is nothing, he deceives himself.' So someone who is nothing can do nothing. Consequently man can do nothing. Second, I will prove that a man can do nothing in this way: because if a man can do anything, it is either by reason of the soul alone, or by reason of the body alone, or by reason of both together. If it is by reason of the soul alone, it is certain that he can do nothing, because the soul without the body cannot gain or lose merit. If it is by reason of the body alone, he can do nothing because the body without the soul is deprived of life and form, and so cannot do anything, because all action is from form. Now if it is by reason of both together, a man can do nothing because if he could do anything, it would be by reason of the soul which is its form. But, as I have already said, if the soul without the body can do nothing, it can do still less when joined to the body, for the corruptible body is a load upon the soul. And I will give you an example of this, Brother Giles: if a donkey cannot walk without a burden, it can walk far less with a burden. And so by that example it is evident that the soul can do less when burdened with the body than it can do without it.

But it can do nothing without it. Consequently it can do nothing with it."

And he made many similar arguments to Brother Giles—in fact he made a good dozen—in order to make him talk. And all who heard those arguments were filled with admiration.

But Brother Giles replied: "You spoke badly, Brother Gerardino. Say your *mea culpa* for all of it."

Brother Gerardino said a *mea culpa*, smiling. But Brother Giles, seeing that he was not saying it sincerely, said: "That is not valid, Brother Gerardino. And when a *mea culpa* is not valid, there is nothing left for a man to gain."

Then Brother Giles said to him: "Do you know how to sing, Brother Gerardino?" And when he answered, "Yes," Brother Giles said: "Now sing with me!" And Brother Giles took from his sleeve a reed pipe such as children make, and beginning with the first note of the pipe and going on, note by note, in rhythmic words he annulled and refuted all the twelve arguments.

Beginning with the first one, he said: "I was not referring to man's being before the Creation, Brother Gerardino, because it is true that he was nothing then and could do nothing then. But I mean the being of man after the Creation, when God gave him free will, by which he could gain merit by consenting to good or lose merit by dissenting. Therefore you spoke badly and offered me a fallacy, Brother Gerardino, because St. Paul the Apostle does not refer to a lack of substance or a lack of capacity but to a lack of merit, as he says: 'If I lack charity, I am nothing.' Furthermore I was not referring to a soul without a body or to a dead body, but to a living man who can do good by consenting to grace, if he wishes to, and who can do bad by resisting grace, which is nothing else than falling away from good. Now as to your asserting that 'the corruptible body is a load upon the soul,' Scripture does not say that a man is thereby deprived of free will, so that he cannot do good or evil, but it means that his understanding and feelings are impeded and also that the soul's memory is preoccupied with temporal matters. Hence the passage continues: 'And the earthly habitation presses down the mind that muses on many things,' for they do not allow the soul to reflect freely and to seek 'the things that are above, where Christ is sitting at the right hand of God.' Therefore the potentialities of the soul are impeded in many ways on account of man's many occupations and physical cares. And so you spoke badly, Brother Gerardino."

And he likewise refuted all the other arguments. So Brother Gerardino said a sincere *mea culpa* and admitted that a creature can do something. And Brother Giles said: "Now your *mea culpa* is valid."

And then he said: "Do you want me to show you still more clearly that a creature can do something?" And climbing onto a box he cried out in a frightening voice: "O damned soul lying in hell!" Then he himself answered for the damned person in a mournful voice in a way that terrified everyone present: "Ah, me! Woe! Ah, me!" And he shrieked and moaned.

Then in another voice Brother Giles said: "Tell us, you unhappy man, why you went to hell?"

And he answered: "Because I did not avoid doing the evil that I could have avoided, and I did not do the good that I could and ought to have done."

And Brother Giles asked him: "Oh, you wicked damned soul, what would you do if you were given time to do penance?"

And he replied for him: "I would throw all the earth in the world bit by bit behind me in order to avoid an eternal punishment, because that would have an end. But my damnation will last for all eternity!"

And turning to Brother Gerardino Brother Giles said: "Do you hear, Brother Gerardino, that a creature can do something?"

Then he said: "Tell me, Gerardino, whether when a drop of water falls into the ocean, it gives its name to the ocean or the ocean to the drop?"

And the other replied that both the substance and the name of the drop are absorbed and take on the name of the ocean.

And after he said that, Brother Giles fell into a rapture before all who were there. For he realized that human nature, in relation to the nature of God, was absorbed like a drop of water into the great ocean of the Divine Infinity in the Incarnation of Our Lord Jesus Christ, who is blessed forever and ever. Amen.

Now the Lady Jacopa, after hearing and seeing these things, went away filled with joy.[6]

### 7 How Brother Giles Removed a Doubt Concerning the Virginity of Mary from the Heart of a Friar Preacher

At the time when the holy Brother Giles was alive, there was a certain great Master of the Order of Preachers who for many years suffered from a serious doubt concerning the virginity of the Blessed Mother of Our Lord Jesus Christ. For it seemed to him impossible that she could have been both a mother and a virgin. Otherwise he had real faith, and therefore he suffered very much from that doubt of his, and he wished to be freed from it by some enlightened man.

Now when he heard that the holy Brother Giles was a very enlightened man, he went to him. But Brother Giles, knowing in advance by the Holy Spirit about his coming and intention and spiritual conflict, went out to meet him. And before reaching him, he struck the ground with a stick that he held in his hand, and he said: "Oh, Friar Preacher, Virgin before bearing!"

And at once a very beautiful lily came up on the spot which he had struck with the stick.

Then he struck a second time, saying: "Oh, Friar Preacher, Virgin in bearing!"

And another lily sprang up.

And striking a third time, he said: "Oh, Friar Preacher, Virgin after bearing!"

And a third lily appeared. And after doing that, Brother Giles ran away.

But that Friar Preacher was immediately freed from his temptation on seeing such an amazing and novel miracle. And when he learned that it had been Brother Giles, from that moment he conceived such a devotion for him that he used to praise both him and his Order in a wonderful way.[7]

To the glory of Our Lord Jesus Christ. Amen.

## 8 *How Brother James Asked Brother Giles How to Act in a Rapture*

The holy and very devout lay brother James of Massa, who had been with St. Clare and many of the companions of St. Francis, had the gift of rapture, and he wished to obtain Brother Giles' advice regarding how he should act when he had such a grace.

Brother Giles answered: "Don't add. Don't take away. And avoid crowds as much as you can."

"What do you mean?" said Brother James. "Explain it to me, Reverend Father."

He replied: "When the mind is ready to be introduced into that most glorious light of God's goodness, it should not add anything by presumption or take away anything by negligence, and it should love solitude as much as possible if it wishes that the grace be preserved and increase."[8]

To the glory of Our Lord Jesus Christ. Amen.

## 9 *How St. Lawrence Appeared to Brother John of Alverna*

Brother John of Alverna was asked by Brother James of Falerone to pray to God concerning a certain scruple of conscience which was sorely tormenting him, namely, certain matters that pertained to the office of a priest. And before the Feast of St. Lawrence he received this answer, as he himself told it. He said that the Lord said to him: "He is a priest according to the order of God."

But when Brother James' conscience still disturbed him, he asked Brother John to pray to the Lord about it again.

Therefore during the night of the Vigil of the Feast of St. Lawrence, Brother John faithfully watched and prayed to the Lord that He might give him some certitude concerning the scruple through the merits of St. Lawrence. And while he was watching and praying, St. Lawrence appeared to him, dressed like a deacon in white vestments. And he said to Brother John:

"I am the Deacon Lawrence, and he for whom you are praying is unquestionably a priest by divine ordination." And then Brother James felt perfect assurance regarding the scruple which he had had, and he was greatly consoled.

Again, while the friars were singing the *Salve Regina* in the evening, St. Lawrence appeared to Brother John as a young man wearing a red dalmatic and holding an iron grill, and said to him: "This grill has brought me glory in Heaven, and the pain of the fire has given me the fullness of God's bliss." And he added: "If you wish to enjoy the glory and bliss of God, bear with patience the suffering and bitterness of the world."

St. Lawrence remained thus visibly with him as long as the friars sang the above-mentioned antiphon. And after they went to rest, Brother John stayed in the choir with St. Lawrence. And the Saint reassured and consoled him, and then disappeared. And he left him so overflowing with affection and divine charity that he did not sleep a bit all that night of the feast, but spent the entire night experiencing marvelous consolations.

Again to this Brother John, once when he was devoutly celebrating Mass, after he had consecrated the host, all the appearance of the bread vanished before his sight, and in the twinkling of an eye Christ appeared there, dressed in a red robe and having a very beautiful red beard, and gave him such sweet consolation that if he had not remained conscious, he would have been rapt in ecstasy. And during that vision he received assurance that the Lord was propitiated by that Mass for the whole world and especially for those whom he commended to Him.[9]

To the praise and glory of Our Lord Jesus Christ. Amen.

### 10 *How Brother John Had the Spirit of Revelation*

When certain persons had some terrible hidden sins which no one could know except by divine revelation—some of them were dead, others were living—Brother John disclosed to the living their hidden sins by divine revelation. As a result they were converted to a life of penance.

One of them said that he had committed the sin which Brother John disclosed before Brother John had been born. And the man to whom he disclosed it told me about it.

And they admitted that what Brother John said about them was true.

It was also revealed to him that some of them who died had perished a temporal and an eternal death, and some only a temporal death. And this was demonstrated to him with certainty. And I saw a trustworthy friar who knew those persons.[10]

## 11 *How a Great Tyrant Was Converted and Became a Friar Minor*

This was a very clear sign that the Order of St. Francis was founded by God: that as soon as it began to increase in numbers, it began to extend to the ends of the earth. So St. Francis, striving to conform himself to Christ in all things, used to send his friars, two by two, to preach in all countries. And the Lord performed such marvels through them that "their sound has gone forth into all the earth, and their words unto the ends of the world."

Once it happened that two of those new disciples of the Saint, while traveling through a foreign land, came to a castle filled with very wicked men. In it was a certain great tyrant who was very cruel and faithless and who was the head and leader of all those robbers and bad men. He was of noble birth, but evil and vile in deeds.

When those two friars came to that castle in the evening, suffering from hunger and cold and fatigue, meekly like sheep among wolves, they asked the tyrant lord of the castle through a messenger to receive them as overnight guests, for the love of Our Lord Jesus Christ.

Inspired by God, he gave them a cordial welcome and showed them great courtesy and compassion. For he had a large fire lit and a meal prepared for them as for noblemen.

While the friars and all the others were resting, one of the friars, who was a priest and had a remarkable gift for speaking of God, noticed that none of the resting men spoke about God or the salvation of the soul but only about robberies and murders and many other evil deeds which they had committed, and that they took pleasure in the wicked and godless acts they had so far done. Therefore that friar, having received food for the body, wished to give some heavenly nourishment to his host and the others, so he said to the master: "My lord, you have shown great courtesy and charity to us, and therefore we would be very ungrateful if we did not try to repay you with some good things from God. So we ask you to have your whole household assemble in order that we may repay you with spiritual presents for the physical gifts which we have received from you."

The lord of the house agreed to their request and had everyone gather before the friars. And that friar began to speak about the glory of Paradise—how there is everlasting joy there, the society of angels, the security of the blessed, infinite glory, a wealth of heavenly treasure, eternal life, an ineffable light, untroubled peace, incorruptible health, the presence of God, and all that is good and no evil. But by their sins and their wretchedness, men lose those great gifts and go to hell, where there is everlasting suffering and sorrow, the society of devils, serpents and dragons, endless unhappiness and life without life, heavy shadows, and the presence of Lucifer; where there is trouble and anger, eternal fire and ice, worms and fury, hunger and thirst; where there is death without death, groaning, weeping, the gnashing of teeth, and an eternity of pain; where there is all that is evil, and all that is good is lacking!

"And," he said, "as I have seen and heard, all of you are hastening and running toward all that evil, for no good appears in your deeds or words. So I advise and warn you, my dear friends, not to lose those highest heavenly good things that will last forever, on account of the vile things of this world and the delights of the flesh, and not to hasten and run this way to such great and bitter sufferings!"

When that friar had spoken by the power of the Holy Spirit, the lord of the castle was stirred and his heart was moved to remorse. He threw himself down at the feet of the friars, and with all the others present he began to weep bitterly, asking and begging the friar to guide him to the way of salvation. And after he had confessed his sins to that friar with many

tears and with sincere remorse, the friar told him that he
should expiate his sins by making pilgrimages to shrines, by
mortifying himself with fasting, by watching and praying,
and by making generous donations to charity and other good
works.

But the lord of the castle answered: "Dear Father, I have
never been out of this province. And I don't know how to say
the Our Father or Hail Mary or other prayers. So please give
me some other penance."

Then the holy friar said: "My dear man, I want to act as
your bondsman and by the charity of God intercede with Our
Lord Jesus Christ for your sins, so that your soul should not
perish. So now I want you to perform no other penance than
to bring me tonight with your own hands some straw for my
companion and myself to sleep on."

He gladly brought the straw and prepared a bed in a room
where a light was burning. And as the lord of the castle reflected how that friar had spoken in such a holy and virtuous
way, he realized that he was a saintly man, and he decided
to investigate carefully what he did during the night. He saw
that the holy friar went to bed to sleep. But when he thought
that everyone was sound asleep, he silently arose in the middle
of the night, and stretching out his hands to the Lord, he
prayed that the sins of him for whom he had become bondsman might be forgiven.

And while he was praying, he was lifted up in the air to the
ceiling of the castle, and there in the air he wept and grieved
over the sins of the lord of the house, asking that they be forgiven in such a fervent way that hardly anyone has ever been
seen weeping for his dead relatives or friends as that friar wept
over that man's sins. And during that night he was raised in
the air three times, always shedding tears of devout compassion. And the lord of the castle secretly observed all this and
heard his charitable grieving and compassionate sobbing and
weeping.

Therefore as soon as he arose in the morning, he threw himself down at that friar's feet and begged him with tears of compunction to guide him along the path of salvation, saying that
he was firmly resolved to do whatever the friar commanded.
Therefore on the advice of the holy friar, he sold all that he

owned, made all the restitution that he owed, and distributed all the rest to the poor in accordance with the Gospel. And offering himself to God, he joined the Order of Friars Minor and lived a holy life with praiseworthy perseverance until he died.

And his companions and associates were inspired by remorse to change their way of life for the better. Such is the fruit that was obtained by the holy simplicity of those friars who did not preach about Aristotle or philosophy, but briefly about the pains of hell and the glory of Paradise, as is written in the holy Rule.[11]

To the praise of Our Lord Jesus Christ, who is blessed forever! Amen.

## 12  How St. Francis Laid a Curse upon a Minister in Bologna

A certain Friar Minor—Brother John of Stracchia—was the Minister of the Province of Bologna in St. Francis' time, and he was a very learned man. And without St. Francis' permission and against his will, while he was away, he founded a house of studies in Bologna.

When it was reported to the Saint that such a house of studies had been founded in Bologna, he immediately hastened there and severely reproved that Minister, saying: "You want to destroy my Order! For I want my friars to pray more than to read, according to the example of my Lord Jesus Christ."

Now after St. Francis had left Bologna, that Minister did not heed him and again organized a house of studies, as he had done before. When St. Francis heard about this, he was deeply troubled, and he laid a heavy curse on him.

Soon after he had been cursed, the Minister fell seriously ill. And he sent some friars to ask St. Francis to withdraw the curse he laid upon him.

But St. Francis answered: "Our Blessed Lord Jesus Christ has confirmed in Heaven that curse which I laid on him. And he is accursed!"

The sick Minister sadly lay in bed and grieved. And all of

a sudden a flaming drop of sulphur came down onto his body and burned up both him and his bed. And that unhappy man died amid a great stench, and his soul was seized by the devil —may Our Lord Jesus Christ who was crucified for us protect us from him! Amen.[12]

### 13 How St. Francis Opposed Retaining Any of the Novices' Property

Once the Saint's vicar, Brother Peter Catani, seeing that St. Mary of the Portiuncula was crowded with friars from other Places and that there were not enough alms to provide them with what they needed, said to St. Francis: "Father, I don't know what to do with so many friars arriving from everywhere! I haven't supplies enough to provide for them. Please allow some of the property of the novices entering the Order to be set aside for our expenses when necessary."

But St. Francis answered: "Dear Brother, put away that kind of piety which impiously goes against the Rule for the sake of anyone whatsoever!"

And Peter said: "Then what shall I do?"

St. Francis replied: "Strip the altar of the Virgin and take away its various ornaments, since you cannot provide for the needy in any other way. Believe me, the Mother of God would rather have the Gospel of her Son observed and her altar stripped than have the altar adorned and her Son scorned. The Lord will send someone who will restore to His Mother what He loaned to us."[13a]

The Saint also often uttered these complaints: "The more the friars turn away from poverty, the more the world will turn away from them. And," he said, "they shall seek and shall not find. But if they had embraced my lady Poverty, the world would nourish them, because they are given to the world for its salvation."[13b]

St. Francis often used to say to the friars: "I recommend these three words to you, namely, holy *simplicity* against an inordinate appetite for knowledge, *prayer* which the devil always tries to set aside by many exterior occupations and worries, and the *love of poverty*, not just poverty itself, the spouse of the Lord Jesus Christ and my spouse, but love and zeal for it."[13c]

### 14 *How Christ Complained to Brother Leo about the Friars*

Once the Lord Jesus Christ said to Brother Leo, the companion of St. Francis: "I grieve over the friars."

Brother Leo answered Him: "Why, Lord?"

"For three reasons," said the Lord; "namely, because they do not recognize My gifts which I have generously given them, as you well know, and which I bestow on them abundantly every day, while they neither sow nor reap; and because they are idle and grumble all day; and because they often provoke one another to anger, and do not return to love and do not forgive the offenses which they have received."[14a]

Once at St. Mary of the Portiuncula, reflecting that the graces obtained in prayer are lost through idle words said after prayer, St. Francis decreed this remedy against the fault of uttering idle words: "Whoever says an idle or useless word must immediately accuse himself and recite one Our Father for every idle word. And I wish him to say the Our Father for his own soul if he first accuses himself of his fault, but if he was first corrected by someone else, he should recite it for the soul of the person who corrected him."[14b]

### 15 *How Brother Leo Saw a Terrifying Vision in a Dream*

Once Brother Leo saw in a dream a vision of the preparation of the Last Judgment. He saw the angels blowing trumpets and various instruments and calling together a vast crowd in a field. And on one side of the field was placed a red ladder that reached from the ground to Heaven, and on the other side of the field was placed another ladder, all white, that came down from Heaven to the ground.

At the top of the red ladder appeared Christ, like an offended and very angry Lord. And St. Francis was a few steps lower, near Christ, and he went down the ladder a bit and shouted loudly and fervently, saying: "Come, my friars, come with confidence. Do not be afraid. Come and approach the Lord, for He is calling you."

On hearing St. Francis' voice and call, the friars went and climbed up the red ladder with great confidence. And when they had all gone up, some fell from the third step, some from the fourth, others from the fifth and the sixth, and all fell down, one after another, so that not one remained on the ladder.

St. Francis was moved to pity by such a fall, and like a compassionate father he prayed to the Judge for his sons, that He might receive them with mercy.

And Christ showed St. Francis His Wounds, all bleeding, and said: "Your friars have done this to Me."

And after the Saint had prayed thus for a while, he went down a few steps and called his friars who had fallen from the red ladder, and said: "Come and get up, my sons and friars. Have confidence and do not despair. Run to the white ladder and climb up, because by it you will be received into the Kingdom of Heaven."

At their father's advice, the friars ran to the white ladder. And at the top of the ladder appeared the glorious Virgin Mary, Mother of Jesus Christ, very compassionately and mercifully. And she received those friars. And without any difficulty they entered the Everlasting Kingdom.[15]

To the glory of Christ. Amen.

### 16   *Concerning a Tribulation of the Order*

The holy Brother Conrad reported—as he heard from Brother Leo—that once St. Francis was praying in St. Mary of the Angels behind the pulpit of the church. And he held out his hands toward Heaven and said: "Lord, have mercy on Your people and spare them!"

Christ appeared to him and said: "You pray well, and I willingly grant your prayer, because they mean much to me and I have paid a great price for them. Nevertheless make a pact with Me, and I will have mercy on all the people, namely, that your Order remain with Me and only with Me. Yet the time will come when it will turn away from Me, but I will sustain the Order for a while for the world's sake, which has faith in it and considers the Order its guide and its beacon. But afterward I shall give power to the devils who will everywhere arouse against it so many scandals and tribulations that they will be expelled and avoided by everyone. And if a son goes to his father's house for bread, he will strike him on the head with a stick. If the friars knew the tribulations of those days, they would begin to flee, and many of them shall flee into the wilderness, that is, those who are zealous for My honor."

And St. Francis asked the Lord: "How will they live there?"

Christ answered: "I who fed the sons of Israel in the wilderness shall feed them there with herbs. And I shall give those herbs different tastes, as formerly the manna. And afterward they shall go forth and rebuild the Order in its first perfect state.

"But woe to those who congratulate themselves on having only the appearance of conversion and who grow inert from idleness and do not steadfastly resist the temptations that are permitted for the testing of the elect, since only those who have been tried shall receive the crown of eternal life, who have meanwhile suffered from the malice of the reprobate."[16]

To the praise of Our Lord Jesus Christ.

## 17   *Concerning the Conversion of a Soldier*

There was a certain strong soldier who had won many victories and later became a Friar Minor. And when soldiers laughed at him because he had joined such an Order rather than the Templars or a similar Order where he could do much good and still fight battles, he replied: "I tell you that when I feel thirst, hunger, cold, and such things, the impulse of pride and concupiscence and such still attacks me. How much worse would it be if I saw my feet shod in armor and I was on a handsome horse and so on!"

And he added: "So far I was strong in fighting others—from now on I want to be strong in fighting myself!"

Thanks be to God.[17]

## 18    *About a Noble Friar Who Was Ashamed to Beg*

At Civitanova there was a certain friar of noble parentage named Michael who simply would not go out to beg because he was ashamed.

Now it happened that St. Francis came there, and he was told about that friar. The Saint scolded him very severely, and under holy obedience he commanded him to go alone, naked with only his breeches, to beg in a certain village that was about a mile away.

He humbly obeyed, and out of obedience went naked to beg, having set aside all shame. And he received enough bread and enough grain and other things, and he returned to the house burdened. And from that day he felt such joy and grace that as long as he lived he did not want to do anything but go and beg.[18]

## 19    *How a Friar Saw a Vision in Which Some Friars Minor Were Damned*

This was told by a friar who visited the Province of England. He heard from the Minister of that Province, a man of great piety and holiness, that a certain friar who was often rapt in ecstasy had once remained in a rapture for a whole day, weeping many tears.

On seeing him, the Minister said: "This friar is dying!" And he said to him: "Brother, I command you under obedience to come out of your rapture."

He immediately came back to himself and asked for some food. And after he had eaten, the Minister said to him: "I order you under obedience to tell me the cause of your weeping, as we have never seen this happen to you before—indeed it seems to be contrary to the nature of a rapture."

When the friar found that he could not avoid revealing it, he said: "I saw the Lord Jesus Christ on a high and lofty throne, surrounded by the heavenly militia, and prepared to pass judgment. And I saw not only lay persons but both clerics and religious of many different Orders being damned.

"Then I saw someone led in wearing the habit of the Friars Minor, very elegantly dressed in a very expensive habit. When he was asked about his state, he declared that he was a Friar Minor.

"Then the Judge said: 'Brother Francis, do you hear what he says? What do you say?'

"He answered: 'Away with him, Lord! For my Friars wear common materials and not such expensive ones.'

"And that unhappy man was immediately cast into hell by the devils.

"And now another came in, an important personage accompanied and honored by many great lay people. And when asked, he said he was a Friar Minor. Again the Judge spoke to St. Francis as before.

"He answered: 'Lord, my Friars seek prayer and spiritual progress, and they flee from the honors and business of worldly men.'

"The same thing happened to him as to the first.

"And now came another burdened with heavy packages of costly and useless books. And the same was done with him as with the first and second.

"And here was another who was completely preoccupied and worried about planning and building large and costly buildings. Like the others, St. Francis denied that he belonged to his Order.

"Finally there came one who was very lowly in habit and appearance. And when he was asked who he was, he confessed that he was a great sinner, unworthy of anything good, and he begged for mercy.

"St. Francis embraced him and led him into the glory of Paradise with him, saying: 'Lord, he really is a Friar Minor.'

"And that was the cause of my weeping," the friar said to his Minister.[19]

## 20  The Canticle of Brother Sun

HERE BEGIN THE PRAISES OF THE CREATURES WHICH
ST. FRANCIS MADE FOR THE PRAISE AND HONOR OF
GOD WHEN HE WAS ILL AT SAN DAMIANO

Most High Almighty Good Lord,
Yours are the praises, the glory, the honor, and all blessings!
To You alone, Most High, do they belong,
And no man is worthy to mention You.

Be praised, my Lord, with all Your creatures,
Especially Sir Brother Sun,
By whom You give us the light of day!
And he is beautiful and radiant with great splendor.
Of You, Most High, he is a symbol!

Be praised, my Lord, for Sister Moon and the Stars!
In the sky You formed them bright and lovely and fair.

Be praised, my Lord, for Brother Wind
And for the Air and cloudy and clear and all Weather,
By which You give sustenance to Your creatures!

Be praised, my Lord, for Sister Water,
Who is very useful and humble and lovely and chaste!

Be praised, my Lord, for Brother Fire,
By whom You give us light at night,
And he is beautiful and merry and mighty and strong!

Be praised, my Lord, for our Sister Mother Earth,
Who sustains and governs us,
And produces fruits with colorful flowers and leaves!

Be praised, my Lord, for those who forgive for love of You
And endure infirmities and tribulations.
Blessed are those who shall endure them in peace,
For by You, Most High, they will be crowned!

Be praised, my Lord, for our Sister Bodily Death,
From whom no living man can escape!
Woe to those who shall die in mortal sin!
Blessed are those whom she will find in Your most holy will,
For the Second Death will not harm them.

Praise and bless my Lord and thank Him
And serve Him with great humility![20]

THIS IS THE END OF THE BOOK ABOUT CERTAIN
WONDERFUL DEEDS OF ST. FRANCIS AND HIS
FIRST COMPANIONS. IN THE NAME OF OUR LORD
JESUS CHRIST, FOR THE HONOR OF OUR MOST
HOLY FATHER FRANCIS. GOD BE PRAISED!

# APPENDICES

## 1  *The Perfect Joy* (*Ch. 8*)

In 1927 Father Bughetti published the following significantly different version of this famous chapter from an early fourteenth-century Latin manuscript (AFH 20, 107):

One day at St. Mary, St. Francis called Brother Leo and said: "Brother Leo, write this down."

He answered: "I'm ready."

"Write what true joy is," he said. "A messenger comes and says that all the masters of theology in Paris have joined the Order—write: that is not true joy. Or all the prelates beyond the mountains—archbishops and bishops, or the King of France and the King of England—write: that is not true joy. Or that my friars have gone to the unbelievers and have converted all of them to the faith; or that I have so much grace from God that I heal the sick and I perform many miracles. I tell you that true joy is not in all those things."

"But what is true joy?"

"I am returning from Perugia and I am coming here at night, in the dark. It is winter time and wet and muddy and so cold that icicles form at the edges of my habit and keep striking my legs, and blood flows from such wounds. And I come to the gate, all covered with mud and cold and ice, and after I have knocked and called for a long time, a friar comes and asks: 'Who are you?' I answer: 'Brother Francis.' And he says: 'Go away. This is not a decent time to be going about. You can't come in.'

"And when I insist again, he replies: 'Go away. You are a simple and uneducated fellow. From now on don't stay with us any more. We are so many and so important that we don't need you.'

"But I still stand at the gate and say: 'For the love of God, let me come in tonight.' And he answers: 'I won't. Go to the Crosiers' Place and ask there.'

"I tell you that if I kept patience and was not upset—that is true joy and true virtue and the salvation of the soul."

The striking minor differences between this shorter and more realistic version and the more elaborate account of Brother James of Massa which is found in the *Actus-Fioretti*, while confirming the substance of his report, point to the priority and greater historicity of the former, which is attributed to Brother Leonard of Assisi, a companion of the Poverello who testified at his Process of Canonization.

Incidentally, the same theme is also found in the Saint's own writings (Fifth Admonition).

Most significant of all are the words, "You are a simple and uneducated fellow," that directly recall another important text in which St. Francis declared that he was a true Friar Minor only if, after preaching at a coming chapter, he could rejoice when all the friars cried out, "We don't want you to rule over us, because you are very simple and uneducated, and we are very ashamed to have a simple and contemptible person like you as our superior," and they drove him away from the meeting (2C145. B6, 5. SP-L38. SP-S64. LA104[83]. Cf. SF 44, 1–17).

Thus the famous chapter on the perfect joy of St. Francis assumes a more profound significance in this older version, for it throws new light on "the dark night of the soul" which the Little Poor Man of Assisi actually experienced when he resigned his office.

## 2  The Wolf of Gubbio (Ch. 21)

*Chi la dice lo primo?* (Who said this first?) reads a challenging note by the critical eighteenth-century Conventual historian N. Papini in the margin of a medieval manuscript account of the famous wolf of Gubbio. Since the story has been questioned by some historians—even Jörgensen did not accept it—we believe the reader will appreciate a summary of all the available evidence concerning this disputed incident.

The fully developed story first appeared in the *Actus* about a hundred years after St. Francis died. A mid-thirteenth-century chronicle of the Benedictine Monastery of San Verecondo at Vellingegno between Gubbio and Perugia supplies the following undoubtedly genuine text (AFH 1, 69–70):

In recent times the poor little man St. Francis often received hospitality in the Monastery of San Verecondo. The devout abbot and the monks welcomed him with pleasure. . . .

Weakened and consumed by his extreme mortifications, watchings, prayers, and fasting, St. Francis was unable to travel on foot and was carried by a donkey when he could not walk and especially after he was marked with the wounds of the Savior.

And late one evening while he was riding on a donkey along the San Verecondo road with a companion, wearing a coarse sack over his shoulders, some farm workers called him, saying: "Brother Francis, stay here with us and don't go farther, because some fierce wolves are running around here, and they will devour your donkey and hurt you too."

Then St. Francis said: "I have not done any harm to Brother Wolf that he should dare to devour our Brother Donkey. Good-by, my sons. And fear God."

So St. Francis went on his way. And he was not hurt.

A farmer who was present told us this.

Another early text that may or may not be relevant is the testimony of Bartholomew of Pisa in his *Conformities* (1399) that on Mount Alverna St. Francis once converted a fierce bandit. The local tradition adds that he was called *Lupo* (wolf) because of his savage cruelty, but that the Saint renamed him *Agnello* (lamb). He is reported to have become a holy friar. It was due more to him perhaps than to the wild animals that Count Orlando sent fifty soldiers to protect the two friars who explored the mountain in 1213 (LV, pp. 270–74). Could this Fra Lupo have been the Fra Lupo who accompanied St. Francis on his journey to Spain in that year and who died in Burgos in 1291 (W1291, n.19)?

In any case, the first clear reference which we have to the story of the taming of the wolf of Gubbio is in the third edition of the Latin *Legenda Sancti Francisci Versificata* by the French poet Henri d'Avranches, dating from about 1290, which reads: "It is said that through his influence one wolf especially was tamed and made peace with a town."

Moreover, the Franciscan Custody of Gubbio adopted the figure of a wolf on its seal perhaps as early as the thirteenth century. A district of the town of Gubbio also took a wolf's head as its emblem in 1349.

Late in the nineteenth century the wolf's skull, with its teeth firmly set in the powerful jaws, was reported to have been found in a small shrine on the Via Globo which was said to be over the wolf's tomb. A stone on which St. Francis preached to the people after converting the wolf is shown to visitors in the Church of San Francesco della Pace.

Finally, in January 1956, press dispatches reported that packs of famished wolves were once again terrorizing villagers in central Italy.

In a letter dated February 8, 1958, the distinguished Conventual historian Giuseppe Abate writes that he is preparing a brief study of the incident based on original research in local archives, and that he considers it "probable" owing to the "great weight" of the 1290 reference, though "perhaps a little embellished" in the *Actus*.

## 3   *The Mystery of the Stigmata*

As a substantial portion of this book deals with the Stigmata of St. Francis, a brief summary of basic facts and principles concerning that baffling subject may be helpful. In the sense used here, stigmata are visible or invisible wounds in the human body that are found in the same (but not necessarily exactly the same) places as those of Christ in His Passion: in the hands, feet, and left or right side, and occasionally around the head or on the shoulders and back. They usually bleed at intervals or continuously. Genuine stigmata are incurable by medical treatment and may last for years or vanish at any time.

The Church is justified in taking an attitude of extreme caution toward all reported cases of stigmatization. It applies at least six technical criteria for the recognition of genuine cases: instantaneous apparition, substantial lesions, unmodified persistence despite treatment, bleeding, absence of suppuration, and complete instantaneous cicatrization.

Genuine stigmata meeting those criteria have never been produced by experiments, despite many attempts by psychiatrists and hypnotists. However, modern research has demonstrated that mental and emotional causes can have visible effects on the skin. For instance, a mother who saw a window nearly fall on her child's neck has developed a sore on her own neck, and a hypnotized person, when told that a coin being applied to his arm is red-hot, has developed a blister on the arm. Such facts may eventually help to supply a partial explanation of the role that natural processes may play in genuine stigmatization, insofar as they play any role at all.

Actually, even the Church's foremost experts on this complex subject which involves medicine, psychiatry, and mystical theology are not in agreement on the basic nature of the stigmata. A Roman physician writing in the *Enciclopedia Cattolica*, while admitting the existence of false stigmata, presents the traditional view that the stigmata of the mystics are beyond all the rules of psychopathology and must therefore be considered preternatural phenomena. But Professor Paul Siwek, S.J., insists that "there are no convincing reasons to hold that stigmatization, considered in itself, necessarily surpasses all the powers of nature or is strictly miraculous." However, he grants that as they are an effect of ecstasy, they would be supernatural in cause if the ecstasy were a supernatural one.

Moreover, the late Father Herbert Thurston, S.J., who studied innumerable case histories of "surprising mystics," claimed that "there are visionaries who have . . . genuine stigmata, but who for all that are by no means saints," and who were "suffering from pronounced and often extravagant hysterical neuroses." It is believed that some pseudo-stigmata have been caused by the devil. Probably some of the neurotic mystics whom Father Thurston mentioned also had pseudo-stigmata. The latest enigma in this still obscure subject is the puzzling case of a non-Catholic German businessman who apparently has the stigmata without being devout!

There is no accurate count of the number of stigmatics in history. Owing to inadequate evidence, estimates covering the last seven centuries range from fifty to over three hundred cases. Relatively few have been beatified or canonized, and very few have been men. St. Francis of Assisi was probably the first stigmatic. Moreover, his Stigmata also had a feature that has never been found in any other case: the protruding nails of flesh, which could only have been produced by a miracle, in the opinion of Agostino Gemelli, O.F.M.

It is clearly the teaching of the Church that the Stigmata of St. Francis were supernatural in the sense that a direct intervention of God was involved. Moreover, the Church has honored them with a special Feast Day in the liturgy. However, mystical theology also stresses that stigmatization, when genuine and supernatural, is a charism, a purely gratuitous gift like prophecies and visions (*gratiae gratis datae*), which is not intrinsically connected with sanctity.

Nevertheless, despite all the reserve and caution with which the Church rightly approaches this little-understood phenomenon, every genuine case of stigmatization in a person whose sanctity has been acknowledged by competent authorities is evidence of extraordinary grace from God. The whole purpose of the phenomenon, as seen in the life of St. Francis and other holy stigmatics, is the vicarious participation in the Passion of Christ and the expiation of the sins of men, through the merits of the Redeemer, by voluntary intercessory suffering of soul and body.

We would certainly fail to understand not only *The Little Flowers of St. Francis* but the whole attitude of the Middle Ages toward the Poverello if we did not grasp the fact that his Stigmata were generally looked upon as the ultimate certification by God of his unparalleled conformity with Christ, as far as is possible to a mere human creature. Dante, writing at the same time as the author of the *Actus*, immortalized that attitude in the famous lines: "Then on that crag between Tiber and Arno he received from Christ the final seal" (*Paradiso* XI, 106–7).

# BIOGRAPHICAL SKETCHES

NOTE: Precise biographical information regarding the companions of St. Francis is generally lacking; even their years of death are often approximate. Surnames were gradually coming into use in the thirteenth century and were usually derived from the name of the father or a place or some striking aspect of the person; for instance, the secular name of St. Francis was Giovanni Francesco di Pietro di Bernardone. The date of commemoration in the Franciscan martyrology is given in parentheses when it is different from the date of death. A few important bibliographical references are included (for abbreviations, see Bibliography).

ANGELO TANCREDI, lay brother: nobleman of Rieti; drafted there by St. Francis in 1210, the first knight to join the Order and probably one of the first eleven companions. Was with the Saint at the Sermon to the Birds, in Rome in 1223, and during his last days in Assisi. St. Francis praised his kindness and courtesy. One of the three companions who wrote their recollections of the Poverello at Greccio in 1246. Was with St. Clare when she died in 1253. Died about 1258 (February 13); buried in the Basilica of St. Francis in Assisi.

ANTHONY OF PADUA (*Antonio di Padova*), Saint, priest: born about 1195 in Lisbon, baptized Fernando. Joined the Canons Regular of St. Augustine in Portugal; probably ordained priest before becoming a Friar Minor in 1220. Sought martyrdom in vain in Morocco. Was present at General Chapter in Assisi in 1221. Taught theology to friars in Bologna; preached in northern Italy and southern France in 1225–27. Elected Provincial Minister of upper Italy in 1227. Died near Padua on June 13, 1231; canonized by Gregory IX a year later; named Doctor of the Church in 1946.

BERNARD (*Bernardo*), lay brother: of Quintavalle near Assisi; member of a prominent family. Became St. Francis' first formal companion on April 16, 1209. Accompanied Giles on first mission to Florence; was leader of the journey to Rome in 1210 and founder of the first friary in Bologna in 1211. Went with St. Francis to France and Spain in 1213–14; returned there the next year. Spent much time in a grotto at the Carceri Hermitage. The Saint praised his faith and love of poverty, and gave him a special blessing before dying. Spent two years in a hut on Mount Sefro near Camerino before Brother Elias was deposed as General. Was visited in Siena in 1241 by the Franciscan chronicler Salimbene. Died in Assisi between 1241 and 1246 (July 10).

CLARE (*Chiara*), Saint, Abbess: born January 20, 1194, in a prominent aristocratic family of Assisi, daughter of Favarone di Offreduccio (not Scifi). Heard St. Francis preach in 1210–11, sent him aid; refused to be married. After secret chaperoned interviews with the Saint, received the habit of the Second Order from him at the Portiuncula on March 18, 1212. Spent six weeks in two Benedictine convents near Assisi; was joined by her sister Agnes; settled at San Damiano at the end of April. Appointed Abbess in 1215. Received Privilege of Poverty from Pope Innocent III in 1216. Sent Agnes in 1219 to be Abbess of Monticelli Convent near Florence. Serious thirty-year illness began about 1224. Her mother, Ortolana, joined the Order in 1226. On October 3, 1226, St. Francis' funeral procession stopped at San Damiano. Pope Gregory IX visited her in 1228 and 1235. Her sister Beatrice joined the Order in 1229. In September 1240 Saracen troops attacking San Damiano were repulsed by her prayers to Christ in the Eucharist. In June 1241 her prayers delivered besieged Assisi. Her last years were troubled by a conflict over the Order's Rule. She fell seriously ill in 1250. Pope Innocent IV visited her in April and August 1253, approving her Rule on August 9. Died August 11, 1253 (August 12); canonized by Alexander IV in 1255. (FS 35, 174–210. EF n.s.4, 5–21. AFH 46, 3–43. AFH 48, 149. VeP 36, 394–404.)

CONRAD OF OFFIDA (*Corrado da Offida*), Blessed, priest: born 1237 in Offida (Marches). Became a friar at fourteen in 1251. Spent ten years in a hermitage; ordained priest. Assigned to Ancona in 1267; spiritual director of Tertiary Blessed Benvenuta. Visited Brother Leo in Assisi. Assigned to Mount Alverna in 1274. Knew Spiritual leaders Jean Pierre Olieu and Ubertino da Casale, then in Florence. As one of five holy hermit friars assigned to dwell near the Chapel of the Stigmata, was in adjoining cell when St. Francis appeared to Brother Matthew of Castiglione in 1281. After 1287 served in Forano with Blessed Peter of Montecchio, then in Sirolo and Offida. In 1295 advised Spiritual leaders to request Pope Celestine's permission to form a separate stricter Order, but after receiving Olivi's letter decided to remain in the Franciscan Order (see Introduction). When accused of separatism, won the lasting confidence and veneration of Minister General Giovanni di Murro. Retired to Rivo Torto; preached at Assisi on Portiuncula Feasts 1304–6. Died in nearby Bastia while preaching Advent, 1306 (December 12). Remains moved to Perugia in 1320; in 1872 to the Cathedral. Cult approved by Pius VII in 1817. (MF 15–17.)

ELIAS (*Elia*), lay brother: born in a village near Assisi about 1180, named Buonbarone. Was a mattress-maker and schoolteacher in Assisi, then student and notary at Bologna University. Joined the Order about 1211–15. Appointed first Minister of Province Beyond the Sea in 1217, founded friaries in Acre, Damietta, and Constantinople. Returned to Italy with St. Francis in 1220. Succeeded Peter Catani as Vicar, 1221–27. Built the Basilica of St. Francis during John Parenti's Generalate, 1227–32. As General, 1232–39, promoted missions and studies, but ruled despotically and oppressed St. Francis' companions Bernard, Masseo, Giles, Angelo, and Riccieri. On complaint of many superiors was deposed by Pope Gregory IX in 1239. Retired to Celle Hermitage near Cortona. Was excommunicated after joining the excommunicated Emperor Frederick II in Pisa. Served 1240–50 as his adviser and emissary to Constantinople and Sicily (where he built fortresses). Spent his last years in Cortona. Died there on April 22, 1253, repentant and reconciled to the Church by a secular priest. (MF 54, 90–139 & 539–635—for bibliography, not conclusions.)

GILES OF ASSISI (*Egidio d'Assisi*), Blessed, lay brother: of a peasant family. When about eighteen, joined St. Francis as third companion on April 23, 1209. Accompanied him on first journey to the Marches in 1209 and to Rome in 1210. Went on pilgrimages to Compostella, Brindisi, Bari, Jerusalem, and Rome. Lived in a grotto at the Carceri. St. Francis, who praised his spirit of contemplation, assigned him to Favarone Hermitage near Perugia. In 1219 sought martyrdom in vain in Tunis. Was in Rieti in 1225; present at St. Francis' death in 1226; then went to Cetona. Deplored relaxation in the Order. About 1234 settled at Monteripido, Perugia; was visited there by "Brother Jacopa," several cardinals, Pope Gregory IX (1234–36), and St. Bonaventure (1260). Present at Brother Bernard's death in Assisi. Died at Monteripido April 22, 1262 (April 23). His remains were buried in San Francesco al Prato in Perugia, moved in 1872 by the future Pope Leo XIII to his archiepiscopal palace, in 1886 to the Cathedral, and in 1920 back to Monteripido. Cult approved by Pius VI in 1777.

GIOVANNI DI CAPELLA, lay brother: of Assisi. Because of the "conformities" theme, the career of this Franciscan Judas is semi-legendary. One of the first eleven companions, as procurator he associated with seculars and introduced the first relaxation of strict poverty by providing overabundantly for the friars (and perhaps by introducing caps or cowls, though *Capella* may be a place name). After St. Francis reproved him sharply several times, he left the Order when the Saint went to Egypt. He then organized a new Order of men and women suffering from leprosy and sought the approval of the Holy See, but was firmly rejected. Having contracted leprosy, he committed suicide by hanging himself.

GREGORY IX, POPE: see HUGOLIN.

HUGOLIN (*Ugolino*), Cardinal, later Pope Gregory IX: born in Anagni in 1170 in family of Counts of Segni, nephew of Pope Innocent III and related to Alexander IV. Studied in Paris and Bologna. Appointed Cardinal Deacon by his uncle in 1198, Cardinal Bishop of Ostia and Velletri in 1206. Served as Papal Legate in Germany and northern Italy. Aided Camaldolese and Cistercian monks and especially the three Franciscan Orders as Cardinal Protector of the First and Second and co-founder of the Third. Was an intimate friend of St. Francis and St. Clare. Elected Pope in 1227. For twenty years defended the Church against the Emperor Frederick II.

Canonized St. Francis (1228), St. Anthony (1231), and St. Dominic (1238). Died in Rome August 22, 1241.

JAMES OF FALERONE (*Giacomo da Falerone*), priest: born about 1215 at Falerone (Marches); family not known. Probably studied in Fermo; was perhaps a secular priest when he became a friar. Knew Brother Masseo. Served as novicemaster at Mogliano; was spiritual father of John of Alverna. Became a leading regional preacher. Not identified as a Spiritual. Died about 1296–1302 (July 25) in Mogliano. (SF 51, 161–172.)

JAMES OF MASSA (*Giacomo da Massa*), lay brother: born in Massa Fermana (Marches) about 1220–30, as he knew Brother Simon. Traveled in Umbria and became acquainted with Brothers Giles, Leo, Masseo, and Juniper. According to his close friend the author of the *Actus* (our only source), he was considered a saintly mystic by them and by his Provincial in the Marches, Matthew of Montone. Undoubtedly a Spiritual, but one who remained in the Order. Apparently still alive when James of Falerone died about 1296–1302.

JOHN OF ALVERNA (*Giovanni della Verna* or *da Fermo*), Blessed, priest: born at Fermo (Marches) in 1259; family not known. At ten joined Augustinian Canons. In 1272 at thirteen became a Franciscan. Had James of Falerone as novicemaster. Served in Massa and Mogliano. Moved to Mount Alverna about 1290 and lived in hut in woods. Probably returned briefly to Marches as he was present at James' death in Mogliano about 1300. Preached throughout Tuscany and Umbria. Opposed the Spirituals. On December 24, 1306, administered last rites to his close friend, the famous friar poet (and Spiritual) Jacopone da Todi at Collazone. On July 24, 1311, testified at Alverna concerning the Portiuncula Indulgence. Often heard confessions in Assisi on Portiuncula Day. In 1322 preached Lenten sermons in Siena. Wrote a one-page essay on "The States of the Soul." Died in odor of sanctity on Mount Alverna on August 9, 1322. Cult approved by Leo XIII in 1880. (LV, pp. 116–155. SF 51, 152–173.)

JUNIPER (*Ginepro*), lay brother: of Assisi; joined the Order about 1210. Sent by St. Francis to found friaries in Viterbo and Gualdo Tadino. Accompanied him on a journey to Rome and Naples. The Saint praised his self-knowledge, perfect patience, and desire to imitate Christ. Was present at St. Clare's death in 1253. Died in Rome in 1258 (January 4).

LEO (*Leone*), priest: of Assisi; probably ordained just before or after joining the Order in 1210. Became the Saint's confessor, secretary, and constant companion in his last years. Francis praised his supernatural simplicity and purity of soul. The only two extant examples of the Poverello's handwriting are notes written to him. Copied a breviary for St. Clare and was present at her death. In 1246 at Greccio wrote his memories of St. Francis with Angelo and Rufino. Also wrote lives of Bernard (lost) and Giles, and probably wrote or inspired the oldest parts of *The Mirror of Perfection* and the *Legenda Antiqua* of Perugia. Was sent by the Poor Clares of Assisi with a message to St. Bonaventure. Spent his last years at the Portiuncula, where he was visited by Salimbene, Conrad of Offida, James of Massa, and Angelo Clareno. Died in Assisi in 1271 (November 15); buried in the Basilica of St. Francis.

MASSEO, lay brother: of Marignano near Assisi. Tall and handsome, joined the Order about 1210. Spent much time in a grotto at the Carceri and at the Cibottola Hermitage. Often traveled with St. Francis; was with him in Perugia in 1216 when he obtained the Portiuncula Indulgence. The Saint praised his pleasant demeanor, common sense, and inspiring speech. Knew James of Falerone and James of Massa. Perhaps the last survivor of the companions, died at the Portiuncula in 1280 (November 17); buried in the Basilica of St. Francis.

PETER CATANI (*Pietro Cattaneo* or *Catani*), Blessed, lay brother: probably belonged to prominent Pecciaroni family of Gualdo Cattaneo, although the surname Catani is found in contemporary Assisi documents. Doctor of law at University of Bologna; perhaps a canon of San Rufino Cathedral in Assisi. Joined the Order with Bernard on April 16, 1209. Served as Vicar during absences of Francis from Assisi 1212–14. Accompanied him to Egypt and Syria and back to Italy 1219–20. Was appointed Minister (Vicar) General in September 1220 when the Saint resigned. Died at the Portiuncula March 10, 1221; buried there.

PETER OF MONTECCHIO (*Pietro da Montecchio or da Treja*), Blessed, priest: born about 1225–30. Became a friar in Montecchio (now Treja) in the Marches. Sent to Ancona about 1270. Knew Conrad of Offida there and in Forano about 1287. Was a leading Spiritual until the crisis of 1295. Preached throughout the Marches. Died at Sirolo February 19, 1304; remains moved to Montecchio-Treja in 1654. Cult approved in 1792 by Pius VI. (MF 34 & 36–37.)

PHILIP (*Filippo Longo*), lay brother: of Costa di San Savino near Assisi. A Crosier monk when he joined the Order in 1209 as one of the first eleven companions, was given the nickname Longo (tall), which was then becoming a surname. Probably preached in the Marches. Served as Visitator of the Poor Clares 1219–20 and 1228–46. Retired to Greccio. Died in Perugia about 1259 (March 14).

RUFINO, lay brother: of Assisi, cousin of St. Clare, his father, Scipione, and her father, Favarone, being brothers. Small in stature. Joined the Order in 1210. Often lived in a grotto at the Carceri. St. Francis praised his constant and powerful spirit of prayer. Was with the Saint on Mount Alverna in 1224. One of the three companions who recorded their memories at Greccio in 1246. Was still living in 1278; year of death unknown (November 14); buried in Basilica of St. Francis. (MF 46, 180. AFH 46, 20.)

SILVESTER (*Silvestro*), priest: of Assisi. An elderly canon of San Rufino Cathedral, joined the Order after the approval of the Rule in 1210—the first Franciscan priest. A great contemplative, lived long in a grotto at the Carceri. Accompanied St. Francis to Arezzo in 1217. Died in Assisi about 1240 (March 4).

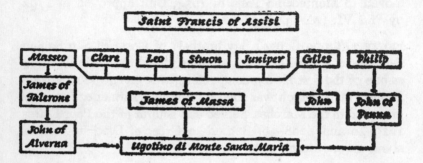

Chart Showing the Oral Tradition of the ACTUS • FIORETTI

Saint Francis of Assisi

Masseo | Clare | Leo | Simon | Juniper | Giles | Philip

James of Talerone

James of Massa

John

John of Penna

John of Alverna

Ugolino di Monte Santa Maria

# NOTES AND REFERENCES

N.B.: Some chapter headings have been condensed. All abbreviations in the references will be found in the Bibliography.

Our subtitle combines those in the *Actus* and the *Fioretti*.

## INTRODUCTION

1. It is a surprising and a regrettable fact that a complete critical biography of St. Francis has not yet been given to the world by his Order, although nearly all available early texts have been printed. Such a work is greatly needed.

2. 3S Ch. 9; cf. MF 9, 38–39; MF 39, 259–61.

3. For Ascoli: 1C62. For the friaries: AFH 1, 19–22.

4. P. Ferranti, *Memorie storiche di Amandola* (Ascoli, 1891), Pt. III, p. 165; R. Foglietti, *Le Marche dal 586–1230* (Macerata, 1907), p. 177, n.1; cf. AFH 14, 326; AFH 49, 3–7. For unpublished data re 1294 and 1342, letter from G. Pagnani, O.F.M., dated January 31, 1958.

5. Sabatier declared in a little-known lecture in London on April 4, 1908: "Those who would set him up as a kind of precursor of Protestantism would be completely wrong. . . . If I have deserved the reproach, I regret it. . . ." British Society for Franciscan Studies *Publications*, Extra Series, v. 1, p. 9.

6. AFH 11, 372.

7. See Note 4 above and AFH 49, 4–5.

8. LV, p. 121.

9. See Appendices 1 & 2; Ch. 37, Note 1; and *The Fourth Consideration on the Stigmata*, Note 15.

10. See *The Third Consideration*, Note 6.

11. First Order: 45,600. Second Order: 13,000. Third Order Regular (men and women): 70,000. Third Order Secular: 1,700,000.

12. LF 1, 5. Blessed Peter Pettinaio (d. 1289) probably knew St. Francis; cf. Dante's *Purgatory* XIII, 128.

## PART ONE: THE LITTLE FLOWERS

### 1 *The Twelve First Companions*

1. The earliest documents mention only eleven companions when St. Francis went to Rome in 1210. Later texts evolved various lists of twelve first or chosen companions.

### 2 Brother Bernard's Conversion

1. "My God and my all!" is only in the Latin text.
2. This revelation is found only in the *Actus*.
3. In earlier versions the church is San Niccolò.
4. This chapter adds details and color to its sources: 1C24; 2C15; 2C109; B3, 3 & 5; 3S Ch. 8 (cf. MF 15, 33–43; EF 49, 476).

### 3 The Humility of St. Francis and Brother Bernard

1. The Place in the woods is the Carceri Hermitage on Mount Subasio above Assisi. The Saint's semiblindness indicates the years after his return from Egypt: 1220–24.
2. Early texts refer to this practice but not to this incident. The first friars did not wear sandals. Later they used to kiss the offended friar's feet (1C53–54. 2C155).

### 4 St. Francis in Spain; The Angel and Elias

1. St. Francis went to Spain with Bernard in 1213–14. This is the earliest mention of his visit to the famous Shrine of St. James the Apostle at Compostella (AFH 4, 796).
2. The Hermitage of Farneto, 12 miles north of Assisi.
3. The chronology is confused. A regulation restricting the eating of meat was passed in 1219 by the two Vicars appointed by the Saint when he went to Egypt, but Elias was then in Syria. The story of Elias and the angel probably evolved during the later conflicts and is considered apocryphal (AFH 2, 357).

### 5 Brother Bernard in Bologna

1. In 1211. The University of Bologna then had 10,000 students. Bernard's mission is first found in the *Actus*.
2. The earliest written Rule (now lost but embodied in the Rule of 1221) was orally approved by Pope Innocent III in 1210.
3. The judge and law professor, Niccolò di Guglielmo dei Pepoli, joined the Order in 1220 and died in 1229.

### 6 The Blessing and Death of Brother Bernard

1. Bernard's trials and death are mentioned in early texts: 2C48; LA11(108); SP-L17; SP-S107.
2. Here two distinct blessings are fused: (1) while lying sick in the Bishop's Palace in Assisi, St. Francis gave Elias a formal blessing (1C108; 2C216; cf. AFH 21, 265); (2) a few days later at the Portiuncula he gave Bernard a personal blessing (LA11[107]; SP-L17; SP-S107), which the *Actus* distorts to suggest that Bernard rather than Elias was the Saint's true heir.

### 7 The Forty Days' Fast

1. Probably the Lent of 1211. First recorded in the *Actus;* earlier texts mention a visit by the Saint to one of the three islands on Lake Trasimene (1C60; B8, 8). All three were inhabited by 1208. The friary existed before 1291 (BF *Epitome,* p. 194).

### 8 The Perfect Joy

1. Dante and Virgil "went on, the one before and the other after, as the Friars Minor walk" (*Inferno* XXIII, 2–3).
2. See Appendix 1.

### 9 How God Spoke Through Brother Leo

1. First found in the *Actus.* On being honored, St. Francis would have a friar "revile" him (1C53).

### 10 How Brother Masseo Tested St. Francis

1. First recorded in the *Actus.* Time: early years.

### 11 Brother Masseo Twirls Around

1. First appears in the *Actus.* A later text locates the crossroad a few miles west of Perugia, but does not mention Arezzo (LF 2, 74). The Saint visited Siena in 1211–12, 1217, and 1226.

### 12 How St. Francis Tested Brother Masseo

1. First found in the *Actus.* Time: early years.

### 13 Brother Masseo Lifted in the Air

1. The meal, Masseo's flight, and the Apostles' apparition are first recorded in the *Actus.* The chronology is confused. Francis had a special devotion to St. Peter and St. Paul (AFH 20, 22).

### 14 St. Francis Talking with His Companions

1. First appears in the *Actus.* Time: early years.

### 15 How St. Clare Ate a Meal with St. Francis

1. First found in the *Actus.* The early friars ate on the ground at the Portiuncula (LA68[33]. SP-S21). Thomas of Celano mentions Francis' reluctance to visit St. Clare (2C205), but he also states in her *Legenda* that she "imprisoned" herself in San Damiano for forty-two years. This problem has not been clarified since 1912–13 when Paschal Robinson, O.F.M., wrote that "the foundation underlying the story is likely to be the slenderest" (AFH 5, 641), while the Capuchin Father Cuthbert regarded the meal at the Portiuncula as "probable" and the fire as an "embellishment" (AFH 6, 670–80). A 14th-century text describes a meal of St. Francis with St. Clare at San Damiano (AFH 20, 106).

### 16 St. Francis Should Preach

1. The Saint may have sent another friar with Masseo (B12, 2).

2. The silencing of the swallows probably occurred at Alviano near Orvieto (1C59. B12, 4). The lay Third Order of the Penitent or Continent was founded in Florence in 1221 (AFH 14, 3–7).

3. The *Actus* adds details and symbolism to the early accounts (1C58. B12, 3). Another friar present was Gerardo da Mutina (Lt141). Franz Liszt composed a sonata on the sermon to the birds.

### 17 A Young Friar Fainted

1. Another *Actus* first. The friars slept on straw (AFH 15, 529).

### 18 The Chapter at St. Mary of the Angels

1. The *Actus* combines features of several General Chapters: Cardinal Hugolin and the Papal Court were at Perugia in 1216; St. Bonaventure (B4, 10) mentions a chapter attended by 5,000 friars (probably in 1221), whose needs were supplied by Providence. An elderly canon told Jean Pierre Olieu in 1261 that he once heard St. Dominic declare he had attended a chapter in Assisi which influenced him to stress poverty in his Order (AFH 17, 300; AFH 20, 155); the most probable year would be 1218. St. Dominic extended his previous conception of poverty about that time. For the instruments of mortification: 2C21; SP-S27.

### 19 God Spoke to St. Francis; The Poor Priest's Wine

1. In recent years scholars have written 500 pages about the events narrated in this chapter (and its parallel texts). The controversy revolves around the question: precisely where and when did St. Francis compose *The Canticle of Brother Sun?* The *Speculum Perfectionis* and the *Legenda Antiqua* of Perugia specify that he composed it during this illness at San Damiano after receiving the assurance of eternal life and before going to Rieti. The testimony of those documents has been rejected by Benedetto and Terzi in favor of the priest's house near Rieti and by Abate in favor of the Bishop's Palace in Assisi, while Fortini has defended the San Damiano tradition (MF 56, 333–415; AFH 50, 142). This student inclines to agree with Fortini.

2. The disputed question here is: exactly where was the Church of San Fabiano—at La Foresta, about 3 miles north of Rieti, or just outside that town? La Foresta had been con-

sidered the correct location since the seventeenth century until A. Sacchetti Sassetti of Rieti examined local archives and reported in 1926 that he found no reference to La Foresta before 1319, but several mentions in thirteenth-century documents of a Church and Poor Clare Convent of San Fabiano on a hillside close to Rieti. Bishop Arduino Terzi, O.F.M., recently made several important archaeological discoveries in the four Franciscan hermitages of the Valley of Rieti, which he described in his monumental work, *Memorie Francescane nella Valle Reatina* (Rome, 1955. 507 pp.). At La Foresta he claims that he found the original Chapel of San Fabiano. Since 1948 Sacchetti Sassetti has published five brochures denying the claim. While awaiting further clarification, this observer agrees with Abate and Pratesi that Sacchetti Sassetti's evidence seems more convincing (bibliography in Terzi & AFH 50, 245–50).

### 20   *A Novice Tempted to Leave the Order*
1. The time must be after St. Anthony's death in 1231.

### 21   *The Wolf of Gubbio*
1. See Appendix 2.

### 22   *How St. Francis Freed Some Doves*
1. First found in the *Actus*. The Place is the Alberino Hermitage near Siena (MF 27, 109).

### 23   *The Devils at the Portiuncula*
1. Similar incident in 2C34.

### 24   *The Sultan and the Prostitute*
1. St. Francis' interviews with the Sultan of Egypt, Malik al-Kamil (1180–1238), during a lull in the Crusaders' siege of Damietta in the Nile Delta in September 1219, are documented by contemporary writers. The Sultan was a cultured Moslem with a taste for mystical poetry, which explains his liking for Francis.

2. Another story of late origin describes a similar incident at Bari; however, such anecdotes about various Saints were current in the fourteenth century. St. Francis volunteered to enter a fire with Moslem theologians or alone (AFH 19, 572, 576).

3. The Sultan's conversion, as first described in the *Actus*, seems to be an echo of St. Bonaventure's report, based on interviews with Brother Illuminato (Francis' companion in Egypt), quoting the Moslem ruler: "'I believe that your faith is good and true.' And from that moment he always had the Christian faith imprinted in his heart" (AFH 19, 572). His Arab contemporaries criticized him for not being a fervent Moslem.

### 25  St. Francis Healed a Man with Leprosy

1. Hansen's disease (leprosy) was endemic in Europe until the Black Death of 1347, and its many victims were strictly segregated. Many Saints and religious gave them compassionate care. St. Francis wrote in his Testament that his conversion began when "the Lord led me among them," and in his First Rule he urged his friars to rejoice at associating with them. Until recently the care of victims of leprosy was almost a monopoly of Christian missionaries. Today medical science considers Hansen's disease only mildly infectious. Patients suffer more from the unjust social stigma than from the bacillus. Realizing this, St. Francis carefully avoided using the hated term "leper" when speaking to them, calling them "brother Christians." In the same spirit the 1948 and 1953 International Congresses on Leprosy strongly recommended that the objectionable words "leprosy" and especially "leper" be abandoned in popular writing.

2. The earliest texts describe several incidents involving victims of leprosy. Another version of this anecdote locates it at the Spedalaccio hospital at Collestrada between Perugia and Assisi (AFH 12, 367). Assisi had several leprosaria (AFH 43, 23).

### 26  The Three Robbers

1. Another version is known (LA111[90]. SP-L43. SP-S66. Cf. AFH 12, 343). The Hermitage of Monte Casale has been in charge of the Capuchins since 1573. The Guardian, Brother Angelo Tarlati of the Counts of Pietramala, should not be confused with Brother Angelo Tancredi of Rieti. His vocation in 1213 is first recorded in the *Actus*. Perhaps he was the Angelo who died as chaplain of the Poor Clares in Cortona in 1237 (BF1, 38).

2. Contemporary chronicles mention a severe famine in 1227 when people ate nutshells and bark (2C53. AF 10, 164).

3. The chronology is confused: the former robber died 15 years after his conversion, i.e., about 1230, but Bernard and Giles lived until 1241–46 and 1262, respectively. This vision is first found in the *Actus*.

### 27  St. Francis Converted Two Students in Bologna

1. The Saint visited Bologna several times between 1213 and 1222; this would be an early visit. See the vivid eyewitness account of his sermon there on August 15, 1222, in JJ, p. 196.

2. Pellegrino died in 1232 at San Severino (March 27). His body was found intact in the sixteenth century.

3. Riccieri was Minister of the Marches in 1225–34. St.

Francis once patched his habit for him (SP-S16). He wrote
the first Franciscan treatise on the spiritual life—a neglected
jewel (MF 8, 113). For his temptation and visit to St. Francis:
1C49; SP-S2. He retired to a hermitage near Muccia and died
in 1234 (March 14). The *Actus* is our main source for both
friars.

### 28   *Brother Bernard's Gift of Contemplation*
1. Once Bernard said jokingly to Giles: "Go out for bread."
Giles retorted: "Brother Bernard, it is not granted to every man
to eat like the swallows, as you do" (AF 4, 182). The mountain is Mount Subasio—also the scene of the next chapter.

### 29   *Brother Rufino's Temptation*
1 & 2. In the *Actus* an Italian expression is used which cor-
responds to the English "four-letter word." Time: early years.
3. First found in the *Actus*. Another diabolic trial of Rufino,
also at the Carceri, was recorded by Conrad of Offida (AF
3, 48).

### 30   *Brother Rufino's Sermon*
1. Appears first in the *Actus*. Time: early years.

### 31   *Rufino Was One of Three Chosen Souls*
1. Another *Actus* first. The friars often had evidence of the
Saint's gift of reading their hearts (1C48; cf. 2C39).

### 32   *How Christ Appeared to Brother Masseo*
1. Another *Actus* first. The Place was probably Cibottola.

### 33   *How St. Clare Imprinted the Cross on Some Loaves*
1. First found in the *Actus;* not mentioned in St. Clare's earliest biography or Process of Canonization. Pope Gregory IX
visited her in 1228 and 1235; Innocent IV had two interviews
with her in 1253. Agnes and Ortolana were in San Damiano in
1253 (FS 35, 203 & 209). The cures are documented.

### 34   *How St. Louis Visited Brother Giles*
1. First appears in the *Actus,* although perhaps current in
1270–95 (MF 16, 110); not mentioned in early lives of either.
There is no record of a journey to Italy by St. Louis (1215–
1270), so probably another Giles was involved. Dominique
Bonin, O.F.M., has suggested, with Livario Oliger concurring,
that it may have been Blessed Gilles, Archbishop of Tyre (d.
1266), who was an intimate friend of the King. Another pos-
sibility is an obscure Blessed Giles who knew St. Francis, was
one of the first friars in France, and was buried at Séez in Nor-
mandy (W1226, n.62); St. Louis gave that friary a thorn from
the Crown of Thorns in 1252. Brother Giles' *Sayings* include
the words: "If you were to go to the King of France . . ." St.

Louis was a Tertiary, and is a Patron of the Franciscan Third Order.

### 35  *How St. Clare Was Carried to the Church of St. Francis*

1. It was her last Christmas, 1252. Three nuns testified and her first biography states that she heard the organ and office and saw the crib in the Basilica "as if she had been present there" (AFH 13, 458, 462, 468). The *Actus* adds the reception of Communion. In direct connection with this incident, St. Clare was named the Patron Saint of television in February, 1958.

### 36  *Brother Leo's Vision*

1. Time: last years. There are three versions of this vision. One, rewritten by a fanatic Spiritual, has St. Francis condemn the use of the breviary by Brother Leo, a priest (AFH 20, 544).

### 37  *How St. Francis Was Very Kindly Received in a Home*

1. Complete Latin text found only in the Little Mss. 54 and a Barcelona codex (AFH 7, 173). The latter confirms the *Actus*. The young man may have been Blessed Guido Vagnotelli of Cortona (d. *ca.* 1245; June 16), although Wadding places the incident in the Marches (W1215, n.31).

### 38  *Brother Elias Was to Leave the Order*

1. Latin text in Lt55. Typical of the confused legends about Elias' death that circulated in the thirteenth century. The Latin has him die in Sicily; the Italian omits the error. The only factual elements in the chapter are his excommunication and his deathbed reconciliation with the Church; see his Biographical Sketch.

### 39  *St. Anthony Was Heard by Men of Different Languages*

1. In his letter authorizing Anthony to teach theology (2C164. FS 31, 135).

2. Anthony's *Legenda Prima* quotes the comment of Pope Gregory IX (probably in 1230). The pentecostal miracle appears later.

### 40  *How St. Anthony Preached to the Fishes*

1. Not in the earliest biographies. Another text gives the town as Padua (AFH 8, 831). The *Fioretti* condenses the *Actus*.

### 41  *Brother Simon of Assisi*

1. Rooks are small gregarious crows that nest in trees. Simon joined the Order in 1210, was one of the early Spirituals, and was probably exiled to the Marches. He died about 1244 at

the Brunforte friary near Sarnano. Ugolino may have known the novice (W1210, n.43).

2. Ugolino's important reference to himself is found only in Lt48 and the Barcelona codex. On its interpretation depends the dating of at least this part of the *Actus* (AFH 49, 4–5).

### 42 *The Wonderful Miracles of Some Holy Friars*

1. Little is known of Lucido (cf. SP-S85).

2. This Masseo of San Severino is not Masseo of Assisi.

3. Bentivoglia de Bonis had three brothers and four nephews who were Franciscans and two sisters who were Poor Clares. Trave Bonanti is now called Ponte La Trave (south of Camerino). He carried the man with leprosy to a lonely hermitage on Monte Sanvicino to the north in order to visit his spiritual father, Blessed Paul of Spoleto, whom St. Francis appointed the second Provincial of the Marches and who died in 1241 (1C77–79. W1232, n.21). Bentivoglia died in 1288 (April 6).

4. Servodeo of Urbino spent his whole life in Ancona.

5. The Crucifix is preserved in the Cathedral of Ancona.

6. See the Biographical Sketches of Peter of Montecchio and Conrad of Offida. The latter's vision occurred on the Feast of the Purification, 1289. In 1307 a commemorative picture was painted in his cell in the woods. Later a large mural of the scene placed in a new chapel became famous and was moved to the Cathedral of Treja (MF 37, 82–85).

### 45 *Brother John of Penna*

1. Blessed Giovanni da Penna San Giovanni was born about 1193, joined the Order about 1213, attended a Provincial Chapter at Recanati, then the General Chapter of 1217 in Assisi, where he was assigned to Languedoc in southern France with a group led by Giovanni Bonelli da Firenze. He returned to the Marches about 1242. In 1248, to settle a civil conflict in Penna San Giovanni, he wrote a recently discovered pact or *charta libertatis* of basic value in the history of Italian law. He died about 1270–75 (April 3); cult approved in 1806. Should not be confused with Giovanni da Penna (Abruzzi) who was sent to Germany in 1217 or with an architect of the Assisi Basilica of like name (MF 42, 133).

### 46 *Brother Pacifico and His Brother*

1. Brother Humble's full name was perhaps Umile di Monte Granaro (MF 10, 109); he died in 1234. Pacifico is not the famous "king of verses" (AFH 20, 395). Soffiano was a grotto high on the steep slopes of Monte Ragnolo, three hours'

climb from Sarnano—a striking example of early Franciscan hermitages.

2. The Place to which Humble's remains were transferred is traditionally the friary called San Liberato da Loro, but our earliest document naming it dates from 1421; see next Note.

### 47 *The Blessed Virgin Appeared to a Sick Friar*

1. This chapter has evolved into one of the most puzzling mysteries in all hagiography. No early Franciscan document names the holy friar of Soffiano (a marginal note on one manuscript is of very late origin). Ugolino did not recall his name, although he lived near Sarnano for three years. The first mention of the name Liberato da Loro occurs in a local civil act of 1421, when the *Clareni* friars were occupying a former hospice at the foot of Monte Ragnolo to which the name became attached; but it is not mentioned in land surveys of 1313 and 1330. One of the early leaders of the *Clareni* was Liberato da Macerata, who died in 1307. The Sarnano *Clareni* joined the Observant Franciscans in 1510. During the fifteenth and sixteenth centuries a biography of a "Beato" or "San" Liberato (Brunforte) da Loro evolved which identified him with the anonymous Soffiano friar; eventually it was included in the Franciscan breviary (October 30), but later omitted. A local cult developed around his tomb, which was said to be in the San Liberato Chapel. Persistent but unsuccessful efforts were made to have him beatified. It was falsely claimed that Pope Honorius IV had canonized him orally in 1286. The Sacred Congregation of Rites in 1697 and again in 1713 ordered pictures of the electuary cure removed and forbade any innovation in the then traditional cult. In the eighteenth century local rivalry between the citizens of Sarnano and San Ginesio produced two documents allegedly dated 1258 and 1269 which proved to be recent forgeries. This obscure conundrum has not yet received the thorough clarification which its inclusion in the *Fioretti* warrants. Until further notice it would appear that this chapter of the *Actus* is the only reliable early data available. See the articles by Giacinto Pagnani, O.F.M., in the Bibliography.

### 48 *The Vision of Brother James of Massa*

1. Another major *Actus* puzzle. Nearly the same text appears in Angelo of Clareno's *Chronicle of the Seven Tribulations*, written in Subiaco about 1325–28. Who then is the author, Angelo or Ugolino? Most scholars, including Sabatier (in his unpublished notes), ascribe the text to the Spiritual leader. However, this is the only reference to James of Massa in the

*Chronicle,* whereas Ugolino mentions him several times and knew him well. Did Ugolino perhaps visit Angelo at Subiaco on his way to Naples? Again further study is needed.

2. St. Bonaventure was not canonized until 1482 (there was no Beatification). See the Introduction for the historical background.

49 *How Christ Appeared to Brother John of Alverna*

1. The reference to his death (in 1322) was added in the *Fioretti.* See his Biographical Sketch.

2. The novicemaster was James of Falerone (see Biographical Sketches).

3. Also added in the *Fioretti.*

4. A significant early medieval instance of devotion to the Sacred Heart of Jesus (not mentioned in Margaret Williams' *The Sacred Heart in the Life of the Church*).

5. The large beech tree was blown down by the wind in 1518. A chapel was built on the spot, and the place where Christ walked is now surrounded by a low stone wall. Nearby is Brother John's cell, also transformed into a chapel.

6. The rest of the chapter appears only in the Latin text.

51 *Brother James of Falerone Appeared to Brother John*

1. The years of death of James of Falerone and James of Massa are not known with precision. Some manuscripts omit the reference to the latter in this chapter.

52 *Brother John Saw All Created Things in a Vision*

1. The entrance of Christ's Humanity into Heaven at the Ascension is meant.

53 *How While Saying Mass Brother John Fell Down*

1. An involuntary interruption of the Mass before the consecration of the wine does not involve irreverence, as the Sacrifice of the Mass requires the consecration of both species.

## PART TWO: THE CONSIDERATIONS ON THE HOLY STIGMATA

### The First Consideration

1. The Italian text—not the Latin—erroneously assigns this incident to 1224. Actually it took place on May 8, 1213, as Count Orlando's four sons declared in a notarized act of confirmation dated July 9, 1274 (CD p. 39). The medieval castle of the Counts of Montefeltro (often mentioned by Dante) is perched on a crag near San Marino; the village is now called San Leo.

2. The armed guard was probably sent to protect the friars from a bandit whom St. Francis later converted; see Appendix 2.

3. The *Actus* passes directly from the choice of companions to the birds' welcome (see Note 7). The Lent of St. Michael probably indicates the last stay of the Saint on Mount Alverna in 1224, but the other incidents and the itinerary belong to his first visit in 1215 (P). The first night was probably spent in the Buon Riposo Hermitage near Città di Castello.

4. The abandoned church is San Pierino, now in ruins, near Caprese (where Michelangelo was born). A similar but different attack by devils occurred near Trevi (2C122. SP-S59). The Saint's way of praying is derived from 2C95.

5. Source: 2C142, with slightly different details.

6. Source: 2C46; CMir15; B7, 12.

7. The birds' welcome is in the *Actus* (cf. LA113[93]; B8, 10). A chapel was built on the spot in 1602, after the oak tree had fallen. Mount Alverna is now a wildlife sanctuary.

## The Second Consideration

1. St. Francis visited Count Orlando in his castle several times. In 1274 the latter's sons gave the friars the tablecloth and wooden dish which the Saint had used there and a leather belt he had blessed when he received the count in the Third Order (CD p. 39). A document of about 1300 states that "the Place of the holy Mount Alverna was accepted" on September 8, 1218 (*Cronica Fratris Salimbene*, Holder-Egger ed., p. 657).

2. See the text of the Saint's Rule for Hermitages in JJ, p. 184 (cf. FS 36, 213). For the poverty contract: 2C70.

3. The revelation about the rocks may belong to an early visit, and the preparation for death to that of 1224.

4. This incident occurred after the Saint received the Stigmata. See the text of his Praise and Blessing in JJ, p. 249. The precious document, with three important notes by Leo, is preserved in the Basilica of St. Francis. Sources: 2C49; 2C118; B11, 9; Lt154; cf. FS 36, 218–22.

5. Sources: A9, 32–35 & A39, 5–7; cf. B10, 4; AFH 12, 369.

6. Several versions of these and other promises regarding the future of the Order are extant (AFH 20, 556). See also *The Third Consideration*, Note 7.

7. This chasm was bridged and the Chapel of the Cross was built on the spot in 1263. Source: A9, 28–31.

8. The marks of his hands were said to be still visible in the rock in 1390 (AF 4, 164). During this fast St. Francis told Brother Leo that if the friars knew how much the devil was persecuting him, they would feel pity for him (SP-S99).

9. The friar was probably Blessed Francesco dei Malefici (d. *ca.* 1290 in Corsica). His 120-foot fall in 1273 may have been accidental, according to another version (LV, p. 82).

10. Source: 2C168; B8, 10. Falcons have nested nearby for the last seven centuries.

11. No source; a similar incident involving a zither occurred at Rieti in 1225 (LA59[24]. 2C126).

## The Third Consideration

1. Source: A9, 37–67; cf. AFH 12, 392. This vision may have taken place during the Stigmatization. See *The Fifth Consideration*, Note 2.

2. Source: 1C92–93; B13, 2. The latter corrects the former.

3. The Feast of the Exaltation of the Cross falls on September 14, while the Invention (or Finding) of the Holy Cross is commemorated on May 3. The Feast of the Stigmata was assigned to September 17. For the probable source of the angel's apparition, see *The Fifth Consideration*, Note 2. The Saint's prayer may be based on the revelation to John of Alverna; see *The Fifth Consideration*, Note 4.

4. Source: 1C94–95; B13, 3. The seraphs before God's throne are similarly described in Isaias 6:2. Thomas of Celano did not specify that the seraph was Christ; later texts did (see *The Fifth Consideration*, Note 1, and *The Life of Brother Giles*, Ch. 10 & 11, with its Note 6).

5. The Latin text (A9, 69) mentions the shepherds; the Italian adds the muleteers.

6. Source: A9, 70–71. The only mention of another *Actus* writer.

7. In *The Second Consideration* (see its Note 6), an angel told the Saint that God would entrust to him the length of time which his less perfect friars would have to spend in Purgatory. Here, based on an unsubstantiated private revelation (see *The Fifth Consideration*, Note 3), this privilege is extended to all the Saint's friends—and their stay in Purgatory cannot last more than a year! As the Church has not formally approved this extraordinary claim, it would be unwise to be guided by it.

8. Source: 1C94–95; CMir4; B13, 3; cf. AFH 3, 427. The Italian text erroneously states that the heads of the nails were in the soles of the feet. See Appendix 3 on the Stigmata.

9. Source: B13, 4. Brother Illuminato Accarino of Rieti was with St. Francis in Egypt (d. 1266); should not be confused with Illuminato of Chieti, Elias' secretary and later Bishop of Assisi, who died in 1282 (LF 1, 136).

10. Source: A39, 8–10. The last paragraph is original and is the only authentic early "Farewell of St. Francis to Mount Alverna." A so-called "Farewell" found in some modern works was invented in the seventeenth century, probably by the unreliable Salvatore Vitale.

### The Fourth Consideration

1. Source: B13, 5 (somewhat expanded).

2. Thomas of Celano places a similar cure in Rieti (CMir-174).

3. Source: 2C98; B10, 2.

4. Source: 1C68; B12, 11.

5. Source: 1C63; B12, 11. One of the Alverna friars was named Peter.

6. Source: 1C70; B12, 10.

7. No source.

8. Source: B13, 7. Place: near Tavernace, north of Perugia.

9. Source: A38, 5–7; cf. AF 3, 68.

10. Source: AF 3, 68 & 676; cf. MF 42, 130. Leo reported this vision in a letter (now lost) to a Minister General.

11. Source: 2C143; SP-S39. The chronology is confused: St. Francis made Peter Catani his Vicar in 1220, not 1224.

12. Source: 1C95–96; 2C135–38; B13, 8; AFH 28, 11–13.

13. Source: 1C109; LA96(64); SP-S121; A18, 1–9.

14. Source: 1C108; LA5(99); SP-S124; A18, 10–13.

15. Source: CMir37–39; AF 3, 687; LA7(101); SP-S112; A18, 14–31; with variants. The first text, written about 1250 and printed only in 1899, confirms the *Actus* account. "Brother" Jacopa dei Settesoli, b. about 1189, married Graziano Frangipani (both of prominent Roman families), had two sons, and became a widow about 1210. She met St. Francis in Rome in 1212 (?) and on several later visits. Her sons were not senators. She was present at the Saint's death and funeral. Spent her last years in Assisi, visited Brother Giles in Perugia, died probably about 1239 (the *Fioretti* errs in stating that she died in Rome and was buried at the Portiuncula); she was

buried in the Basilica of St. Francis (February 8). See references in AFH 21, 375.

16. Source: B15, 4. The prominent knight Jerome is mentioned in several Assisi documents of 1228–37 (AFH 33, 219. MF 15, 131).

17. Source: 1C116. St. Francis died on the evening of October 3, 1226. The Poor Clares were not present at his funeral in the Church of St. George, but venerated his remains at San Damiano when the funeral procession stopped there (see JJ, p. 122).

### The Fifth Consideration

1. See *The Life of Brother Giles*, Ch. 11 and Note 6.
2. The text of this revelation in the Provincial's report places the three coin-offerings during the stigmatization and interprets them as symbolizing the Saint's three Orders (see *The Third Consideration*, Note 1). Conrad of Offida was in the adjoining Chapel of the Cross when Brother Matthew had this vision in May, 1281 (AF 3, 641; cf. AFH 12, 347; AFH 20, 553).
3. Other texts: AF 3, 635; AF 5, 397; SV119. See *The Third Consideration*, Note 7. Cf. LV, p. 384–89.
4. No source for the confirmation of the Purgatory revelation. John's touching the Stigmata appears in a contemporary biography.
5. Source: AFH 12, 393. The reference to the two friars in the last sentence is only in the Latin.
6. Source and texts: AFH 12, 362; AFH 20, 561; cf. AFH 17, 548.
7. Source: AF 10, 627; CD, p. 17–36 & 40–41. The Popes are Alexander IV (1254–61) and Nicholas III (1277–80).

### PART THREE: THE LIFE OF BROTHER JUNIPER

Source of the entire Part (except Ch. 6): AF 3, 54–64.
1. Ch. 3. The tyrant, Niccola di Giovanni Cocco, was a ruthless leader in Viterbo's bitter civil conflicts in 1224–27. After betraying the city to the Romans, he was "hacked to pieces" in 1227; see Niccola della Tuccia's "Cronaca di Viterbo" in *Documenti di storia italiana* (Florence, 1872) v. 5, pp. 16–17. In another version of this chapter, the tyrant became a good friend of Brother Juniper, who sent him small gifts. This account also states that the torture by cord left Juniper with "a weak head" (AF 4, 245; cf. W1232, n.26; AFH 2, 76).

2. Ch. 5. The ringlets (*campanellae*) were not small bells (AFH 20, 423). The frontal was probably a gift of Pope Gregory IX (W1258, n. 15).

3. Ch. 5. The General's name, found only in the Latin, gives the approximate years 1230–32, as the Basilica opened in 1230.

4. Ch. 6. Source: LF 2, 201.

5. Ch. 11. Here, as in Ch. 8, the Italian omits the Latin "without breeches." Time: perhaps 1222 (MF 17, 158).

6. Ch. 13. Brother Tendalbene ("Strive-for-Good")—real name Giovanni Atti of Todi—joined the Order about 1230, cured a blind man and a paralytic, and died at Santa Illuminata near Alviano in 1255 (May 9). He is the "friend" in Ch. 10.

## PART FOUR: THE LIFE OF BROTHER GILES

1. Ch. 1. Some early texts place Brother Giles' first meeting with St. Francis at Rivo Torto. The hospital and crossroad are halfway between there and the Portiuncula (AFH 43, 13 & 37).

2. Ch. 4. Some Latin and Italian versions give the place as Ancona, but this sentence, found in only a few Latin codexes, indicates a Palestinian background.

3. Ch. 5. This Cistercian Cardinal Nicholas of Clairvaux (d. 1227–28) almost became a Franciscan but was dissuaded by Pope Honorius III. He was in Rieti with the Papal Court in 1225–26 (AFH 19, 289).

4. Ch. 6. San Paolo di Favarone (sometimes confused with Fabriano in the Marches) was a small temporary hermitage near Perugia; later the friars moved to Monteripido.

5. Ch. 8. San Bartolommeo di Cibottola, south of Lake Trasimene, was visited by St. Francis, Brother Masseo, and (perhaps) St. Bonaventure. St. Francis also lived in the nearby Hermitages of Cetona and Sarteano on Mount Pesulano.

6. Ch. 11. Brother Giles apparently reflects a general impression that the seraph was not Christ Himself. Writing just after Giles' death, St. Bonaventure declared that it was Jesus (see *The Fifth Consideration*, Note 1).

7. Ch. 13. The other friar was Brother Leo (W1262, n.23). See also Giles' *Sayings*, Ch. 13.

8. The last paragraph was added by a copyist.

## PART FIVE: THE SAYINGS OF BROTHER GILES

1. Ch. 7. "For he used to call sins and bad examples bad money, and virtues and merits good money" (AF 3, 107).

2. Ch. 13. See Giles' *Life*, Note 7. St. Bonaventure refers twice to this saying of Giles (*Opera Omnia*, Quaracchi ed., v. 7, p. 231; v. 9, 269; cf. v. 8, p. CXIV). St. Anthony may have communicated it to Abbot Thomas Gallus, who used Giles' words in a famous treatise on contemplation (CF 5, 494).

## PART SIX: ADDITIONAL CHAPTERS

N.B.: the numbers of the Notes correspond to the chapters.

1. A17; Lt74. Minister General John Parenti (1227–32) decreed that no friar should be called "master" or "lord" (*Cronica Fratris Salimbene*, Holder-Egger ed., p. 659).

2. A25; Lt15; cf. 2C82; AF 5, 163; MF 8, 97.

3. A33; Lt26; cf. AF 3, 48; AF 4, 201.

4. A38, 8–12; Lt29. See Part One, Ch. 26, n.2.

5. A40; AFH 12, 336 & 363. Another version places the incident near Avignon and has Pope Benedict XII (1334–42) go to see the mural and stop the flow of blood by vowing to institute the Feast of the Stigmata (AFH 3, 169).

6. A44. The name of the disputatious friar is corrupt. It could be Guardianus. If it is Gerardino, perhaps he was the famous Joachimist Gerardo di Borgo San Donnino, who may have visited Perugia about 1248.

7. A45.

8. A47. Note that these three chapters are not in Leo's life of Giles or in the Little Manuscript *Actus*.

9. A55; Lt43; cf. AF 3, 440.

10. A58; Lt46.

11. A60. Lt38. AF 4, 560.

12. A61; AFH 20, 102; cf. AF 3, 364. St. Francis made the friars leave the house of studies in Bologna, until Cardinal Hugolin declared it the property of the Church (2C58; SP-S6). Pietro Giovanni Stracchia, an expert in Roman law, was appointed Minister of the Province of Bologna in 1217 and suspended in 1221. Various accounts of his being cursed and his death are found in late texts.

13. A62 has 3 parts: (a) 2C67. (b) 2C70; cf. AFH 20, 103. (c) Lt146; AFH 17, 568; AFH 20, 98—these few lines are one of the brightest and fairest jewels in all Franciscan literature.

14. A63 has 2 parts: (a) SP-S52; AFH 20, 99. (b) 2C160; SP-S82.

15. A64; cf. AF 3, 71.

16. A65. AFH 17, 567. Last paragraph: 2C157.

17. A66.

18. A67. Lt94. Place: probably Civitanova north of Fermo.

19. A70. AFH 12, 350 & 400. As Chapters 61–64, 66 & 70 of Sabatier's *Actus* (our Additional Chapters 12, 13a–b, 14, 15, 17 & 19) are not in the Little Manuscript, they may not have been part of Ugolino's original *Actus*.

20. *The Canticle of Brother Sun* has in recent years been the subject of another learned controversy in addition to the one concerning the time and place of its composition (see Part One, Ch. 19, Note 1). In 1941 Luigi Foscolo Benedetto advanced the theory that its repeated *per* meant "by" or "through," not "for," e.g., "Be praised, my Lord, by Brother Wind . . . by Sister Water." Over a dozen scholars have since debated the matter, but the majority tends to favor the traditional sense. Perhaps St. Francis, like other poets and mystics, had several senses in mind. See Giovanni Getto's *Francesco d'Assisi e il Cantico di Frate Sole* (Turin, Stab. Tip. Editoriale, 1956. 70 pp.).

The *explicit* following the poem appears in a fifteenth-century *Actus* manuscript (AFH 1, 409).

# BIBLIOGRAPHY

NOTE: A comprehensive (but little-known) current bibliography of Franciscana has been published since 1930 in *Collectanea Franciscana*, Istituto Storico dei Cappucini, Via Boncompagni 71, Rome.

## I. GENERAL WORKS AND PERIODICALS

A      See *Actus* entry in next section.

AF      *Analecta Franciscana.* Quaracchi, Collegio di San Bonaventura, 1885–1941. 10 v.

AF3      *Chronica XXIV Generalium Ordinis Minorum (1209–1374) cum pluribus appendicibus.* Quaracchi, 1897. 748 pp.

AF4-5    *De Conformitate Vitae Beati Francisci ad Vitam Domini Iesu,* auctore Fr. Bartholomaeo de Pisa. Quaracchi, 1906–12. 2 v.

AFH      *Archivum Franciscanum Historicum* (Quaracchi) 1, 1908+

B      *Legenda Maior S. Bonaventurae.* AF10, pp. 557–652.

BF      *Bullarium Franciscanum,* Giovanni G. Sbaraglia, ed. v. 1–4, Rome, 1759–68; Conrad Eubel, O.F.M. Conv., ed. v. 5–7, Rome, 1848–1914; *Epitome et Supplementum* (Quaracchi, 1908).
     *Carte topografiche delle diocesi italiane nei secoli XIII e XIV.* Vatican City, Biblioteca Apostolica Vaticana, 1932–52.

1C      Thomas de Celano, *Vita Prima S. Francisci Assisiensis.* AF10, pp. 1–117.

2C      ——, *Vita Secunda S. Francisci Assisiensis.* AF10, pp. 127–268.

CD      *Codice Diplomatico della Verna e delle SS. Stimate di S. Francesco d'Assisi,* Saturnino Mencherini, O.F.M., ed. Florence, Tipografia Gualandi, 1924. 759 pp.

CF      *Collectanea Franciscana* (Rome) 1, 1930+

CMir    Thomas de Celano, *Tractatus de Miraculis.* AF10, pp. 269–330.

EF     *Etudes Franciscaines* (Paris) 1, 1899+
       Fortini, Arnaldo, *Nova vita di San Francesco;* new
       ed. Florence, Vallechi, 1958. 3 v.

FF     *Frate Francesco* (Assisi; Rome) 1, 1924+

FS     *Franziskanische Studien* (Muenster in W.) 1, 1914+
       Huber, Raphael M., O.F.M. Conv., *A Documented
       History of the Franciscan Order (1182–1517).* Mil-
       waukee, Wis., & Washington, D.C., 1944. v. 1.
       1028 pp.

JJ     Jörgensen, Johannes, *Saint Francis of Assisi.* Garden
       City, N. Y., Image Books, 1955. 354 pp.

LA     *La "Legenda Antiqua S. Francisci," Texte du Ms.
       1046 (M.69) de Pérouse,* Ferdinand-M. Delorme,
       O.F.M., ed.; (a) AFH 15, 1922, 23–70 & 278–
       382; (b) Paris, Editions de la France Franciscaine,
       1926. 70 pp. We cite (a) first, then (b) in paren-
       theses.

LF     *La Franceschina,* Nicola Cavanna, O.F.M., ed. Flor-
       ence, Leo S. Olschki, 1931. 2 v.

Lt     See "Little" entry in next section.

LV     *La Verna, Contributi alla Storia del Santuario (Studi
       e Documenti).* Arezzo, Cooperativa Tipografica,
       1913. 397 pp.

MF     *Miscellanea Francescana* (Foligno; Rome) 1, 1886+
       Moorman, John R. H., *The Sources for the Life of S.
       Francis of Assisi.* Manchester, Manchester Univer-
       sity Press, 1940. 176 pp.
       Oliger, Livario, O.F.M., "Spirituels." In *Dictionnaire
       de Théologie Catholique* (Paris, 1941), v. 14, col.
       2522–49.

SF     *Studi Francescani* (Florence) 1, 1914+

SP-L   *Speculum Perfectionis (Redactio I),* Leonardus Lem-
       mens, O.F.M., ed. Quaracchi, 1901. 106 pp.; in his
       *Documenta Antiqua Franciscana,* Pars II.

SP-S   *Le Speculum Perfectionis,* préparé par Paul Sabatier.
       Manchester, The University Press, 1928–31. 2 v.

3S     *Legenda Trium Sociorum.* In MF 8, 1908, 81–107;
       & 39, 1939, 325–432.

VeP    *Vita e Pensiero* (Milan) 1, 1915+
       Von Auw, Lydia, *Angelo Clareno et les Spirituels
       Franciscains.* Lausanne, Université, 1952. 59 pp.

W      Wadding, Luke, *Annales Minorum.* Quaracchi,
       1931–56. 31 v.

## II. *ACTUS-FIORETTI* TEXTS AND EDITIONS

### 1. ACTUS

*Speculum Exemplorum*. Deventer, 1481 (cf. AFH 20, 1927, 109–115)

*El Floreto de Sant Francisco*. Sevilla, 1492.

*Speculum Vitae B. Francisci et Sociorum Eius*, Fabian de Igal, comp. Venice, 1504. (I have used the 1752 Györ edition.)

*Chronica XXIV Generalium* . . . In AF3.

*Actus Beati Francisci et Sociorum Ejus*, Paul Sabatier, ed. Paris, Librairie Fischbacher, 1902. LXIII, 271 pp.

*De Conformitate* . . . In AF4–5

Kruitwagen, Bonaventura, O.G.M., "Descriptio nonnullorum codicum MSS. quibus insunt libelli 'Speculum Perfectionis' et 'Actus B. Francisci,'" AFH 1, 1908, 300–412.

"La Question Franciscaine. Vita Sancti Francisci Anonyma Bruxellensis; d'après le Manuscrit II.2326 de la Bibliothèque Royale de Belgique," A. Fierens, ed. *Revue d'Histoire Ecclésiastique* (Louvain) 9–10, 1908–9.

Little, Andrew George, *Description of a Franciscan Manuscript Formerly in the Phillipps Library*. In British Society of Franciscan Studies *Collectanea Franciscana* (Aberdeen, 1914) v. 5, pp. 9–113.

——, *Un nouveau manuscrit franciscain, ancien Phillipps 12290, aujourd'hui dans la bibliothèque A. G. Little*. Paris, Librairie Fischbacher, 1919. 110 pp. (*Opuscules de critique historique*. Fascicule 18.)

Delorme, Ferdinand M., O.F.M., "Descriptio Codicis 23.J.60 Bibliothecae Fr. Min. Conventualium Friburgi Helvetiorum," AFH 10, 1917, 47–102.

Bughetti, Benvenuto, O.F.M., "Descriptio Novi Codicis 'Actus Beati Francisci' Exhibentis (Florentiae, Bibliotheca Nationalis Centralis II, XI, 20)," AFH 32, 1939, 412–38.

### 2. FIORETTI

*I Fioretti di S. Francesco*, Arnaldo della Torre, ed. Turin, Paravia & C., 1909. lvi, 285 pp.

——, Benvenuto Bughetti, O.F.M., ed. Florence, Adriano Salani, 1925. 423 pp.

——, Fausta Casolini, ed. Milan, Casa Editrice Giacomo Agnelli, 1926. 368 pp.

——, Filippo Graziani, O.F.M., ed. Assisi, Tipografia Porziuncola, 1931. 326 pp.

——, Mario Casella, ed. Florence, G. C. Sansoni, 1946. 143 pp.

——, Agostino Gemelli, O.F.M., ed. Milan, Società Editrice "Vita e Pensiero," 1945. 218 pp.

——, G. M. Bastianini, O.F.M. Conv., ed. Rome, A. Signorelli, 1950. 267 pp.

——, Mario Ruffini, ed. Turin, G. B. Paravia & C., 1953. 188 pp.

*Gli scritti di San Francesco e "I Fioretti,"* Augusto Vicinelli, ed. Milan, Arnoldo Mondadori Editore, 1955. 427 pp.

*The Little Flowers of the Glorious Messer St. Francis and of His Friars,* W. Heywood, tr. London, Methuen, 1906. 207 pp.

*The Garden Enclosed,* M. Mansfield, tr. Florence, n.p., 1911. 67 pp. (Eleven *Fioretti* Additional Chapters)

*Les petites fleurs de saint François d'Assise (Fioretti),* traduction nouvelle d'après les textes originaux par T. de Wyzewa. Paris, Perrin & Cie., 1912. 374 pp.

*Les Fioretti de saint François . . . Edition complète,* Omer Englebert, tr. Paris, Editions Denoel, 1945. 420 pp.

*Les Fioretti . . .* traduction nouvelle d'après l'Incunable de Milan par le R. P. Godefroy, O.F.M. Cap., Paris, Editions Marcel Daubin, 1947. 314 pp.

*Les Fioretti de saint François . . . Edition complète,* Alexandre Masseron, tr. Paris, Editions Franciscaines, 1953. 509 pp.

*Franz von Assisi. Legenden und Laude,* Otto Karrer, tr. Zurich, Manesse Verlag, 1945. 811 pp.

*Florecitas del glorioso señor San Francisco y de sus frailes.* Madrid, Apostolado de la Prensa, 1913. xlv, 403 pp.

## III. *ACTUS-FIORETTI* STUDIES

Alvisi, E., "I Fioretti di San Francesco, Studi sulla loro compilazione storica," *Archivio storico italiano* (Florence) s. 4, v. 4, 1879, 488–502.

Avanzi, Gianetto, "Le Edizioni del secolo XV dei 'Fioretti di San Francesco,' Indice Bibliografico," MF 40, 1940, 29–48.

Bughetti, Benvenuto, O.F.M., "Alcune idee fondamentali sui 'Fioretti di San Francesco,'" AFH 19, 1926, 321–33.

——, "Bibliographia," AFH 20, 1927, 386–407.

——, (Mario Negretti, pseud.), "Dai Fioretti di San Francesco secondo la lezione di un nuovo codice," FF 1, 1924, 230–43 & 374–86; 2, 1925, 133–44.

——, "Intorno ai Fioretti di San Francesco," FF 4, 1927, 235–57.

——, "Una parziale nuova traduzione degli *Actus* accopiata ad alcuni capitoli dei *Fioretti*," AFH 21, 1928, 515–52; 22, 1929, 63–113.

Camerano, Anna Maria, "Su la francescanità del traduttore dei Fioretti," FF 4, 1927, 262–64.

Cellucci, Luigi, *Le Leggende francescane del Secolo XIII nel loro aspetto artistico*. Rome, Società Editrice Dante Alighieri, 1929; see pp. 162–98.

Chiminelli, Piero, "Paolo Vergerio critico dei Fioretti," *Conscientia* (Rome) June 14, 1924.

Cuthbert, O.F.M. Cap., "The Teaching of the 'Fioretti,'" *The Catholic World* (New York) 89, 1909, 189–202.

Damiani, Quinto, O.F.M., "Origine Marchigiana dei Fioretti," SF 16, 1944, 197–99.

Facchinetti, Vittorino, O.F.M., "Attorno ai Fioretti," FF 3, 1926, 165–72.

——, *Il più bel fiore della leggenda francescana*. Quaracchi, 1918. 93 pp.

Faloci-Pulignani, Michele, "I 'Fioretti' di San Francesco," *San Francesco d'Assisi* (Assisi) 7, 1927, 57–60 & 78–83; cf. FF 4, 1927, 235; MF 26, 1926, 96; 27, 1927, 174.

Ferretti, Francesco A., "Ricerche sui Beati: Giacomo da Falerone, Giovanni da Fermo o della Verna, e sui primitivi conventi di Montolmo, di Mogliano e di Massa Fermana," SF 51, 1954, 152–73.

Garavani, Giunio, "Il Floretum di Ugolino da Montegiorgio e i Fioretti di S. Francesco. Studio storico-letterario," R. Deputazione di storia patria delle Marche *Atti e Memorie* (Ancona) n.s. 1, 1904, 169–242 & 265–315; n.s. 2, 1905, 11–58.

——, "La questione storica dei Fioretti di San Francesco e il loro posto nella storia dell'Ordine," *Rivista storico-critica delle scienze teologiche* (Rome) 2, 1906, 269–90 & 578–99.

Gardner, Edmund G., "The Little Flowers of St. Francis." In *St. Francis of Assisi: 1226–1926. Essays in Commemoration* (London, University of London Press, 1926) pp. 97–126.

Innocenti, Benedetto, O.F.M., "Teologia e Bibbia nei Fioretti di San Francesco," SF 12, 1926, 331–54.

Leandro de Bilbao, O.F.M. Cap., "Nostalgía y partidismo en 'Las Florecillas,'" *Estudios Franciscanos* (Barcelona-Sarriá) 51, 1950, 305–28.

Manzoni, Luigi, "Studi sui Fioretti di San Francesco," MF 3, 1888, 116–19, 150–52, 162–68; 4, 1889, 9–15, 78–84, 132–35.

Marconi, Angelo, O.F.M., "Attorno agli autori dei 'Fioretti,'" SF 12, 1926, 355–65.

———, "Chi fu il giardiniere dei Fioretti?" FF 4, 1927, 112–20 (cf. SF 14, 1928, 364–66 & 533).

Pace, Camillo, "L'autore del 'Floretum,'" *Rivista abruzzese di scienze, lettere ed arti* (Teramo) 19, 1904, 85–89.

Pagnani, Giacinto, O.F.M., "Contributi alla questione dei 'Fioretti di San Francesco,'" AFH 49, 1956, 3–16.

———, "Ricerche intorno al B. Liberato da Loro Piceno. A proposito di un viaggio di San Francesco a Sarnano," MF 57, 1957, fasc. 3.

Pellegrini, Leo, "I Fioretti del glorioso Messere Santo Francesco e de' suoi frati," *Annali della Scuola Normale Superiore di Pisa* (Pisa) ser. II, 21, 1952, 131–57.

Petrocchi, Giorgio, "Dagli 'Actus Beati Francisci' al volgarizzamento dei Fioretti," *Convivium* (Turin) n.s., 1954, 534–55 & 666–77; and in his *Ascesi e mistica trecentesca* (Florence, Le Monnier, 1957) pp. 85–146.

———, "Inchiesta sulla tradizione manoscritta dei 'Fioretti di San Francesco,'" *Filologia romanza* (Turin) 4, 1957, 311–25.

Quaglia, Armando, O.F.M., "Il 'Floretum' e i 'Fioretti' del Wadding," SF 50, 1953, 107–12.

———, "Perchè manca un' edizione critica dei Fioretti di San Francesco," SF 52, 1955, 216–23.

Staderini, Giuseppe, "Sulle fonti dei Fioretti di S. Francesco," Società Umbra di storia patria *Bollettino* (Perugia) 2, 1896, 339–64.

Terracini, B. A., "Appunti su alcune fonti dei Fioretti," *Bollettino critico di cose francescane* (Florence) 2, 1906, 21–30.

Tosi, Gianna, "Il 'Cursus' negli Actus Beati Francisci," R. Istituto Lombardo di scienze e lettere *Rendiconti* (Milan) ser. 2, 68, 1935, 659–68.

———, "I 'Fioretti di San Francesco' e la questione degli 'Actus Beati Francisci.' Contributo alla ricerca del testo latino dei 'Fioretti,'" *Ibid.* ser. 2, 69, 1936, 869–83.

## IV. THE LIFE AND SAYINGS OF BROTHER GILES

Bughetti, Benvenuto, O.F.M., "Ricostruzione di due capitoli aggiunti ai Fioretti," AFH 13, 1920, 355–87.

Bulletti, Enrico, O.F.M., "De Vita B. Aegidii Assisiensis auctore Fratre Leone iuxta novum codicem," AFH 8, 1915, 12–22.

Lemmens, Leonard, O.F.M., "Vita Beati Fratris Aegidii," in *Scripta Fratris Leonis Socii S. P. Francisci,* Pars I of his *Documenta Antiqua Franciscana* (Quaracchi, 1901) pp. 37–63.

Seton, Walter W., *Blessed Giles of Assisi.* Manchester, The University Press, 1918. 94 pp. (British Society for Franciscan Studies *Publications* v. 8.)

*Vita brevis B. Aegidii Assisiensis,* Ferdinand M. (Delorme), O.F.M., ed., AFH 1, 1908, 274–77.

*Dicta Beati Aegidii Assisiensis.* Quaracchi, 1905. 123 pp. (Bibliotheca Franciscana Ascetica Medii Aevi, v. 3.)

*Leben und "Goldene Worte" des Bruders Ägidius,* Paul Alfred Schlüter, tr.; Lothar Hardick, O.F.M., ed. Werl-Westf., Dietrich-Coelde Verlag, 1953. 176 pp. (Franziskanische Quellenschriften, Band 3.)

Miles    0   5   10      20

○ Town  • Village  ✦ Hermitage

ADRIATIC

SEA

MARCHE

METAURO R.
CESANO R.
MISA R.
Ancona
Sirolo
ESINO R.
MONTE SAN VICINO
MUSONE R.
Recanati
Forano
Traja
Macerata
Civitanova
Fabriano
POTENZA R.
CHIENTI R.
San Severino
Montegranaro
TENNA R.
Loro
Mogliano
Fermo
MONTE SEFRO
Camerino
Massa
Montegiorgio
MONTE
Muccia
Ponte La Trave
Falerone
Monterubbiano
ASO R.
Sarnano
Penna S. Giovanna
S. Stefano
Offida
TRONTO R.
Ascoli

**ASSISI REGION**

TIBER R.

Monte Ripido
Perugia
Favarone
Collestrada
Bastia
Portiuncula
Rivo Torto
San Damiano
Bettona
Miles  3

MT. SUBASIO
Carceri
Assisi

**SARNANO REGION**

San Ginesio
San Liberato
Brunforte
Soffiano
Sarnano
MONTE RAGNOLO
Brunforte Castle
Miles  3